The word *blat* refers to the system of informal contacts and personal networks which was used to obtain goods and services under the rationing which characterised Soviet Russia. Alena Ledeneva's book is the first to analyse *blat* in all its historical, socio-economic and cultural aspects, and to explore its implications for post-Soviet society. In a socialist distribution system which resulted in constant shortages, *blat* developed into an 'economy of favours' which shadowed an overcontrolling centre and represented the reaction of ordinary people to the social constraints they faced. In social and economic terms, *blat* exchanges became vital to the population, and to the functioning of the Soviet system. At the same time, however, *blat* practices subverted the ideological and moral foundations of Soviet rule, and the study of *blat* provides concrete evidence of the tendency of the Soviet system to subvert itself. Finally, the book shows that the nature of the economic and political changes in contemporary Russia cannot be properly understood without attention to the powerful legacy of the *blat* economy.

ALENA V. LEDENEVA is a Research Fellow at New Hall, University of Cambridge. She previously lectured in sociology and social theory at Novosibirsk University

# RUSSIA'S ECONOMY OF FAVOURS

**Cambridge Russian, Soviet and Post-Soviet Studies: 102**

*Editorial Board*

*Cambridge Russian, Soviet and Post-Soviet Studies,* under the auspices of Cambridge University Press and the British Association for Slavonic and East European Studies (BASEES), promotes the publication of works presenting substantial and original research on the economics, politics, sociology and modern history of Russia, the Soviet Union and Eastern Europe.

# Cambridge Russian, Soviet and Post-Soviet Studies

*Series list continues at back of book*

# RUSSIA'S ECONOMY OF FAVOURS
## *Blat,* Networking and Informal Exchange

ALENA V. LEDENEVA

PUBLISHED BY THE PRESS SYNDICATE OF THE UNIVERSITY OF CAMBRIDGE
The Pitt Building, Trumpington Street, Cambridge CB2 1RP, United Kingdom

CAMBRIDGE UNIVERSITY PRESS
The Edinburgh Building, Cambridge, CB2 2RU, United Kingdom
40 West 20th Street, New York, NY 10011-4211, USA
10 Stamford Road, Oakleigh, Melbourne 3166, Australia

First published 1998

Printed in the United Kingdom at the University Press, Cambridge

Typeset in Palatino 10/12.5pt [CE]

*Library of Congress Cataloging in Publication data*
Ledeneva, Alena, V. 1964–
Russia's economy of favours: *Blat*, networking and informal exchange /
Alena V. Ledeneva.
    p.  cm. – (Cambridge, Russian, Soviet, and post-Soviet studies: 102)
Includes bibliographical references and index.
ISBN 0 521 62174 7 (hc). – ISBN 0 521 62743 5 (pbk.)
1. Business ethics – Soviet Union.   2. Exchange – Soviet Union.
3. Black market – Soviet Union.   4. Business networks – Soviet Union.
5. Bribery – Soviet Union.   6. Soviet Union – Moral conditions.
7. Business ethics – Russia (Federation)   8. Exchange – Russia (Federation).
9. Business networks – Russia (Federation.   10. Bribery – Russia (Federation).
11. Russia (Federation) – Moral conditions.   I. Title.   II. Series.
HF5387.L436   1998
306.3'0947–dc21   97–29949   CIP

ISBN 0 521 62174 7 hardback
ISBN 0 521 62743 5 paperback

# Transferred to
# Digital Reprinting 1999

# Printed in the
# United States of America

To my mother

# Contents

# Cartoons

# Figures and tables

# Acknowledgements

I am indebted to a number of people who, at various points and in various ways, significantly influenced my ideas. I owe most to the people whose knowledge and experience shaped the content of this study – my Russian friends and my interviewees who were good enough to talk to me about their personal connections and their views on *blat*.

I am especially grateful to Anthony Giddens for support and inspiration throughout the period of preparing the book. John Barber and Zygmunt Bauman also made many valuable comments. Caroline Humphrey gave me much support and counsel about anthropological aspects of research. I have greatly benefited from discussions with Marilyn Strathern; her challenging comments at the very early stage of my work sharpened my vision and guided my fieldwork.

Many other fortunate encounters contributed to the project. Professor Steven White and Professor Bill Miller gave advice on data and illustrations and supplied most helpful recommendations for the revision of the manuscript. Professor Teodor Shanin commented extensively on the project and helped me in many other ways. I am grateful for the opportunities I was given to present my work. Rachel Walker organised a panel on informal practices at the 1997 BASEES conference which was very stimulating. Jonathan Gershuny and Ray Pahl ran the discussion and provided invaluable comments. I deeply appreciate the help and enthusiasm these scholars expressed for my work.

This book would never have been written without the support and cooperation of Rosemary Mellor. She read all my drafts and chapters and helped enormously with her comments, advice and proofreading.

An exceptional opportunity to discuss my research with historians and to defend my ideas at the Workshop of Russian Studies at the University of Chicago was provided by Sheila Fitzpatrick. I am also extremely grateful to her for drawing my attention to an important document dealing with *blat* circa 1940 which she came across in the Soviet archives. Other American collegues have contributed to the book. Gregory Grossman supplied me with a detailed bibliography about the Soviet informal economy. John Ackerman was extremely stimulating. Nancy Ries provided a most scrupulous report on the manuscript. Finnish collegues Risto Alapuro and Markku Lonkila shared their data on networks of St Petersburg teachers and organised a discussion of my work at the University of Helsinki. Thanks also go to Vladimir Yadov and Lena Danilova for inviting me to give presentations in Moscow.

A continuous exchange of ideas with Vadim Volkov has been a significant part of my postgraduate work. Oleg Kharkhordin wrote the most detailed and critical review on the manuscript which guided me in my revisions. Other Russian colleagues, Natalia Lebina, Boris Firsov and Grigorii Khanin advised me on materials and data for the book. I shall always be indebted to Inna Ryvkina and Tat'yana Zaslavskaya for teaching me sociology when it did not officially exist, and other collegues in Siberia, among whom Gagik Mkrtchyan, Irina Kozachok and Irina Davydova have contributed most deeply to the book.

Without the financial and organisational assistance of several institutions, this book would not have been possible: I thank the people in them who supported my project. For research grants, I am grateful to the Cambridge Overseas Trust; New Hall and Newnham College, Cambridge. For institutional affiliation, I thank the Institute of Economics in Novosibirsk, the Novosibirsk University, the European University at St Petersburg, the Institute of Sociology in Moscow and the Faculty of Social and Political Sciences, University of Cambridge.

All the halftone illustrations in the volume are taken from *Krokodil*, and are published by kind permission of the Chief Editor, Aleksey Pyanov.

My mother, Nina Anisimova, supported me throughout the research and took care of my daughter Maria. She stoically bore the obsessiveness of my study and the frequency of my travel. This book is dedicated to her.

# Introduction

A Russian phrase 'nel'zya, no mozhno' (prohibited but possible) offers a summary understanding of Soviet society with its all-embracing restrictions and the labyrinth of possibilities around them. In a society in which, according to the *Guardian* reporter Martin Walker (1989: 17), 'nothing is legal but everything is possible', these possibilities were called *blat*. *Blat* is the use of personal networks and informal contacts to obtain goods and services in short supply and to find a way around formal procedures. The word is virtually impossible to translate directly into English. As J. S. Berliner, one of the earliest observers of *blat*, remarked (1957:182) 'the term *blat* is one of those many flavoured words which are so intimate a part of a particular culture that they can be only awkwardly rendered in the language of another'. The ubiquity of *blat* was obvious to every citizen of the ex-Soviet Union and was also reported by Western researchers, who first described the phenomenon in the 1950s (Dallin 1951; Crankshaw 1956; Berliner 1957). Crankshaw referred to it as 'an extremely elaborate and all-pervading "old-boy" network . . . Everyone, including the most ardent Party members, deals in it' (1956: 74). Yet although *blat* has long been recognised, there has been no attempt to study it directly.

It is perhaps surprising that among the works of Sovietologists who have concerned themselves with the detailed analysis of Soviet society, there are so few which have treated *blat* with the attention it deserves. Partly it is the ambiguous character of *blat* connections, their small scale and elusiveness, that gives the impression that very little of any substance can be said. It is also due to a certain attitude of disdain towards *blat* which, it may seem, was not significant for the functioning of the 'command' society. When social scientists involved with Russian studies today reflect on the shortcomings of Sovietology, which proved unable to predict and analyse the transition to the post-communist order, they are forced to acknowledge that *blat*, among

1

other overlooked aspects, is of cultural, economic and political importance:

> We have been unable to understand scarcity and bargaining. We have found it difficult to comprehend the politics of survival in economies that are dominated by nonmarket forces and that reward *blat*, stability, conformity, and material equality rather than work, risk, creativity, and personal achievements. Because we live in consumer-oriented societies where virtually all goods and services are available to those who have the money to pay for them (i.e., societies with no nomenclatura elites), we have brought too many Western economic, social, and psychological assumptions to our analyses of Communist systems. (Fleron and Hoffman 1993: 374)

The present work is the first attempt to trace the contours of *blat* as a social phenomenon, to capture the nuances, paradoxes and dynamics of *blat* relations – the core of the day-to-day workings of the Soviet state – and to explore some of its consequences for the post-Soviet transformation. It is based on 56 in-depth interviews (these appear in the text numbered [1]–[56], according to the list of respondents provided in appendix 1, p.215).

The window of opportunity for such research occurred after people ceased to be inhibited from discussing *blat*, while still having a fresh memory of the Soviet past. Before *perestroika* people were unwilling to talk because of fear of the consequences or because of a basic lack of practice in speaking openly. The political and economic reforms of the 1990s resulted in dramatic social changes, which to some extent made the phenomenon of *blat* a matter of the past. Now that life has changed people have lost their inhibitions and even become nostalgic in talking about *blat*. This provided a great deal of material which would otherwise have been inaccessible to a researcher. The fact that while still remembering the social workings and mechanisms of Soviet society people had already had enough time to reflect on the changes in post-Soviet conditions also contributed to the understanding of the nature of *blat*. These materials are unique because the phenomenon of *blat* has been changing so much in recent years that its parameters and specifics may quickly be forgotten.

The theoretical account offered in the book is concerned with those institutional characteristics of Soviet society which caused a gradual expansion of *blat* networks, and with the ways in which these networks were interwoven with other forms of power – both economic and political – and how they have been used by social actors to pursue their aims and interests. A central argument of the book is that *blat* should be considered as the 'reverse side' of an overcontrolling centre, a reaction of ordinary people to the structural constraints of the socialist system of distribution – a series of practices which enabled the Soviet system to function and made it tolerable, but also subverted it. The book contributes to the debate among social historians about the self-subversive nature of the Soviet system (e.g. Fitzpatrick 1992; Kotkin 1995; Rittersporn 1991), seeking to transcend the totalitarian concept of the Soviet system. I argue that the phenomenon of *blat* – aimed at acquiring desired commodities, arranging jobs and the outcome of decisions, as well as solving all kinds of everyday problems – became a pervasive feature of public life. Understanding *blat* as grounded in both personal relationships and in access to public resources sheds light on its elusive character and the contradictory nature of its contribution to the functioning of the Soviet regime.

In developing my arguments I also draw on the studies of 'informal practices' in later periods of Soviet history. In the massive literature on the 'second economy' (e.g. Grossman 1992), the informal practices pervading the Soviet command system were identified and thoroughly examined. The characterisation of these practices as 'informal' testified to the Soviet regime's ability to ensure that for the most part they contributed to rather than undermined the formal targets and activities of society. The informal economy took care of many needs which were not met by the command economy, and thus contributed to the functioning of the Soviet system. According to Jowitt, however (1983:275), at some stage informal practices subverted more than they contributed to the party's formal goals and general interests. Defining *blat* as ties of reciprocity in contrast to impersonal, strictly accountable, exchanges of standardised value, Jowitt interpreted it as another expression of the charismatic–traditional quality of the Soviet polity/economy: 'In this respect, Soviet social organisation resembled primitive economies where "reciprocity demands adequacy of response not mathematical equality" (Polanyi 1957: 73), and traditional peasant communities where "reciprocal favours are so dissimilar in quality that accountancy is difficult" (Campbell 1977: 254).' Although one can agree that 'the status and personal nature of exchange involving deference, appreciation, generosity, and loyalty became defining parts of social transactions', it seems insufficient to consider *blat* as an exchange, 'based on mutually exclusive status; e.g. nobles/serfs, big men/small boys, or Soviet cadres/Soviet citizens', as Jowitt (1983: 682) suggests.

The fact that *blat* is bound up with many other concepts, such as 'second economy', 'black market', 'bribery', 'political corruption' and 'neotraditionalism', reflects its pervasive nature. To some extent this indicates that *blat* does not really fit any of them and must be conceptualised as a distinctive phenomenon in its own right. The intricate interrelations between *blat* and other practices of circumventing formal procedures through informal contacts requires a thorough examination, and I undertake to trace how *blat* is both distinct from and similar to other informal practices in Russia and analogous practices in the West.

Notwithstanding the Soviet origins of *blat*, its consequences for post-Soviet society are far-reaching. In the book I analyse recent changes in *blat* practices and their contribution to the post-Soviet social order. *Blat* stands now as one among several available possibilities for influencing decision-making and obtaining access to all kinds of resources, but in many contexts retains its unique importance. Of course, many goods and services which could formerly have been obtained only through *blat* may now be acquired by the use of money. Market mechanisms have to some extent replaced *blat* transactions to do with everyday consumption, but *blat* is proving to be both durable and, surprisingly, to some extent functional for the emergence of market mechanisms. In other ways the continued existence of *blat* is a barrier to the generalising of a money economy, because *blat* was and still is a non-monetary way of doing things. Just as *blat* had a double relation to the old Soviet economy, perhaps it has also to the new market system.

## Methods and perspectives

To a Western eye, practices of informal exchange are a kind of art (see both Wedel 1986 and Yang 1994), conferring an ability 'to read between the lines which Westerners are lacking' (epigraph in Wedel 1986) while for natives they are neither artistic nor artificial. They are nothing special at all – just a daily routine, habitual and therefore fairly automatic. I grew up in such an environment, and took most of it for granted. What made me think about *blat* as something specific was my experience in the West, where I felt things were done differently. Then I became alert to 'Russian ways' and undertook to explicate them. In so doing I tried to combine the participants' view of the subject and their self-understanding, on the one hand, and the descriptive discourse which would make it clear for an outsider, on the other.

Between August 1994 and April 1995 I spent a great deal of time travelling and interviewing people. I met some of them at random in trains and other places, talked to them and asked to record our conversation. Some of these interviews were particularly interesting, for people expressed their views to a 'stranger': a casual place, no names, no responsibility or social control involved. For the same reason, however, such responses were more difficult to interpret because I could not judge the sincerity of the respondents or visualise the contexts of their information. In the interviews with people who trusted me and were ready to disclose their *blat* contacts, we discussed *blat* in personal terms, in concrete situations, talked about common acquaintances and their *blat* networks, etc.; these interviews were particularly revealing in dealing with such a delicate topic. It is not surprising, therefore, that a large number of my respondents were my acquaintances, friends of friends or friends' contacts. In this sense the subject-matter of my study predetermined its method: the network of respondents (similar to *blat* networks) was largely inter-twined with personal networks and, due to the latter, turned out to be really effective.

To assure the quality of my data base I selected respondents of different status, occupational strata, gender, age and location, and of diverse personal experience or expertise. I approached some respondents formally, mostly those who (I thought or was told) could make good informants on the topic. There were only a few refusals, but the character of the interviews with those who agreed to be interviewed varied a lot: from a competent expertise on *blat* to the most refined strategies of misrecognition (see chapter 2, p.60). It is also worth mentioning that not all the information was obtained in organised interviews. Apart from 56 recorded interviews, I drew upon many discussions which happened spontaneously as people reacted to the topic with amusement and enthusiasm. In these cases, I took notes of conversations afterwards.

People varied in their attitudes to *blat* in general according to their environment and personal dispositions. Some people were more cynical than others and less inhibited in revealing their strategies and reflecting on them. For some people, to say 'got it by *blat*' became a matter of pride, for others a matter of routine. The fact of such recognition, however, was not very helpful, for it did not imply any further explication. It terminated the conversation, creating a self-explanatory effect in approximately the same manner as 'Fine' in reply to the question 'How are you?' As an explanation of 'how' something was done by someone, the expression 'by *blat*' did not provide an answer, but rather concealed the matter.

The most conspicuous feature of all the interviews was that the informal deals were called '*blat*' when practised by others but described in terms of friendship or mutual help in the case of personal involvement. The assumption that '*blat* is everywhere' was universally accepted by respondents, but most of them avoided accepting their own involvement in *blat* or refrained from naming it as such. The paradox created by the majority saying '*blat* is everywhere but not near here' resolved itself in the course of the interviews. Respondents repeatedly claimed that they had nothing to do with *blat* at the beginning of the interview and had come up with clear examples from their own experience by the end. Many interviews followed the same pattern. The initial reaction was:

> Why me? I am not an expert on *blat*, I was not involved in *blat* relations. Can't remember anything from my own life. If there was something, it was not significant, nothing to do with *blat*'.

By the end:

> Well, I had to. A room in a communal flat some time ago was acquired by *blat*. A hoover was obtained through friends. About the bed my sister rang me: 'Go and get it, I arranged it for you.' [39]

Often people remembered things only when asked directly: 'How did you get this fridge or TV?,' 'Whom did you bring a souvenir for after your holidays or tour abroad?,' 'Did you ask your friends to get some medicine or plane tickets in cases of emergency?,' and provided details about their contacts and channels. It seemed as if *blat* functioned most effectively on condition that its logic remained misrecognised. I therefore learned to talk in terms of the 'misrecognition game' of the respondent when appropriate. It was also crucial (1) to ask about personal experiences retrospectively; (2) to ask about others, not the self; and (3) to follow a 'swapping experiences' pattern rather than a 'question–answer' one.

The most effective way of understanding *blat* in personal terms was through taking a detailed interest in life histories: the organising of one's wedding banquet; getting oranges out of season for the children; a ticket for a resort at Yalta; medicine for a relative; a seat on the Trans-Siberian; high-quality clothes; spares for the television set and car; a new electric stove; exemption from compulsory *kolkhoz* work or presence at a party meeting; caviar when there was no caviar in the shops; a new edition of Dostoevsky sitting on the shelf; seed potato for one's allotment, etc. These interviews enabled understanding of people's ways of dealing with everyday problems, revealed their needs and expectations and were informative about the networks they maintained.

These materials enabled me to develop an ethnography of *blat* – that is, to present it as a distinctive form of social relationship or social exchange articulating private interests and human needs against the rigid control of the state – 'an everyday form of resistance', as James Scott (1985:12) would perhaps call it. A distinctive feature of this study is that I was particularly concerned with the perspective of 'common people'. I was always explicit about the subject of my study: rather than observing and describing what is done and how, I let my respondents observe, describe and speak for themselves. It was their talk and opinions that turned out to be so revealing and constructive. A detailed study of the participants' points of view uncovered daily problems experienced by Soviet people – problems which represent the ex-Soviet system in a light not readily seen by an outsider. Such a perspective also gave me an insight into the paradoxical nature of *blat* – a phenomenon which people know but do not recognise, which people perform but also repudiate.

This study is not an alternative to study of the institutional system; rather it is a necessary complement to it, as *blat* was embedded in both individual action and the structural characteristics of the Soviet system. The phenomenon of *blat* implies both 'explicit rules' and limits that invert them, both institutional restrictions and personal ways of circumventing them. The structural conditions do not only restrict but also enable and organise the practices (Giddens 1984: 21), while these practices, in turn, penetrate, transform and thus shape the system. *Blat* practices have to be grasped in an everyday context at the same time as being related to the structural conditions of the Soviet system in order to analyse both its impact on *blat* practices and the impact of *blat* practices on the system.

This study focuses on the texture and principles of the day-to-day workings of society, rather than providing statistical evidence for the pervasiveness of *blat* practices. I believe that although my sample was not of a representative nature, it does in fact represent Russia quite well – after all, *blat* practices and idioms are commonplace and common knowledge. Some supporting quantitative evidence, however, is available from the results of the sociological survey conducted by the All-Russian Centre of Public Opinion among the

**Table I.1** *Allocation through connections, 1992, per cent*

In the last year or two, have you or anyone in your household gone to someone to get things you couldn't get in the ordinary way?

| Age | Up to 29 | 30–59 | 60+ | Total |
|-----|----------|-------|-----|-------|
| Yes | 64 | 50 | 24 | 49 |
| No | 36 | 50 | 76 | 51 |

**Table I.2** *Used connections for (per cent answering 'yes'):*

| Age | Up to 29 | 30–59 | 60+ | Total |
|-----|----------|-------|-----|-------|
| Doctor | 18 | 18 | 23 | 19 |
| Medicine | 47 | 54 | 74 | 53 |
| Getting house, repairs | 14 | 15 | 14 | 14 |
| Consumer goods | 43 | 42 | 15 | 39 |
| Clothes, food | 62 | 51 | 47 | 55 |
| Car repairs | 12 | 13 | 9 | 12 |
| Holidays | 9 | 8 | 4 | 8 |
| Hospital | 8 | 12 | 7 | 10 |
| Kindergarten | 8 | 7 | 3 | 7 |
| Private teacher | 2 | 1 | 1 | 1 |
| Better school | 1 | 5 | 1 | 3 |

urban population of the Russian Federation – a large-scale representative sample of 2,106 respondents. Consider the data on allocation through connections in tables I.1–I.2.[1]

These findings aimed at comparing the generations and covered only the period of the 'last year or two'.[2] They are probably understated (49 per cent of respondents admitted the use of connections, but this does not mean that the other 51 per cent do not have connections, or did not use them at all, or are not going to use them when an urgent need arises). Quantitative data are also insufficient to grasp the cultural aspects of *blat*. A random sample and large-scale survey interviewing

[1] I. Boeva and V. Shironin, 'Russians Between State and Market: The Generations Compared', *Studies in Public Policy*, 205 (1992), Centre for the Study of Public Policy, University of Strathclyde.
[2] In both 1992 and 1996 surveys younger generations use connections more, which probably means that at the earlier stages of a life cycle needs/wants are more urgent (housing, children, etc.), and that older generations must have used their connections before 'last year'.

techniques are not designed for the deeper study of connections, because people would not normally describe their contacts or share *blat* techniques. Such data would be interesting in a longitudinal analysis, for the use of connections has significantly decreased since the early 1990s, but unfortunately such statistics were not available before 1992. The relative proportion of goods and services, for which connections were used in 1991–2 (see table I.2) is, perhaps, the best proxy one can get for the pre-1990s period: 'clothes, food' and 'medicine' were the most needed items (55–53 per cent), then consumer goods (39 per cent), medical services (19 and 10 per cent), repair services (14 and 12 per cent), holidays (8 per cent) and needs connected with children (7, 3, 1 per cent). The more recent survey results of *New Russia Barometer IV* (1995) also provide a statistical evidence for the trends I describe, namely that the use of connections decreases (from 49 per cent in table I.1 to 24 per cent in an analogous survey in 1995), and especially among younger groups of respondents.

### Structure of the book

In chapter 1, I introduce the term '*blat*' and its euphemisms, illustrate and discuss main use-contexts of *blat* both historically and as it appeared by the 1990s before the era of market reforms. The multiplicity of contexts in which *blat* is considered a relevant term makes it rather difficult to define and conceptualise. I formulate a range of features characteristic of *blat* situations and more or less common for all of them and offer a working definition of *blat* on that basis.

In chapter 2, I suggest some contrasts which might be made between *blat* and notions more established in the sociological and anthropological literature, such as bribery, corruption and other informal practices. I start with the discussion of the connections and contrasts between *blat* and other phenomena in Russia and move on to analogous practices in other cultures, such as patron–client relationships in the Mediterranean region and 'fiddling' in market economies. In conceptualising the phenomenon further, I argue that the aspects of the 'misrecognition game' – in which *blat* remains obscured by the rhetoric of friendship, etc. in one's own case, but could easily be recognised in the case of someone else – turn out to be essential for understanding the nature of the legitimacy of *blat* and its relation with the Soviet regime. I also explain why such a pervasive phenomenon could also be so elusive.

Chapter 3 focuses on the political and socio-economic conditions which restricted yet also enabled the development of *blat* practices. The analysis concentrates on how *blat* merged with the Soviet system as seen from the perspective of ordinary people – that is, how people dealt with policies and ideological demands of the state and how the realities of social life shaped their experiences and actions. I discuss the impulse *blat* received from Stalin's policies concerning the ruralisation of cities, privileges in distribution and the return of traditional (middle-class) values, and move on to consider the role of characteristics of the Soviet regime – the ambivalent character of constraints and personalisation of bureaucracy, perennial shortage and increasingly expanding system of privileges and closed distribution – in creating the social order in which unwritten rules and practices prevailed.

Chapter 4 is concerned with the social basis of *blat* practices – *blat* networks and the principles of their formation. Although pervasive, *blat* practices were not universally or evenly distributed across society. Hence I look at differences in personal attitudes towards *blat* of different types of individuals – from *blatmeisters* to *blat* non-users – and consider aspects of stratification in relation to *blat*: different social and occupational groups, gender aspects in constructing *blat* networks and its urban–rural specifics.

In chapter 5, I provide an ethnography of *blat* as a form of exchange. I am concerned with the internal logic of *blat* relations, the forms of reciprocity, mutual trust and obligations it involved, as well as with its ethical foundations. I make use of narratives or statements from those rare experts who 'recognised' their strategies despite generally misrecognised involvement with *blat* in their own case. Despite the fact that one cannot be sure how general were the opinions quoted, they are crucial to understanding the spirit of *blat*. These data largely relate to the Soviet past, and thus form a starting-point for the analysis of the ongoing economic and social transformation in post-Soviet Russia presented in chapter 6.

If the thesis that *blat* was fundamentally a phenomenon of the Soviet system is correct, then *blat* was bound to become transformed under post-Soviet conditions. A variety of new contexts has replaced the Soviet contexts of *blat*, thus reflecting the shape taken by the recent reforms. In chapter 6, I analyse the role *blat* has played in economic and social restructuring and in the formation of post-Soviet society, and the impact which social changes brought by the reforms had on *blat*. I also consider contemporary forms of *blat*-like networks and suggest some implications of my research findings for the likely future of socio-economic development of Russian society.

# 1 *Blat*: the unknown commonplace

*Blat* is higher than Stalin.                     (A folk saying)

### The origins of *blat*

It is almost a commonplace, especially among younger generations, that *blat* was especially prominent in the 1970s, a period of 'raised needs but obvious shortages'. [29] The most improbable folk version of the origins of the term that I came across was also related to this period of stagnation:

> As I heard from my relatives, native Muscovites, Brezhnev's Minister of Trade had a surname Blatov. The word '*blat*' derived from his name. He developed all this personally. People used to say 'from Blatov' or 'by Blatov' which then came into jargon as 'by *blat*' and spread all over. [38]

Most people, however, when asked could not tell precisely about the entry of *blat* into common usage: 'When I first arrived in Russia from Armenia, the word was already common. This was in 1967. To obtain, to arrange, everything was by *blat*'. [36] One respondent remarked that 'at the end of 1940s, when I was nine, the word was in the air. I heard it from childhood, it was a common word in my parents' conversations, in school, etc.' [37] Another remembered *blat* at the beginning of the 1930s. [33]

It turned out that '*blat*' is an old word which developed a new meaning at the very beginning of the Soviet era. It does not appear, however, in any of the three editions of the *Great Soviet Encyclopedia* published in 1927, 1950 and 1970, although it can be found in dictionaries of the Russian language at least since the 1930s (Ozhegov 1935; Ushakov 1935). For while the term was in wide currency in an informal way, it was banned from official discourse and the practices involved in *blat* were condemned by the Soviet authorities. As Berliner

(1957: 184) concluded: 'if we were totally reliant upon the written sources of Soviet society, we might hardly have guessed at the importance of "*blat*."'

Most dictionaries of the Russian language contain the pre-revolutionary meaning of *blat*, which refers to criminal activity – although it was generally used to mean less serious kinds of crime, such as minor theft. The criminal underworld spoke a jargon of its own which was referred to as '*blatnoi* jargon', or 'thieves' jargon'. The word acquired a 'new common vulgar' usage in early Soviet times (Ushakov 1935); in the expression *po blatu* it means 'in an illegal manner'.[1] In its current meaning, the term appears only later. The *Dictionary of Literary Russian Language* defines *po blatu* as 'illicitly, by protection, by patronage'.[2] Another dictionary, *Collection of New Words and Meanings*, based on the press and literature sources of the 1960s, mentioned the word in a few literary contexts, but the vernacular usage of the word was emphasised. Appearing in the phrases 'there is *blat* everywhere', 'there is leather *blat*, shoe *blat*, etc.', 'people with different kinds of *blat* get together' (Berliner 1957:192), the term '*blat*' is more often turned into the wording 'by *blat*' (*po blatu*) by native speakers. 'By *blat*' means approximately 'by acquaintance' (*po znakomstvu*) and would be used to mean ways of obtaining (*dostat'*) or arranging (*ustroit'*) something using connections.

According to dictionaries of etymology (Vasmer 1964; Shansky 1965) the term '*blat*' came into Russian from Polish '*blat*', meaning 'someone who provides an umbrella, a cover' (*ukryvatel'*), which in turn is taken from Jewish '*blat*' which means 'close, familiar' (*svoi*).[3] In its original meaning, in phrasing '*Svoi? Stuchish' po blatu?*' meaning 'Are you one of us? Do you speak our *blat* jargon?', it was already used at the beginning of the century.[4] *Svoi* is a pronoun, but in such contexts it became used like an adjective and noun[5] . It was used as a

[1] D.N. Ushakov, (ed.), *Tolkovyi slovar' russkogo yazyka* (Interpretative Dictionary of the Russian Language). OGIZ, 1935.
[2] *Slovar' russkogo literaturnogo yazyka* (Dictionary of Russian Literary Language). Tom 2. Moskva, AN SSSR, 1950.
[3] As opposed to Polish–Jewish, there is a German version of the etymology which connects 'blat' with German 'Blatt'. According to Vasmer (1964), 'blatt' means a bank note or a list. Russian historians of language suggested that the term *blat* comes into usage after 1918 when Russian prisoners in Germany returned to Russia. Prisoners in the German camps were given favours and privileges in supplies according to their work record, behaviour, etc. – such list of privileges was called 'Blatt'. 'According to blatt' became later spread as 'by blat'.
[4] Trachtenberg, *Blatnaya muzyka*, SPb, 1908.
[5] The connotations of '*svoi*' are different from '*nash*', even though both mean 'one of us' and can sometimes be used interchangeably ( for example, '*svoi sredi chuzhikh, chuzoi*

label to signify belonging to the *blatnoi mir*, and was also adopted by modern Russian language as synonymous with *blatnoi* in its second meaning.

Like many other idioms, the word first became widespread in Odessa.[6]  A second meaning was also mentioned in relation to Odessa. According to the report of a correspondent from there, one could only live there '*po bukve Z*' (by 'letter Z', Z for *znakomstvo* (acquaintance)), another euphemism for *blat* (*Krokodil* 1931, 27: 10).

The word '*blat*' was widely used in the vernacular, but it was not a 'polite' word and many people in 'polite society' were embarrassed to use it. In official discourse *blat* was regarded as an 'un-Soviet' phenomenon. Therefore people either pretended to have nothing to do with it or referred to it in euphemistic terms. The multiplicity of euphemisms and their extensive use explains the fact that there are few sources where the term '*blat*' is used explicitly. Another reason why *blat* was usually spoken of only indirectly derived from its ambiguous nature: *blat* often had to do with minor things and services which in themselves were not worthy of attention but, precisely for this reason, it expanded to such an extent that people tended to take *blat* for granted as part of their environment. Consequently, the best available sources are those representing everyday life: memoirs, diaries, letters, novels, films, satirical periodicals, etc. Such sources provide a solid evidence of the multifarious details and contexts in which *blat* occurred in different historical periods.

I shall proceed with the analysis of *blat* as portrayed in the satirical periodical *Krokodil* in the 1920s and 1930s. The euphemisms used most often were 'by acquaintance', 'by protection', 'I am from Ivan Ivanovich', '*svoi lyudi*' (people of the circle), '*ty – mne, ya – tebe*' ('You help me, I help you', the closest English idiom being 'I'll scratch your back, you scratch mine'), '*vyruchit*' (helping out), etc. As early as 1933, the cartoon entitled 'Subtleties of Language' reflected a general shift from buying (*kupil*) to obtaining (*dostal*) in everyday discourse. The cartoon illustrates two people meeting in the street; one is holding a variety of packs, sacks, boxes and other things including fish, game, a gramophone and a bicycle. 'Have you bought all this?', asks one. 'Obtained', answers the other (*Krokodil* 1933, 12: 4).

---

*sredi svoikh*', a title of Nikita Mikalkov's film). Generally, '*nash*' or '*nashi*' sound inclusive and patriotic, while '*svoi*' or '*svoii*' imply an element of exclusion and conspiracy.

[6] Odessa, Russia's southern port, is known as the leading conduit for linguistic imports. See A. Polivanov, *O slavyanskom slovoobrazovanii*. Moskva, 1931, p.154.

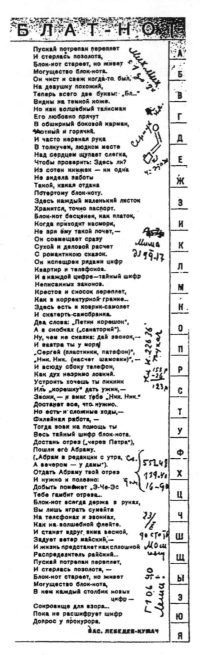

**Figure 1.1** *Blat-not*

Euphemisms for *blat* were widespread, but the word ' *blat'* itself was hard to find. It first appeared in *Krokodil* in 1933 in the poem *Blat-not* written by the poet Lebedev-Kumach (see figure 1.1). The pun *'blat-note'* referred to *'bloknot',* a note-pad for *blat* contacts. The Russian version of the poem contains *'blat'* only in the title, elsewhere the word is implied by the usage of *'bloknot'* (note-pad in our translation). The poem represents *blat* as a powerful way of approaching any problem:

> **Blat-not.**
> The note-pad is used and rather old
> The writing on its spine has faded from gold,
> But while its pages are frayed and it has aged
> Its power has grown undiminished like a maturing sage.

The efficiency of the note-pad depends on how old and used it is. The more contacts, telephones, addresses accumulated in it, the more value it has:

> There was a day the note-pad was new,
> A day where there was little it could do
> It is today that it is loved,
> Kept safely like a dove.
> It is no ordinary book
> At which we merely look
> Then to leave it idle as a pond
> The note-pad exists to function, it is a paper wand.

*Blat* is not presented in the poem as a calculated exchange between people, but as a romanticised practice of mutual favours, care and help, implying special techniques and being ruled by unwritten codes:

> Its every page is a document
> A useful testament
> In that it combines necessary calculations
> With romantic tales and wild exaltations.
> It's covered by the rows numeric,
> Of flats and addresses telephonic
> Where every figure represents
> Unwritten codes a secret presence.

The magic of *blat* consists in the power of connections which facilitate almost anything (I will consider this in detail in chapter 4). There is no direct indication in the poem as what sources are used for such magic. *Blat* simply acts as a magic wand providing luxurious holidays, fashionable music, train tickets and foodstuffs without any difficulty:

> You want a picnic party?
> For celebration day?
> You ring Nik.Nik. and he will find
> The necessary way.

The poem also refers to the indirect return of favours, and gives a hint at the distribution system which underpins such transactions:

> Sometimes it's a more demanding task
> to tie the codes up,
> then only fantasy applied
> can give you the result:
> Obtain fabric (through Peter)
> And send it to Abram,
> Who will return the favour
> That's wanted by the Dame.
> You try to manage all the calls,
> To contact them in turn,
> And winter turns into spring
> Of a distribution system.                    (*Krokodil* 1933, 28: 3)

The character of the favours (leisure, travel, fashionable music, fine fabric, foodstuffs for banquets) granted by *blat* implies the involvement of a specific group: urban, refined in its demands and having access to a telephone (in the 1930s in Stalinist Russia!). The Jewish name Abram, the bourgeois term 'Dame' (as opposed to the gender-neutral 'comrade') and the nomenclatura sounding of Nik.Nik. (Nikolai Nikolaevich) conveys the idea of *blat* as something alien to the mass of the people involved with building socialism (see cartoon 1). Such an image can be considered as an ideologically charged construction of '*blat*'. I will argue that *blat* usage was not linked to one group or stratum, as was sometimes implied in satire. *Blat* was also embedded in intimate relations which resulted in mutual help, help which could prove crucial in conditions of scarcity.

## *Blat* from the 1920 to the 1940s

Unfortunately, there are not enough secondary sources to provide a detailed picture of *blat* in the past. As far as I can judge from a careful analysis of the documentary section '*Vily v bok*' in *Krokodil*, *blat*, even though the term was not often used, was practised by all social groups, and covered both routine and more unusual goods and services. In the second half of the 1920s the following themes were persistent:

*People who have nothing to do with factories often come to the resorts for workers.*

**Cartoon 1**
– Which workshop is he from?
– As a matter of fact, from the most harmful, procuring.

(*Krokodil* 1931, 23–24: 8)

ТОЖЕ ПОМОГАЕТ

*Рис. К. Елисеева*

— Неужели пы через биржу устронлись?! Как же вам
это удалось?!
— Очень просто, — биржей мой дядя заведует...

**Cartoon 2**
– I can't believe you got a job through the job centre?! How did you manage?
– Very simple, my uncle is the director there . . .

(*Krokodil* 1928, 15: 3)

**Cartoon 3**
– How are you going to exterminate me as class, yeah?
– Very simple! Re-register you as *serednyak*, that's all!

(*Krokodil* 1930, 4: 9)

**Cartoon 4**

*Guest*: – And why do you, Aleksey Stepanovich, cross your son at home, not in the church?

*Priest*: – He is, sorry to say, a party member. And party members are not supposed to go to church.

(*Krokodil* 1928, 48: c. 6)

**Cartoon 5**
– There happen to be some good [people] among Communists . . . Look at our housemanager – he's been so good to us! He's obtained ration tokens for us, helped with exemption from the reduction of living-space and takes minimum rent as from the unemployed. It's a pity there are not enough such people in the party!

(*Krokodil* 1930, 3: back cover)

getting jobs for friends and relatives (see cartoon 2);

exemption from different campaigns such as the 'Specialists – to the provinces!' (connections had to be used to retain positions in Moscow and to avoid appointments in the provinces), or the 'All *kulak*s must be *raskulacheny* [deprived of property and exiled]!' campaign (connections could be used to conceal one's status and arrange registration as *serednyak* ('*perepisat'sya iz kulakov v serednyaki*') (see cartoon 3);

the right to maintain religious rituals (under a husband's protection the wife of a party leader could christen her child if the priest was trustworthy and discreet) (see cartoon 4);

exemption from reduction of living-space; paying minimum rent (as for unemployed) (see cartoon 5);

obtaining ration tokens (*zabornye kartochki i knizhki*) for goods and things of primary necessity (soap, cotton, socks) through personal contacts.[7]

In the 1930s *blat*-usage became increasingly associated with matters of consumption. Lebedev-Kumach, the writer of '*Blat-not*', working for *Krokodil*, portrayed a social type formed in conditions of shortage and allegedly opposed to every true Soviet person (*Krokodil* 1931, 34: 5). He points out that to possess something that was not accessible to the majority, to obtain things that were sold out and were not available, or to enjoy goods in short supply became auxiliary motives for *blat* connections. While most of the population were involved in obtaining things of primary necessity, such as shoes, boots, coats, fabric, kerosene lamps and train-tickets, there was increased demand for things which were considered particularly prestigious: books, records of American music, vacations (*putyovki*) to particular resorts, foreign goods and other items of status consumption as described by Vera Dunham (1976) in her analysis of Soviet 'middle-class' values.

The most conspicuous evidence of the prevalence of *blat* is provided by the letter of a citizen of Novgorod found in the correspondence of Vyshinsky, the head of the People's Deputies Soviet.[8] It was written to call attention to this pervasive phenomenon and as early as 1940 posed basic questions about *blat* to the authorities.

The letter starts with the obligatory praising of the regime and reproduces all the features of Soviet official discourse: approval of state policies and optimism about the 'bright' future (even at the cost of sacrifice); claims for equality and justice; acceptance of the norma-

---

[7] Extracted from *Krokodil* throughout the 1920s, particularly the years 1928–9.
[8] The State Archive of Russian Federation, f. 5446, op. 81a, file 24, p.49.

tive character and primacy of the state ('we must not have idlers . . ., our state order is incompatible with these people'); and exposition of the required attitude to the shortcomings of the political and economic order. These shortcomings are supposedly grounded in the nature of particular individuals and thus to be countered ('there remains one unresolved issue'):

> The entire Soviet nation applauds the Decree of the Presidium of the USSR Supreme Soviet 'On the duration of the working day, the introduction of the seven-day working week and on the prohibition of voluntary leave from enterprises and organisations'. This Decree will implement a genuine order in all our organisations and enterprises.
>
> We must not have idlers, trouble-makers, absentees and the like in our enterprises. Our very system, our state order is incompatible with these people. Every campaign aimed at strengthening the power of our Motherland is a campaign for improving the everyday life and well-being of every worker. All our state enterprises, public and cooperative organisations must work perfectly. The same should be demanded of every employee of these enterprises and organisations. The Soviet nation has never tolerated and will never tolerate different kinds of slackness, swindling, sabotage, etc. For this is directed against honest labourers. But there remains one unresolved issue that must be resolved, because it gained an illegitimately wide popularity among some employees and, as they say, came into fashion and practice.

Emphasising the negative connotations of *blat*, the author arrives at the seemingly paradoxical conclusion that to have no 'close connection with a swindler, speculator, fiddler, thief, flatterer and the like . . . is equal to having no civil rights . . . and [to be] deprived of everything':

> The word '*blat*' has entered the Russian lexicon. I cannot give you a literal translation of this word because it probably derives from a foreign term. Nonetheless I understand it well in Russian and can interpret it with literal precision. In Russian the word '*blat*' means swindling, dodging, pilferage, speculation and carelessness, etc. But what does it mean to say 'I have *blat*'? This means that I have a close connection with a swindler, speculator, fiddler, thief, flatterer and the like. To have no *blat* is equal to having no civil rights though, for it means that everywhere you are deprived of everything. You can obtain nothing in the shops. In response to your legitimate demands you will get a simple and clear answer 'no'. If you appeal, they are all numb, deaf and mute.

The letter outlines the basic use-contexts of *blat*, such as obtaining foodstuffs, housing, promotion at work and influencing official decision:

> If you need to obtain, that is, to buy stuff in the shop, *blat* is what you need.
>
> If it is difficult or impossible for a passenger to obtain a train ticket, it is easy and possible by *blat*.
>
> If you have no apartment, never go to the housing department or anywhere similar, try to have a little *blat* and an apartment will become available.
>
> If you want an excellent promotion at work, at the expense of others, with no justice and legality, again you need *blat*.
>
> Finally, if you address a representative or executive of a state, mass or cooperative organisation in order to solve some personal problem just try to achieve a decision without *blat*! You'll break yourself but gain nothing.

The document indicates the pervasiveness of *blat*, and brings into focus the problem of its legitimacy:

> *Blat* ensnared many employees. As if it were legalised. It came into fashion, received a civil right and became dominant. A high percentage of employees are enveloped in *blat*. It is such a common thing that people do not feel shy to apply it in their petty deals and do not fear to use it in the grand ones. People stopped feeling shy of speaking of having *blat*, that is, a connection with swindlers and dodgers, and became instead rather proud of it.

The author emphasises the subversive influence of *blat* on Soviet institutions, on the legal system, on social justice and, as a result, on confidence and trust in the Soviet system:

> *Blat* engenders speculation. Everyone who speculates does it using *blat*. *Blat* harms the plan provision. *Blat* corrodes and demoralises the work and employees of state, mass and cooperative organisations.
>
> It is an enemy of all justice and legality. *Blat* is a slyly disguised but direct road to every disgrace and slovenliness. *Blat* undermines authority and fills people with distrust of honest employees who are not enveloped by it.

Posing the question 'Why does the party and the state tolerate such outrage?', the author provides his own answer by suggesting another campaign of purges in which *blat* would be 'killed and buried' (apparently, together with people involved in it).

> It is foreign and inimical to our society, to our state. Why does the party and the state tolerate such outrage? It can and must be executed at one firm Bolshevik blow. We must put an end to it. *Blat* has to be killed and buried.

The author has astutely recognised *blat* as a specific form of relationship in which the one providing a favour is not easy to catch or punish. He does not spell out the reasons for, or understand the human roots of, this phenomenon, but he comes close to the central theme of this book, that is, the interrelation between *blat* and the Soviet system.

> You might say that there is an article of law which makes provision for a punishment for such swindling and dodging. I do not dispute this!
>
> *Blat*, however, is a new, particular, disguised form of swindling, which causes a reprimand, reproach, discontent of a third party but never leads to the dock. For this new form of shiftiness and slovenliness there should be a new law making a punishment specifically for this *blat*. Such a law must exist. It will be applauded by our entire great Soviet nation. We must have humanism, equal rights, honesty and justice.

The development of *blat* in the post-war period and in the 1950s can be characterised as its further merging with the Soviet system. Speaking about *blat* in a narrow, economic sense – as 'the sphere of illicit economic activity, a giant network of unlicensed and unplanned business as opposed to the "PLAN"' – Dallin (1951: 182) referred to *blat* as 'His Majesty *Blat*', pointing to its growth, expansion and flourishing. *Blat* became more transparent and institutionalised with the appearance of a hero of Soviet industry '*tolkach*', a professional *blat* dealer (Berliner 1957). The word derives from a verb meaning 'to push' or 'to jostle', and *tolkachi* were people who 'pushed' for the interests of their enterprise in such matters as the procurement of supplies. Their 'professional' role was to support the Soviet command economy, to enable it to work, which paradoxically could be done only by violation of its declared principles of allocation. In the command economy, in which the fulfilment of five-year plans was the main criterion of efficiency, success depended upon the setting of output targets. Faced with the need to achieve these targets, and because their bonuses were linked to such achievements, the chiefs of factories had *tolkachi* ('pushers') on their payroll, who essentially were engaged either in practices of reducing plan tasks or procuring necessary resources:

> It was their job to bypass bureaucratic snarl-ups. A *tolkach* earned his keep by having good contacts: by being skilled in manipulating people, procedures and paperwork; by being powerful enough to obtain a reduction in the targets and by speeding up or even increasing essential supplies to ensure that targets are achieved. (Nove 1977)

The *tolkach's* competence and skills are perfectly grasped in the poem
of Vladimir Mass and Michael Chervinski:

### The Irreplaceable Anton Fomich

Anton Fomich is irreplaceable,
One feels safe with him, comfortable with him,
However much the official estimates interfere,
He always finds a roundabout way
Of arranging this, of fixing that,
Of working out any business problem,
Of getting from the warehouse, without an allocation order,
Everything that is needed and even what is not needed,
And having received a carload of this,
Of exchanging it for that,
Of reducing the plan, of writing something off,
Of concealing resources, and accepting rejects.

. . . One hand, he knows, rubs the other.
And therefore, of all the sciences,
He has mastered one above all,
The interrelations of sordid hands.
This science says that one good turn
Deserves another in return.
If he has done something for you, why not
Do something for him in return?
It is not difficult to do a favour,
A favour is not illegal
For nothing criminal has been done,
No order has been broken:
A favour is not a bribe,
And you can't be put on trial for that!

. . . Without him management often
Cannot move a step.
Management is so comfortable with him.
Always, in every kind of weather,
He dives into the deepest water for management,
And always emerges dry.

Involuntarily a question arises,
It is indeed difficult to understand how,
In this day and age, he always manages
To worm his way into an institution,
Such as Anton, such as Fomich!
For the door has long since been closed to him:
Plan, Estimate, Fund, Account, Limit

Have closed the door with a hundred keys
Against all Anton Fomiches.
But, imperceptibly, he gnaws
A little hole there
And finally he crawls through one of them,
Slowly, but wholly.[9] (*Krokodil* 1952, 27: 3)

A convincing indicator of the integral place of *blat* in the Soviet system was the rise of a number of widely quoted folk sayings about it. The most common ones collected by Berliner in his study of *Factory and Manager in the USSR* (1957) were '*Blat* is higher than Stalin' or 'You've got to have ZIS'. ZIS in this context is a pun referring to the Soviet automobile of that name, and also standing for the first letters of the expression 'acquaintances and connections' (*znakomstva i svyazi*). The necessity of ZIS in everyday life was grasped in another neologism *blatmeister*,[10] which denoted *tolkach* for individual rather than industrial needs. In the case of *tolkach* collective purposes justified the means and the phenomenon, even if criticised, was tolerated for the sake of production. *Blatmeistership*, sometimes referred to as the new entrepreneurship of the 1960s, signified a further step in official tolerance. In Brezhnev's era, known for a certain acceptance of individualism and the adoption of the values of 'welfare society', this tolerance was extended and this period was the one where *blat* seemed to flourish most widely.

### Common *blat*-usage in later periods

Although my respondents disagreed somewhat about its historical origins, all of them admitted the pervasiveness of *blat* and provided a variety of contexts in which it was used: 'It is very unlikely that there is a person who has not used *blat* connections. Even if people were not involved in such practices in a routine way the hardships of life forced them to use their personal and business contacts.' [44]

When asked in which spheres *blat* was most important, respondents remarked that particular spheres became more important in moments of particular need and thus one needed to keep contacts in all of them. The question: 'To what extent did you depend on your personal contacts, help or the favours of others?' was answered with reference

---

[9] Quoted abridged from the translation in Berliner (1957: 207–9).
[10] *The Collection of New Words and Meanings* (derived from literature and press in the 1970s).

to needs – regular, periodic, life cycle needs – satisfied with the help of contacts (see chapter 4).

### Blat in daily life

In its most frequent use, *blat* was about obtaining goods in short supply, of better quality, or at lower prices by providing access (*dostup*) to foodstuffs and other goods of everyday consumption:

> In Soviet times the main role of *blat* was to obtain foodstuffs. It was the basis of life. If you had an acquaintance working in shop, you were able to buy products in short supply. You paid the same price, but an acquaintance meant that you knew when to come, could buy more or even jump the queue. It is difficult to remember now, now we can buy everything, if there is money. In those days 'to obtain' was crucial to feed a family, to entertain guests. Shortages and queues were omnipresent. I regularly sent butter and meat to my mum. She lived in Krasnodar where general provisioning was much worse than in Moscow. I have been living in my block for 25 years already, and all these years I went to the same butcher in the shop downstairs. He always gave me the best cuts. I never paid above the price. He just liked to talk to me and wanted me to come. Perhaps, it was not right that he did it or that I used to send 10 kg meat parcels to Krasnodar, but this was how people survived. One needed *blat* to have meat in the freezer, and to take it out when necessary, rather than going into the queue. [13]

*Blat* flourished not only in the state shops, but also in the canteens of organisations: 'A barmaid I knew always kept a best cut or a nice chicken for a boss and her acquaintances.' [31] Meat was mentioned as a usual item on the *blat* agenda, not only because it was the most scarce staple of the Soviet diet but also because of conspicuous injustice in how butchers distributed it. Those respondents who happened to queue for meat emphasised the unfairness of butchers, leaving best cuts for their acquaintances whereas people in the queue had to pay the same price for bones and fat: 'They did not even care to hide it, shortage made them kings, rude and shameless.' [31, 38] In tune with state propaganda, however, people used to blame butchers, but not the system. When ration tokens for foodstuffs were introduced, they also became objects for exchange: 'My students, sportsmen of the regional team, were affiliated to a special shop and occasionally obtained ration tokens for me as a friendly gesture.' [28]

In the 1970s and 1980s, there was a high demand for such industrial consumer products as tape recorders, colour televisions, sewing machines, washing machines and refrigerators: 'I had to obtain a stereo system, a fridge, a TV. It was impossible to buy an automatic washing machine when they appeared in 1980s. One had to have a contact in a shop or warehouse to obtain it.' [38]

Through official channels, these brand-name products could be bought only with specific allocation slips, which were given to every organisation or enterprise, and then distributed by every work unit to selected employees each year. If one had *blat* in the organisation, one could get to the top of a long waiting-list at one's work unit.

Items of everyday consumption, such as foodstuffs or clothes, could also be significant as indicators of social status: 'Not just basic products and consumer durables in short supply, the prestigious products and things such as chocolates, lemons, smoked fish, good cognac, had also to be obtained. It was necessary to catch up with others, to be able to entertain guests properly.' [40]

Goods from 'the other side of the iron curtain' (like jeans at the end of the 1970s) or from the elitist distribution system (including 'Beryozka' shops trading imported goods for special currency available only to those who worked abroad) became fashionable, which gave another stimulus to *blat*. The acquisition of these commodities was more often oriented at 'conspicuous' consumption and led by considerations of prestige, particularly among youth. A car, a prestige symbol for adults, was one of the most difficult *blat* items. Everything relating to cars – spares, tyres, service, garages – was also in short demand and obtained by *blat*.

### Maintaining health and other services

Those who had a job or a residence permit generally had access to low-cost health care provided by the state. Getting into a good hospital, a hospital already filled to capacity, or the hospital with the right specialisation for one's illness still required *blat*. Surgical operations at the best medical centres were, and still are, organised by *blat*: 'When I had this problem, my friend arranged that I be hospitalised in the regional clinic where he worked and not in the city hospital to which I was affiliated.' [28] To arrange an appointment with a well known doctor also implied a personal contact or acquaintance. Doctors were important people with whom to cultivate relationships because, in addition to providing access to hospital beds, *blat* with the doctor could sometimes make the difference between whether he or she listened seriously to the patient and gave a good diagnosis during a visit or only dealt with the matter perfunctorily. Doctors were also a potential source of rare and potent medicines that were generally hard to obtain, and they could also write sick leave permissions slips so that one could take some days off from work. 'To have an acquaintance in a pharmacy was of extreme importance. Pharmacies were specifically *blat* places. Often one couldn't get medicine there even with a prescription unless there was a contact. Doctors used to have contacts there, and I obtained medicines through a physician, for whom I had repaired a tape-recorder, many times.' [38] This applied to spheres much less serious than health:

> One doesn't want to run the risk of seeing the first person one comes across in a hospital or even in a hairdressing salon. One goes to those recommended by friends. If one respects oneself, one has to have one's own dentist, gynaecologist, hairdresser, masseuse, tailor. If these are friends, it's the best. It is much more pleasant to socialise than just to get rude service. [13]

*Blat* referred not only to goods and services as such but also to their quality. By *blat* one received a service for free, or for the usual price, and of a higher quality and without waiting. Goods and services of more prestige, of better quality and more variety, at lower prices, were the desired 'objects' in *blat* transactions.

### Obtaining housing and household upkeep

Most urban housing in Russia was allocated either by local Soviets or by one's work unit. Through state subsidies, rents were kept very low, so that rents were a relatively minor proportion of a household's income. Housing was always in short supply. Regardless of whether one obtained an apartment from one's own work unit or from the local Soviet, the practice of *blat* enabled one to attain success in a shorter time. In situations of choice, for example, in the distribution of apartments, the one allocated by *blat* would be of better location, with a telephone, etc. To have a private telephone line was a particular privilege; it was normally supplied to those occupying high professional positions or had to be arranged by *blat*.

For house repairs, dacha and garage construction, one also had to establish and maintain good connections. The difficulty of obtaining a prestigious place for a dacha or garage was insurmountable without connections: 'Formally, permits for construction were given by dacha or garage cooperatives, but in fact informal relations with a chairman or a powerful member of the neighbourhood could settle the problem. The construction materials could always be bought at the price of a substandard product, if there were contacts.' [11]

### Enjoying leisure activities

Everything connected with leisure activities required *blat* contacts. Booking places in prestigious resorts and medical resorts, tickets (train, airplane) for travelling, tickets to concert halls and performances were obtained through *blat* channels: 'To look at the audience at premieres in the popular theaters or guest performances, a large proportion of those sitting at the best places were tradespeople. One couldn't buy these seats, they were distributed by *blat*.' [26] 'The demand for culture was enormous, every week I obtained theatre tickets for somebody. Not only tickets, but free passes. This was a regular activity,' remarked a journalist writing on culture. [29a]

People with a hobby had to be and still must be well-connected: 'I obtained books and music for people. These were not easy things to obtain but I had my own contacts. Now one can buy almost everything. Then every popular record was in short supply.' [16]

One of the most prestigious activities was going abroad as a tourist. *Blat* was needed to get a place in a tourist group, permission from one's organisation and to get to the top of the waiting list for a travel passport: 'A tourist tour was the only way to go abroad and see the world but it also improved one's material wealth. With currency supplied for a tourist trip one had the possibility to bring back prestigious clothes and consumer durables, which created another stimulus to go.' [26] Those people who were in charge of distribution of such opportunities became frequent targets of *blat* overtures.

In the Soviet system one could achieve a decent life-style for no money. This was predicated upon either privileges or *blat* connections – not only because everything was in short supply, but also because some activities, connected with the use of state property, could not be bought in principle:

> Money could not have been possibly involved. My father could never have afforded his hobby to hunt from a helicopter, which he did every year. It was only possible through connections. There were three other bosses and the chairman of the airport who went altogether. They were friends but also interrelated in their work. So they always had a chance to be useful to each other. [11]

*Obtaining employment, job transfers, and promotions*

*Blat* was often essential in getting a job. Transfers between organisations and promotion also presented difficulties, often solved by recourse to 'pulling connections'. Most problems of employment could be solved by *blat*:

> It is illegal but commonly known that pregnant women are not accepted for jobs. This is because an organisation has to pay maternity welfare and keep the place for her while she is on maternity leave. I arranged by *blat* that my pregnant wife was employed. Thus in my case the lawful decision was made by *blat*. [9]

'It was often the case that bosses receive their positions by *blat*. They were not necessarily the most competent specialists and skilful managers, which was a problem for other employees.' [31] *Blat* was never, however, sufficient in itself: '*blat* was necessary to obtain an employment or to have a promotion. But one had to prove oneself worthy of an appointment. In fact, *blat* was just a means of access, whereas everything else depended on one's abilities.' [13] *Blat* at work did not necessarily imply protection, however. The same respondent disclosed her horizontal contacts:

> In my post as secretary I could arrange a publication of an article, an introduction to useful people, etc. My job [organising conferences, events, etc.] demanded a lot of contacts everywhere. I would never have been able to organise conferences at Dagomys [a Black Sea resort], if my father had not worked there long ago and my friend did not work there now. To organise a conference one had be able to book hotels, conference premises, restaurants, banquet halls, etc. which was never possible without *blat*. [13]

*Bringing up children.*

*Blat* was essential for bringing up children. It is not only foodstuffs and children's goods which were always in great demand but in short supply. *Blat* was useful in getting a child into a nursery, especially into one with well trained staff and better facilities, or into a specialised school. At the stage of graduate exams or high school entrance examination those parents who did not have acquaintances to influence grades directly were involved in a search for a package of written examination papers: 'My father, a head of a taxi car park, was approached regularly by his friends, because everyone knew that my mother was a teacher of literature and I was excellent in writing

compositions.' [15] When the topics of examination papers were
announced by the Ministry of Education in Moscow, parents rang
Moscow or other Western cities to get know the examination topics
(because of the time lag the topics were known earlier there). At the
entrance exams *blat* was again needed. The efforts of parents could be
decisive in choosing between two students having the same grades.
The struggle for entrance into a high school was especially dramatic
for the parents of boys, hoping to exempt their sons from military
service (by regulation, students were freed from military service if
they were at high schools or universities with military departments).
In such high schools and universities the entrance examinations were
especially competitive.

The military were also a target for *blat*, for the difference between
conditions and terms of military service were considerable: 'I passed
my military service at a military plant in Leningrad, my native city.
We were allowed to go home every night. The director of the plant
called us "generals' sons" and we were treated correspondingly. I got
there by mistake, I guess, others told me that their parents paid a lot
or had good connections.' [8]

The contacts in police (*militsia*) were also important. If a child was
in trouble or there was a burglary or accident problem, one had to
have contacts in the militia. Through militiamen other problems could
be settled, for they were basically in control of everything.

The least visible but most ubiquitous 'object' of a *blat* exchange was
information. It was information, more than anything else, that routinely maintained *blat* networks. Information was not only an 'object',
but also an indispensable channel for *blat* chains and *blat* networks. In
an economy of shortage, information on what, where or when could
be bought or who was to be approached was very important.

## On the definition of *blat*

Given the multiplicity of its use-contexts, *blat* is not easy to define:
'*Blat* seems an obvious word, it does not need definition,' remarked
one respondent. Interestingly, everybody knows what *blat* is about but
few grasp its essence. One reason is that the term means different
things in different contexts, irreducible to some common ground: *blat*
is an acquaintance or friend through whom you can obtain some
goods or services in short supply, cheaper or better quality. Also, *blat*
is a reciprocal relationship which people call '*Ty – mne, ya – tebe*' (You
help me, I help you). *Blat* is about using informal contacts, based on

mutual sympathy and trust – that is, using friends, acquaintances, occasional contacts. *Blat* also takes place where one arranges a good job for another, or where, on otherwise equal conditions, the one who is known or recommended gets chosen. Sometimes *blat* means influence and protection, all kinds of 'umbrellas' (*kryshi*), using big names – so-called 'I am from Ivan Ivanovich ' – introductions. Facing this variety of contexts in which *blat* or *'po blatu'* is considered a relevant term, one faces the question what are the shared characteristics of situations referred to as being solved 'by *blat*'. The question cannot, however, be answered satisfactorily because it is often the case that some characteristics present in one case are lacking in another: for instance, getting access to goods and services in short supply is different from getting access to positions providing income (jobs or educational courses). The variety in regularity of favours, kind of relationship between the parties, type of need, character of reciprocity, participation of an intermediary makes *blat* situations almost irreducible to any clear-cut classification. Rather, these situations are tied together in the way which is best grasped by the notion of 'family likeness' or 'family resemblance' enunciated by Wittgenstein in his *Philosophische Grammatik* (1969: 75, 118, hereafter *PG*) and developed in the *Blue Book* (1958, hereafter *BB*). Entities which we commonly subsume under a general term, Wittgenstein wrote, need not have anything in common:

> they form a family the members of which have family likenesses. Some of them have the same nose, others the same eyebrows and others again the same way of walking; and these likenesses overlap. The idea of a general concept being a common property of its particular instances connects up with other primitive, too simple, ideas of the structure of language. (*BB* 17, see also *BB* 87, 124, *PI* 1, 67)

In what follows I shall explicate a range of such family features which may not be available in every particular *blat* situation but which altogether can be associated with *blat* practices.

First, *blat* is a distinctive form of non-monetary exchange, a kind of barter based on personal relationship. It worked where money did not. In the planned economy, money did not function as the main element in economic transactions, things were sorted out by mutual help, by barter. In his autobiographical story, an émigré Soviet writer described his temporary position on the editorial board of a journal as a source for such exchanges:

I finally realised what kept these capable people on the editorial board. One would think why they need all this? Superfluous efforts, troubles, administrative cares. Only for 250 humble rubles? Why not just write books? It is not as simple as that. The journal – is a kind of property, currency, an exchange fund. We publish *N* from another journal. *N* publishes us . . . Or pays compliments to our work in the party regional committee . . . Or does not criticise . . . We give a possibility of earning to *B*. *B* in his turn . . . And so on . . . *C* was responsible for the business trips abroad. *D* brought me batteries for my transistor radio. *E* arranged a swimming pool for my daughter . . . Things went on and on. (Dovlatov 1993: 79)

Thus, apart from official rations and privileges allocated by the state distribution system to different occupational strata, every employee had a particular kind of access (*dostup*) which could be traded in *blat* relations. The relative unimportance of money in the command economy brought into being this specific form of exchange, intermediary between commodity exchange and gift-giving.

The objects obtained in *blat* relationships were rarely exchanged in a straightforward manner. It should be emphasised that *blat* involved relationships and not merely goods. The *blat* favours bear, as it were, a non-alienable character. They are marked by the personal stamp of the donor. This can be best imagined as the occasional lending or borrowing of one's access (*dostup*) but the access itself is never alienable. Just as in gift exchange, where debt cannot be paid by a different kind of gift, a received favour is never equivalent to that which the recipient can provide in return. The original favour leaves a 'memory' even if an unlike return has been made. Thus, access could be 'lent', 'borrowed' or 'exchanged'. In this sense *blat* is a 'favour of access' (*usluga dostupa*) which someone chooses to provide.

Favours of access became possible because they demanded no one's own resources and were perceived as 'sharing', 'helping out', 'friendly support', 'mutual care', etc. Such help derived not from one's own pocket, but rather was given at the expense of state property or someone formally entitled to this resource. Sharing access with friends and acquaintances became so routine that the difference between *blat* and friendly relations became blurred: one almost became consequent upon the other. The use of public resources for private (even if not selfish) purposes reflected another paradoxical feature of the Soviet regime, the character of state property. State property was declared to be public and supposed to be guarded by everyone: the slogan 'Everyone – to guard public property!' (*Vse – na*

*okhranu obshchestvennoi sobstvennosti!*) was one of the most common.
But 'public' could also be interpreted as quasi-private, which was
grasped in the everyday sayings: '"public" means that part of it is
mine,' 'one has what one guards' (*'kto okhranyaet - tot imeet'*). The
trickle-down of public property, through the access provided by those
who 'guard' it, to a wider circle of people was a common practice,
either denied or sincerely 'misrecognised' by the rhetoric of mutual
help used to speak of personal relationships. Being not just mutual
help or friendly support but help given at the expense of the state or
others, *blat* therefore referred to a wider system of possibilities and to
one's influence within it.

The functioning of informal contacts and connections was predicated upon the structural characteristics of the Soviet-type system.
Soviet *blat* was similar to *guanxi* in China (Yang 1994) or *zalatwic
sprawy* in Poland (Wedel 1986) but had no direct analogy in the West.
One reason for this was that the use of informal channels in Soviet-
type society was not a matter of choice, it was an enforced practice
necessitated by perpetual conditions of shortage. One could argue
that not every society characterised by scarcity and shortage generated
*blat*, and this may be so. *Blat*-like phenomena resulted from the
particular combination of shortages and, even if repressed, consumerism; from a paradox between an ideology of equality and the
practice of differentiation through privileges and closed distribution
systems. In so far as those who had no privileges in the state
distribution system could by-pass rationing and queueing it had an
equalising as well as a stratifying effect. It therefore had a bearing on
the society's egalitarian claims and its actual inequalities.

*Blat* was oriented to different needs in different historical periods (it
was already flourishing in the 1930s) but it always – directly through
obtaining goods and services or indirectly through obtaining jobs and
status – related to personal consumption and thus the distribution of
material welfare: '*Blat* was simply a necessity for a decent life. You
couldn't eat or wear what you bought in the shops, everything was in
short supply, queueing and bad quality of services were appalling. To
live normally, one *had to* have acquaintances and informal access to
every sphere where needs arose,' many respondents remembered.
*Blat* therefore became an everyday pattern of behaviour and mentality,
penetrating personal relationships, such as friendship, etc. and
shaping specific attitudes towards legality.

Another characteristic feature of *blat* was that it remained 'misrecognised' in one's own case, but could easily be recognised in the case

SHAME?

of the other. While practising *blat*, which was, in a sense, a necessity for everyone, people refrained from declaring it. They knowingly or unknowingly withdrew the term from describing their own contacts and personal relations while the informal contacts of other individuals or groups were described in such a way. Personal contacts through which a formal procedure was circumvented, or access to public resources received, could not be seen by participants themselves as *blat* relations, because they were either personal and already perceived as kin, intimate or friendly relations or mediated by them. These were the relations in which *blat* was embedded and which made it 'mis-recognisable' for those involved.

In contrast to personal relations and simple barter, *blat* relations were not necessarily dyadic. *Blat* transactions could be circular: *A* provided a favour to *B*, *B* to *C*, *C* to *D*, and *D* to *A*, and the last chain might not have taken place. What was important is that there had to be no immediate repayment – reciprocity was to be masked by the delayed return. Mediated favours were even more efficient for avoiding practical and social constraints against immediate repayment. Psychologically, mediation was very important because 'it was terribly difficult to ask on behalf of oneself. It was much easier to ask for a friend, or for an institution, just to put in a word for somebody'. It looked respectable when an intermediary asked to help somebody 'unselfishly', or when a donor helped an unknown person just for the sake of the relationship with the intermediary. Everyone helped 'unselfishly' but this constructed an efficient system called '*blat*' by outsiders.

To summarise all these features, I offer the following working definition of *blat*:

*Blat* was an exchange of 'favours of access' in conditions of shortages and a state system of privileges.

A 'favour of access' was provided at the public expense.

It served the needs of personal consumption and reorganised the official distribution of material welfare.

*Blat* exchange was often mediated and covered by the rhetoric of friendship or acquaintance: 'sharing,' 'helping out,' 'friendly support,' 'mutual care,' etc. Intertwined with personal networks *blat* provided access to public resources through personal channels.

The resemblance of *blat* and some other ways of circumscribing formal procedures – manipulating access to resources through direct purchase as in bribery or diverting of state property for personal profit – makes *blat* a member of a wider family of informal practices and complicates the matter of drawing the boundaries between them.

The problem can be exemplified with reference to another metaphor about 'family resemblance' discussed by Wittgenstein in his *Philosophische Grammatik* (1969: 75, 118): 'Think of ball games alone: some, like tennis, have a complicated system of rules; but there is a game consisting just in throwing the ball as high as one can, or the game which children play of throwing the ball and running after it. Some games are competitive, others not' (*PG* section 68).

This thought was developed in a famous passage of the *Philosophical Investigations* in which Wittgenstein denies that there was any feature – such as entertainment, competitiveness, rule-guidedness, skill – which formed a common element in all games: board games, card games, ball games, Olympic games, and so on. Instead we find a complicated network of similarities and relationships overlapping and criss-crossing (*PII*, sections 66–67). There is a family of informal practices among which *blat* is but one subfamily (e.g. ball games), itself consisting of the whole variety of ball skills and rules about them presented above. In chapter 2, I will consider whether it is possible to distinguish between *blat* and other informal practices and thus to clarify the boundaries of the phenomenon and find out more about its nature.

# 2 Understanding *blat*

## *Blat* and its extended family

I shall start with a discussion of the connections and contrasts between *blat* and other phenomena in Russia, such as bribery, corruption and the informal economic practices with which it is sometimes confused. The main difference derives from the fact that although *blat* was often associated with shady aspects of the state command system it had positive features which led to its acceptance and toleration. Embedded in 'human' relationships (friendship, kin relations, acquaintance), *blat* differed from more negative forms of exchange and power. On the other hand, it did have those negative overtones which distinguished it from mutual help or support in personal relations and made it closer to morally reprehensible practices. These negative connotations are rooted in the use of access to public resources for private, even if not selfish, benefit. Let me consider the distinctions of *blat* in more detail.

### *Bribery*

Certain criteria for a distinction between *blat* and bribery were suggested by Berliner (1957: 191). One element of difference appeared to be 'the nature of the entree into the arrangement'. In *blat* there is some personal basis for expecting a proposal to be listened to sympathetically, either because of past friendship, or because of the trust developed after a long business association (a subject–subject relation). In bribery it is only the offer of a bribe which links the two persons involved (an object–object relation). Hence bribery has a more cynical quality than *blat* and is a more dangerous practice. Bribe-giving should never be witnessed and does not imply trust or continuity in relations. Bribery is illegal according to a statute in the Criminal Code while *blat* is not mentioned at all. According to respondents who were asked how a person could accomplish a given end, *blat* was usually acknowledged to have high potential, whereas bribery was considered unsafe.

In contrast to bribery, *blat* is a matter of belonging to a circle. *Blat* favours are normally provided to *svoim* (people of the circle, one of us). In such long-term relations, all kinds of favours are possible and not normally paid for directly (*za mnoi ne propadet*). It is thus another difference between the two that a direct and immediate payment is usually implied in bribery, whereas in *blat* the reciprocation may or may not take place some time in the future and may take any form. In contrast to bribes, 'money etc. offered to procure action or decision in favour of the giver',[1] *blat* does not imply a straightforward offer and normally excludes money or any other immediate and equivalent repayment.

It should not be thought, as Crankshaw (1956: 74) observed, that

> *blat* has anything in common with simple bribery. It is essentially the product of an under-the-counter mentality which causes friends and acquaintances to combine together to defeat the shortages, and the unlimited, obstructive, entangling red tape of the bureaucratic machine. The motive is self-defense; and the most incorruptible individuals deal in it freely. There is no other way to come through in a land where there is still far from sufficient goods to satisfy all needs, even for a price. Straight bribery is quite another matter. *Blat* stands for the exchange of personal favours and is human and warm. Bribery stands for impersonal corruption.

Bribery implies a conflict of interests where one is to be 'compensated' for doing something one would not do otherwise, while *blat* is a form of cooperation and mutual support with a long-term perspective, implying trust rather than compensation for risk. In daily life, 'by *blat*' implies ordinary people using their contacts, which may be justified by the situation of urgent need and by their aims if they do not exceed modest norms of personal consumption, while 'bribery' implies a bribe-taker using their public office and their power for their own material gain, which is reprehensible.

It follows that *blat* and bribery have different implications for a person's self-image. In the case of bribery, one draws a profit (not necessarily pecuniary) from his or her position.[2] In cases of *blat*, even

---

[1] The *Concise Oxford Dictionary*, seventh edition. Oxford: Clarendon Press, 1982.
[2] *Vzyatka* (bribe) refers to somebody who *vzyal* (took a bribe), that is, somebody who is in a decision-making position, while if you have *blat* or you are *blatnoi* implies that you are well connected but not necessarily powerful yourself.

if the position is used, it is done not for immediate profit, but to help a friend, a relative or a good person, and the self-image is altruistic: 'It could be considered as bad by outsiders, but my conscience is clear. It is not like bribery, it is help. You help this person because you know well that she or he deserves it. I know this person won't get it without my help and I give him or her an opportunity,' said a high-status university boss. [36] A younger ex-academic, now a businessman, added:

> In *blat*, one's self-image is positive also because no money is involved. People often provide favours in anticipation of some return favours in order to create a certain image: 'no need to pay, it is a sign of friendship, no calculations between friends, I could be in the same situation myself, one day you'll prove useful.' [22]

*Blat* is more pervasive than bribery, for it penetrates spheres where money is not applicable (either because of an ethic of personal relationships, or because the favour is so petty or so large that it cannot be repaid). Within the same circle everything can be solved by *blat*, although to enter another circle one may need money, paid directly or through *blat* contacts. *Blat* is widespread both among the poor who have no money to pay premiums and among those who would not dare to receive a bribe, but would protect or promote someone or something by *blat*. For those who prefer to pay, *blat* is therefore restrictive. New businessmen seem annoyed:

> If it were possible to bribe, *blat* would not be necessary. You pay and get what you want. But there are spheres closed to bribery, and at a certain level *blat* is the only available means for getting what you want. Also, to give a bribe, one has to know whom to bribe and how much is to be given. Such information can only be obtained informally: to give a bribe one has to be recommended as a reliable person to guarantee the safety of a bribe-taker, that is, *blat* relations mediate bribery. [27]

One needs a chain of *blat* contacts to work out how and who has to be approached in every particular case. With good contacts bribery may not be necessary at all, everything can be decided by *blat*. If there are people in the chain who are not tied by close personal relations, a bribe may quite often be paid in some form. Thus, some links in the chain are *blat* ones, some must be paid off. The cases where *blat* approaches or mediates bribery create juridical problems as well as everyday confusion. This is but one reason why struggle against bribery and corruption cannot be fully effective – only one link (bribe-

**Table 2.1** *Bribery and* blat: *differences and similarities*

| Differences | Similarities |
|---|---|
| 1 No personal basis for a request, no continuity in relationship after transaction, no network | 1 Bribery sometimes makes use of *blat* channels |
| 2 Explicit exchange, usually immediate payment, money is normally involved | 2 Goods and services obtained by *blat* may involve extra payment |
| 3 More limited areas of application | 3 Areas of application may overlap, e.g. allocation of scarce resources (apartments, cars, etc.) |

giver–bribe-taker) in the chain is involved in the case while the greater part of it – to do with *blat* and personal networks – is not targeted.

To summarise (see table 2.1), *blat* is not based on immediate payment. Rather, it implies a personal basis for and continuity in relationships. *Blat* is embedded in personal networks and disguised by altruistic motives of friendly help. It is thus capable of pervading a wider range of areas of social life – people resisting bribery for ethical reasons would use their connections or 'help' their close people. The use of *blat* is less morally reprehensible and defended by the mechanisms of 'misrecognition'.

### 2.1.2 Corruption

Both in literature and conversations *blat* is often referred to as corrupt practice. This may be acceptable in everyday usage, but it is also misleading, for neither '*blat*' nor 'corruption' have an agreed meaning, nor are these terms independent of moral judgements. According to one of the basic approaches (Palmier, 1983), corruption is defined as the use of public office for private advantage (the latter term being understood not only in a pecuniary sense but also in terms of status and influence). However, as Friedrich (1966: 74–5), following Weber, has pointed out, the use of public office for private advantage is not always widely perceived in a given society as corrupt. Particularly if an individual making personal gains is simultaneously making a positive contribution to the society, many will see such actions as at least acceptable and sometimes even a 'just reward'. Thus although corruption usually implies a form of betrayal of public confidence, the significance of that betrayal can not be universally assessed. Because of the clash that can arise between an abstract definition of corruption and its application to a complex real world, some authors have distinguished between what can crudely be called 'good', 'bad' and 'ambiguous' – or white, black and grey – corruption (Heidenheimer 1970: 26–7).

According to Lampert (1984: 371), cases of corruption have a ranking specific to the society. The Soviets clearly felt that bribery and embezzlement on whatever scale were worse forms of corruption than small-scale use of public resources for private ends (such as using workers to do private jobs in enterprise time). This is in tune with the distinction drawn between various forms of corruption in the Criminal Code and the different penalties applied for engaging in them. *Blat* is not on the criminal scale at all and cannot strictly speaking be characterised as illegal (by reason of its small scale or recognised necessity), thus falling into the category of 'good' or 'ambiguous' corruption.

Scott (1972: 4) suggests defining corruption in Communist societies as: 'behaviour which deviates from the *formal* duties of a public role because of private-regarding (personal, close family, private clique) wealth or status gains; or violates rules against the exercise of certain types of private-regarding influence.' What is designated as 'private-regarding' here conceals a whole dimension of horizontal relations, such as kin and friendship or relations of mutual understanding (*voiti v polozhenie*), which are not necessarily self-oriented. These horizontal, non-hierarchical chains of relations also embrace *blat* relations, in which favours are done not for a material reward but for the sake of relationships: 'she is my friend', or 'he is a good man', 'he is one of us', or just because one cannot reject a request of an acquaintance. These relations imply non-bureaucratic, human codes of behaviour at any level of social hierarchy. These codes occur in a hierarchical, repressive or totalitarian system or under similar constraining conditions as compensatory codes or codes of hidden opposition. It is this horizontal dimension of personal relations with their internal codes that is overlooked in the analysis of corruption as a systematic phenomenon. Most corruption studies focus on bureaucracies, while *blat* is rather about common people. Concentrating on the phenomena of corruption, that is the advantages bureaucracy enjoys at the public expense, we leave out those informal practices which contribute to corruption without being identified as corrupt, as well as the advantages over the system gained by common people.

Western definitions of corruption can be very misleading when applied to Soviet conditions. Definitions focusing on public and private interests or purposes have to confront differences in the economic system and the system of property rights. As Lampert (1984: 370) concluded of the USSR: 'it is appropriate to interpret some typical abuses as "organisational" rather than "individual"; the purpose of illegal practices is to further the overall aims of the organisation, not the personal interests of individuals within it.' The distinction between the organisation and the individual, however, becomes blurred, both because organisational success will often lead to status and/or material rewards to the individual, and because individual offences may be rationalised in terms of 'good for the organisation'. It is this confusion of organisational and personal (which resulted from the ideological norm of self-identification with the purposes of the organisation, the Party, the Soviet state) that contributed to the creation of an appropriate environment for *blat*.

Another distinctive characteristic of corruption is what Palmier (1983: 208) calls 'moral condemnation'. A given act may not be clearly illegal, but if there is evidence that many people see it as improper (illegitimate), then such evidence is included in the analysis of corruption. As opposed to corruption, *blat* is related to mundane (and legitimate) favours. People were forced to engage in *blat* practices to obtain things which were legal to have – obtaining medicine for an ill person or sausages to feed a family, arranging places in schools and hospitals could not have been seen as improper. Similarly, enterprises had to obtain the resources to fulfil plan tasks, thus meeting the demands of the command economy through informal channels of *tolkachi* ('pushers' responsible for obtaining supplies so that the enterprise could meet the plan tasks). In this sense, the acceptance of *blat* or any form of economic informal practices was a forced necessity for people, and the morality of these practices was an issue only when one was not involved in them. A moral position which seems relevant for the case was expressed by Zinoviev:

> You, of course, will think that . . . the behaviour of [the] *Homososes*[3] in such a situation is amoral. But we look at it differently. It is easy to be moral if you live in conditions which do not force you into morally reprehensible actions. You are well fed and clothed; you

---

[3] *Homosos* is an abbreviation for Homo Sovieticus, a stereotypical Soviet person, outlined in *Homo Sovieticus* (Zinoviev 1985).

have a nice house with books and other ways of enjoying yourselves. And it seems to you that to be moral is natural and not in the least bit difficult . . . Everything is simple and clear-cut. But if a man finds himself below the bread-line, beneath the minimum that is indispensable if moral norms are to be considered applicable in real life, then it is senseless to apply moral criteria to his behaviour. A man in such a position is not only freed *ipso facto* from normal norms, he is freed from them by these moral concepts themselves. It is immoral to expect a man to be moral if he lacks the minimum living conditions that permit society to demand morality from him . . . *Homososes* are born, are educated and live in such conditions that it is just ridiculous to accuse them of immorality. (Zinoviev 1985: 48, 63)

In his study of corruption, Simis describes the activities of his friend, a lawyer, and his contacts named in a list of chores he had to get through a week (see figure 2.1). These cases, to do with everyday needs and necessities, are what is ordinarily called '*blat*'.

1. Food – Lyubov' Lazarevna
2 Dry cleaning – Big Lyuda
3 Toilet paper – Little Lyuda
4 Dostovesky – Olga Nikolaevna (candy)
5 Concert tickets – Irina Mikhailovna
6 Flowers – Ivan Kirillovich (bottle)

**Figure 2.1** Weekly *blat* chores

'For an old Muscovite like me,' writes Simis, 'it was easy to see that the left-hand column was the list of chores to be accomplished and on the right were the names of the people who helped my friend to circumvent the immense complexities presented in Moscow by each one' (Simis, 1982: 146–74). Simis explicates various strategies his friend applied in these situations: in the case of food or services – paying above the price, jumping the queue, going via the backdoor; in the case of books and tickets – greetings and gifts (French perfume or magnificent boxes of chocolates that you cannot buy in ordinary stores) several times a year on special occasions. By categorising *blat* as corruption, however, he ignores a distinction significant for a better understanding of *blat* practices. It is clear from the above examples that for some favours (concert tickets and a Dostoevsky volume) pecuniary return is not possible. Return favours, if any, are determined by the relationships with people providing the original favours. Some (particularly in trade) would value extra money, some would appreciate attention and socialising. The personal relations form a basis for *blat* relationships as

much as access provided by formal structures. The embeddedness of
*blat* in both formal institutions and informal relations constitutes its
essential nature. *Blat* is grounded not only in the use of one's position
or working place (which is implied in corruption) but also in personal,
often altruistic, incentives.

What is significant in Simis' argument is the idea of forced corruption for both those who give bribes and those who take them – the
very system of services (such as, for example, free medical care) forces
a patient to look for either personal contacts or possibilities of bribery
and a doctor to accept 'candy, perfume, caviar, sausages, meat and
anything else the patients can think of' (Simis 1982: 158). Structural
(both economic and cultural) forces or constraints of the Soviet overcontrolling centre resulted in flourishing *blat*: life became impossible
*unless* the rules were broken. Despite the extent and frequency of *blat*,
however, it received little formal acknowledgment. When publicised it
was treated as deviant acts of atypical people. In practice, the reverse
seemed nearer to truth – in many jobs indeed it was often abnormal
*not* to be involved in *blat*. Simis tried to identify the structural
conditions of the socialist system that brought these practices into
being.

In Soviet conditions *blat* and other informal activities can also be
considered as compensatory mechanisms against the planned
economy and ideological pressure against the legitimacy of private
gain. *Blat* articulated private interests and 'human' needs against the
rigid constraints of the State order, allowed people to meet harsh
conditions, to maintain their social comfort and enjoy a sense of
'beating the system'. *Blat* also implies a transgression of social
boundaries predetermined by the system, not least by redistributing
goods and services to which middle-ranking or senior officials of the
regime had nearly or totally exclusive access, such as foreign consumer goods, special shops, exclusive hospitals etc. to the less
privileged.

Despite the similarities between *blat* and corruption, *blat* is restricted by its domain of everyday life, unlike that of corruption to do
with politics and bureaucratic organisations (see table 2.2). Although
it implies access to public resources and so-called 'workplace crime',
as does corruption, *blat* is more legitimate, since it is oriented to
satisfying everyday needs and basic necessities. Recourse to *blat* is
normally enforced by hard conditions, inefficiency of formal procedures and the inability of state institutions to cope with day-to-day
demands. In contrast to corruption, *blat* derives from personal net-

**Table 2.2** *Corruption and* blat: *differences and similarities*

| Differences | Similarities |
| --- | --- |
| 1 Mainly involves misuse of high official positions | 1 Use of the workplace and influence over accessible resources |
| 2 Implies private wealth on a fairly substantial scale | 2 *Blat* falls into the category of 'good' or 'white' corruption |
| 3 Transactions concerned with elevating one's economic status above that of others | 3 Misrecognition is also characteristic of corruption |

works which govern, control and regulate *blat* on an ethical, rather than a legal, basis.

### *Informal economic practices*

Apart from being seen as corrupt, *blat* is also sometimes described in the literature as an economic practice. Most approaches to informal economies are oriented towards calculating the share of informal practices in national economies, as a drain of resources from the workplace, fiddling of all kinds. If mentioned in economic studies at all, *blat* is regarded a part of a broader phenomenon of the 'second economy' complementary to the Soviet central planning system. It is then considered in economic terms, that is, as a channel for the flow of resources from the formal into the informal economy, or as a way of gaining extra income. In this section, I shall consider what the differences between *blat* and informal economic practices are, and what they have in common. A discussion of research on the informal economy is also relevant for understanding the conditions under which *blat* developed and acquired its semi-legal status, and which necessitated its correlation with illegal economic practices.

The study of informal practices goes under a variety of names: 'submerged', 'parallel', 'hidden', 'informal', 'unofficial', 'underground', 'black', 'shadow', 'illegal' economy, etc. The most widespread term for Soviet-type economies is the 'second economy'. This derived mainly from the work of Grossman (1977), who used it to refer to economic phenomena 'ideologically alien to the Soviet system'. In particular, Grossman suggested that the second economy comprised production and exchange activities that fulfilled at least one of the two following tests: (1) being directed for private gain, (2) being in some significant respect in knowing contravention of existing laws (1977: 25). Although this definition has proved useful, there is something inherently unsatisfactory in its combination of two quite disparate elements: private gain and illegality. Apart from this, the term 'second economy' seems strictly divided from the 'first economy' – a distinction which in fact does not exist – on the one hand, and from non-economic aspects of analysis, necessary for the analysis of *blat*, on the other.

Gabor (1979: 292–3) defines the second economy as 'activity aimed at earning and redistributing income outside socially organised production and distribution'. In this sense, the second economy comprises all those activities for the production of income that escape the direction and control of the state and are performed by families or individuals independently from the organisations of the socialist sector. Although *blat* is not 'an activity for the production of income', it is an activity aimed at redistributing socially organised access to resources, rewards and privileges through individual or family channels, and thus indirectly connected with 'the non-regulated aspects of activity within state- and cooperative-operated organisations and all forms of private, semi-legal and illegal activity'. This definition of the second economy includes, apart from the regular private sector, 'not officially recorded' activities in the private sector itself, earnings deriving from tips and other types of undeclared remuneration, the clandestine use – including theft – of state property (raw materials, semi-finished articles, machinery, spare parts, finished products, labour, services) for personal advantage and, finally, illegal financial and commercial transactions.

The term 'economic activities' displays some inherent vagueness not only in respect to *blat*. For example, the regular and routine theft of liquid fuel by professional drivers, who resell it to private car owners, is a well known phenomenon in Russia. It should be regarded as an economic activity which forms part of the second economy. The occasional theft of a can of fuel by a bystander is not an economic activity, although the totality of all such thefts will have a measurable effect on the economy. From the perspective of *blat*, the same transaction has to be viewed in terms of relations between a professional driver and a private car owner. It can occur between relatives without any visible payment, between friends it can be paid off symbolically by a bottle of vodka. In this sense, the study of *blat* provides a way of understanding the situation in terms of participants, to find out their 'non-economic' reasons. As Douglas (1978: 6) put it: 'there is a link between the social environment of jobs and what can be called their cosmology – that is, the ideas, values, attitudes and beliefs that are appropriate to them. People at work or elsewhere need a fit between what they do and the justifications, explanations and excuses they can give for doing it.'

It would not be, therefore, helpful to use a terminology that refers primarily to the legal character of the activities concerned. In other words, 'black market', 'illegal economic activities', and similar designations are unsuitable. The economic activities of the informal economy, such as selling goods and making garments, are legal, but carried out illegally by avoiding one or more applicable state regulations. It is worth mentioning that the common element in the provisions in the Soviet Criminal Code directed against specific economic activities was that they covered activities that are legal and universal in most countries and times and in which people will engage more or less spontaneously as long as they are not specifically prevented from doing so. The most important among these were the provisions of the Criminal Code against speculation (article 154), the exercise of forbidden professions (article 162), commercial middlemen (article 153) and foreign trade transactions and foreign currency speculation (article 88) (Feldbrugge 1989: 301). The term 'speculation' in this context may be misleading because the Criminal Code defined speculation as buying and selling with the purpose of making profit. The various offences known as 'official crimes' (articles 170–175 of the Criminal Code) received their peculiar Soviet colouring from the fact that there was no private sector in the Soviet economy, in education, services, and so on. Therefore, almost anybody in any position of authority in Soviet society was an official.

In a state-controlled economy of the Soviet type, state property was omnipresent, and every working citizen was in direct contact with it at her/his place of work. Most reliable sources agree that theft of socialist (state) property was almost as widespread as state property itself (see p.136 on theft in *kolkhozy*). A comparatively innocent and universal form of it was the taking home of small quantities of goods, or goods of little value, such as tools or materials, stationery, etc. At a more serious level, there was the more substantial theft of building materials by persons who had access to them, especially store attendants and transportation workers. These phenomena are known as *vynos* (siphoning off, carrying out or diversion of state property). These are covered by another general practice of *pripiski*, whereby truck drivers, for example, systematically falsify their fuel consumption sheets and dispose of the surplus through routine channels. Store personnel, particularly in shops selling clothing and foodstuffs, were traditionally low paid. They would supplement their incomes by putting aside part of the store supplies to be sold from under the counter. In these various manifestations of *vynos* theft was usually, but not always, the central offence. The most characteristic element of *vynos* was that goods belonging to the state were diverted from their official destination by persons who had some amount of control over these goods and who re-routed these goods to other sectors of economy. Thus, managers and other high-ranking staff of an enterprise might have houses or dachas built by enterprise personnel and from materials belonging to the enterprise. Or such work might be carried out by friendly business partners. To get something done through these channels would be called *blat* in everyday life, and it is the task of this study to find the cultural roots of these phenomena.

From a legal perspective, *blat* could be most adequately viewed as 'anti-systemic' behaviour (Wiles in Feldbrugge 1989: 305), which is not to be branded as unlawful (against the law), but as unjust towards the others or, perhaps, simply contrary to the prevailing system. Or it could be referred to as 'semi-legal' activity. Generally speaking, this term may be applied to activities and transactions that contain an element of illegality but for one reason or another do not attract serious governmental repression. Although those in informal activities are frequently harassed, informal practices as a whole tend to develop under the auspices of government tolerance. Governments tolerate and even stimulate informal practices as a way to resolve potential social conflicts or to promote political patronage. The transaction may have been on behalf and in the interest of a state enterprise; it may have been private and legal but unrecorded and thereby in avoidance of taxation; or it may have been officially encouraged but lacking a firm basis in law. A well known example of the first category is the practice of *tolkachi* (pushers) already mentioned. The second category embraces the letting of apartments and holiday houses, private tuition, paid services by doctors, dentists, nurses, lawyers (although such services are in principle available free of charge), and numerous other privately produced services. *Blat* practices do not appear in such a categorisation, rather these practices are about networks, channels and ways through which all these operations are accomplished. *Blat* is thus not in the list, but in fact shapes most of transactions which can be placed in the second economy.

The availability of resources and goods to some economic agents and consumers and not to others fosters the growth of an 'irregular market' for their exchange. This market is irregular, either because it entails corruption or because it discriminates among purchasers in terms of availability, quantity or price of the goods traded; or else because it is not open to all on an equal footing but restricted to a more or less extended group of people with special characteristics (acquaintances, relatives, those willing to pay a 'bonus' on top of a price, provide other scarce articles or to grant favours). These aspects are not readily grasped by quantitative methods, but rather lend themselves to analysis in terms of social and cultural context. The latter are predicated upon the role of *blat* as a way of life and an economic necessity, the importance of contacts in certain areas and for certain activities, and the population's distrust of the state and the government: a distrust which, in their eyes, legitimates *blat*. In this sense, the lines of analysis of *blat* and other informal practices correspond: these phenomena are not exceptional but endemic; not marginal but integral to organisation and the rewards of work.

It should also be emphasised that, contrary to informal economic practices, *blat* practices relied on unwritten laws according to which 'by *blat*' ways were normal and unproblematic. No analysis of such unwritten codes is available. The fact that the informal economy makes use of non-contractual but binding relationships, for which kinship is often the base, is difficult to represent in quantitative economic analysis. Families often find in the informal economy the flexibility and accessibility that the formal economy does not have. By pooling resources, by engaging in informal practices, by self-provisioning, and by the skilful use of social networks and families, it can be argued, people avoided entrapment in the Soviet regime. They became actors who engaged in relations with others to get what they can out of the existing system.

To conclude, *blat* cannot be adequately grasped in terms of informal economic practices (see table 2.3). It implies ties of reciprocity within personal networks, rather than profit-oriented activities and market-type exchanges, on which informal economic practices are often based. The study of *blat* therefore requires a socio-cultural analysis of personal relationships and their impact on *blat* exchanges (see chapter 5).

**Table 2.3** *The second economy and* blat: *differences and similarities*

| Differences | Similarities |
|---|---|
| 1 Runs counter to the law | 1 Both are non-regulated activities |
| 2 A regular activity for the production of income | 2 Use of access to state property and public resources |
| 3 Based on economic exchange (rather than ties of reciprocity) and implies a 'market' for such exchanges (rather than networks) | 3 Both practices are functional in some ways and subversive in others |

To summarise the relation between *blat* and other related practices presented in tables 2.1–2.3, *blat* should be viewed as:

(1) less morally reprehensible and therefore more pervasive than any of these other practices;

(2) a specific form of social relationship embedded in personal (horizontal, non-hierarchical, compassionate and warm) networks;

(3) a culturally grounded pattern of mentality and behaviour, a form of exchange based upon certain ethical and cultural codes;

(4) in some ways quite specific to the Soviet system and therefore not amenable to explication apart from such characteristics as perennial shortage and the state system of distribution.

### *Blat* and its further relatives

I lack space here to consider all of the extended family of *blat* – its 'relatives in the West', such informal practices as 'patronage' in Italy, 'pilfering', 'fiddling' and 'old-boy' networks in England, 'skimming' or 'gypping' in the USA, *'le piston'* in France or 'plug in' in Spain. It would also be a daunting task to consider differences and similarities between *blat* and the ways connections work in the West. Every society has its specific patterns of conduct in these poorly explored matters. Not enough research has been carried out internationally to make such a comparison possible. On the other hand, it is important to discuss this, because every reader will make such comparison in his or her mind when reading the book. In this section I will focus on patronage and fiddling in Western societies.

*Patron–client relationship*

The role of personal relations in formal institutions is strongly emphasised in studies of patronage. 'Patronage' may be defined as a political system based on personal relations between unequals. Clients offer patrons their political support and also deference, expressed in variety of symbolic forms (gestures of submission, language of respect, gifts and so on). For their part, patrons offer clients hospitality, jobs and protection. There are, however, some difficulties inherent in the notion of a patronage system. Some degree of patronage exists in every society, however 'modern'. In societies where 'bureaucratic' norms are weak and 'vertical solidarity' particularly strong, the social order may be described as based on a patronage system. However, the assumption that the links between patron and client are fundamental encourages the observer not to notice horizontal solidarities or conflicts between rulers and ruled.

The intersection of institutional hierarchies and personal relationships within patronage systems is relevant for the analysis of *blat*. Different approaches to the question of patronage see these in varying ways. For anthropologists the relations between patrons and clients are viewed either as a particular type of social relation between two individuals taking the form of a contract, exchange in a dyad (Scott 1972), or a result of particular political and economic conditions under which people are operating. In each of these senses patronage is interesting for the present study. In contrast, political scientists have regarded patronage as an attribute of the political system and have shown less interest in the internal structure of such relations (see, for example, Weingrod 1968; Willerton 1992). Political science focuses primarily on political machines – patronage as a mode of political organisation, or party-oriented patronage. Here clients are no longer individuals but social or territorial groups which trade off their votes for the resources the party machine provides.

Some *blat* transactions may look similar to the relations of clients with those above them creating chains of patronage and networks of influence, but *blat* is normally a relation of equal parties, no matter what the official position of each is and to what kind of hierarchies they belong. It is a basic principle of *blat* chains that the relations in dyadic links are horizontal, but they can yield favours not readily available through primary horizontal contacts. The search for an appropriate intermediary, setting informal contexts and establishing friendly contacts are thus distinctive features of *blat* (the role of vodka as lubricator of *blat* relations is often emphasised: Dallin 1951; Douglas 1988).

The following examples given by Boissevain from his research in Sicily (1966) can be used to demonstrate the similarities and dissimilarities between *blat* and patronage. A student needing permission to get his thesis accepted after the closing date used intermediaries to obtain an introduction to the appropriate professor. In Russia this would be a typical *blat* situation. The following comment on the return of the favour that 'student promised to help the professor's electoral campaign and in return his thesis was accepted and he passed his examination' constructs the case of patronage (Boissevain 1974: 150–3). Another example is of an older man who wanted a job in his town's council offices. The appointment was approved by the town council but had to be confirmed by a provincial committee. In order to secure confirmation the man applied to his commanding officer from army days, and to a lawyer: these two applied 'pressure' to the members of the provincial committee, and the man got his job (Boissevain 1966: 27; 1974: 159–60). These cases are identical with what would be seen as the use of *blat* in Russia. It is always the case that an agreement is mediated by the present ('Here is a friend of my friend of my friend') or absent ('I am from Ivan Ivanovich' or by the preliminary telephone call of Ivan Ivanovich himself) party whose personal influence is involved when one's own is not enough.

Viewed within the political context, however, the dissimilarities come to the fore: Boissevain places these examples in the context of electoral and voting support. *Blat* in Soviet conditions cannot, strictly speaking, be regarded as a patron–client relationship. Let us emphasise here just one reason why the terms of patronage can hardly be relevant for Soviet conditions. In circumstances with no free interplay of political power, party-directed patronage involving the repayment of goods and services in return for electoral votes is out of the question. According to Tarkowski who summarises an analogous Polish experience of patron–client relationships, patrons at the party level do not obtain any tangible advantages from the benefits they confer. The motives inclining patrons to act are found in the psychological make-up of patrons and in the cultural norms of the society. These involve the display of respect, recognition and gratitude paid to the patron, receptions given in their honour. At times patrons are given presents (there was a special museum of presents given to Stalin). It would be erroneous, however, to treat these presents as repayment for services rendered (Tarkowski, 1981: 182). According to

Tarkowski's analysis, they are rather symbolic tokens, in much the same way as a box of chocolates or a bottle of cognac given to doctors for a successful operation or particular care and attention. In these cases, it is not the present but the sentiment that counts.

As a political arrangement, patronage is extremely significant in the Mediterranean region as it is based on the personalisation of political institutions and mediates formal state authority. Submission to a patron in order to gain access to resources is regarded as more common and widespread than bureaucracy, or fascism, or communism, or any of the varieties of democracy: it can exist without any of them, and coexists with all of them. It is argued to be a *sui generis* mode of political representation (Davis 1977: 146). The hard core of patronage, Davis comments, is a contractual act of submission which has chameleon characteristics, taking shape as well as colouring from its surroundings. Moreover it affects more areas of life than formal politics or bureaucracy do. All these features seem similar to the characteristics of *blat* and thus can be taken into account. *Blat* is, however, a matter of personal consumption or personal demands, and thus marginal to the political sphere.

From an anthropological perspective, patronage is sometimes said to be an extension of friendship or kinship or some spiritual relation. What is similar between *blat* and patronage is that the resources obtained through patrons do not belong to them personally but constitute public property. In patronage the access to resources can be gained by exerting moral pressure from below – the pressures of acceptance, deference, friendliness, etc. This kind of relationship has been thoroughly analysed by Mediterranean ethnographers (Davis, 1977), and also researchers of the European and the Third World varieties of political clientelism (Clapham 1982; Eisenstadt and Lemarchand 1981). Studies of Mediterranean patronage emphasise a series of restrictions imposed by clients on their patron's use of power: it may be real, fictitious or spiritual kinship (friendship). In some communities all these are available to clients; in others, some may be conventionally excluded. This is an expansion of Bailey's point that 'it is the supplicant who seeks to make the relationship diffuse: to make it a moral relationship . . . because it is in his interest to do so' (1966: 395). When there are no adequate bases for social obligations the ties are created through spiritual kinship, gift-giving or friendship (Campbell 1964: 246). Friendship is initiated and maintained by a continuing exchange of favours and goods, which are carefully noted. Berliner provides a similar observation in his study of

Table 2.4 *Patronage and* blat: *differences and similarities*

| Differences | Similarities |
|---|---|
| 1 Form of political order grounded in personalisation of political institutions | 1 Both involve institutional positions and personal relations |
| 2 Based on vertical type of relationships | 2 Both provide a favour of access to public resources |
| 3 Implies personal favours in return for electoral or voting support, in order to achieve political ends | 3 Both imply informal influence and power of the recipient |
| 4 Patrons are not associates by choice as *blat* partners | |

Soviet managers (1957: 192): 'although friendship is considered the basis of *blat*, great care is often taken in cultivating the friendship by means of little gifts.'

Gaining access to resources usually coexists with other forms of patronage (for example, moral support or defence), and is influenced by them: that is to say that while the content of patronage varies, naturally enough, with the kinds of resources which are at stake, it varies, too, with the general political context in which it exists (Davis 1977: 134). Even though patronage makes use of personal relations for political ends in a similar way as *blat* does for personal consumption their implications are different. In patronage it is the political power of the stronger that is controlled by the weak, in *blat* often equal parties exchange their access to resources for personal needs. The emphasis on political and hierarchical aspects of patronage systems, the view of patronage as a personalisation of political institutions therefore determines its difference from *blat*.

Finally, there is a certain difference 'in the flavour' of both practices. *Blat* can be recognised by the flavour of 'beating the system' in which being smart and efficient, people cooperate and try alternative ways and possibilities. In a patronage system there is no alternative, for patrons are the system itself. Mingioni suggested that it is a more feudal-type relationship in which everything is supposed to be gained from the same patron. Change of patrons or avoidance of dealing with a patron are penalised.[4] In *blat* there is no such strictly inflicted

---

[4] Comments from Enzo Mingioni and Jonathan Gershuny given at the Colloquium 'Informal/Expolary Economies', Moscow, 10–14 January 1997.

obligations. It is based on free associations of agents in which sanctions are imposed by 'people of the circle' where one wants to belong rather than 'family' where one belongs with no choice.

### Fiddling

In this section I will consider the logic of fiddling which seems similar to the logic of *blat* in several aspects. First of all, both practices occur in hard living conditions. In his analysis of fiddling, Ditton (1977: 14) expresses some understanding and sympathy for 'fiddlers' stemming from consideration of their harsh employment conditions. He tries to explain that good people do dirty work not because they are really bad people, but because, under the circumstances, dirty work is what good people do. Describing a group of salesmen who break the law by overcharging customers, and yet at the same time believe themselves to be ordinary, good citizens, Ditton comes to the conclusion that such divisions are false. He refers to our ability, as Mead (1934: 142) puts it, to 'divide ourselves up in all sorts of different selves with reference to our activities'. The identity develops separately from the real 'me' that each person constructs out of work hours, and as 'elementary self' is not aggregated with other moral experiences in the production of a 'complete' self. Thus, fiddling is an activity supported by the part-time self at work, and thus has auxiliary or *partial* status in the development of each person's identity (see pp.59–63 below on the 'misrecognition game'). Ditton emphasises one irreversible effect, however: once he has fiddled, the salesman can never look at the world in quite the same way again. He may stop fiddling, but he cannot stop knowing about it (Ditton 1977: 20). Mars (1982) has also shown how deep fiddling penetrated into workers' culture: 'It influence[d] their relationships with one another and with their wives, affected their reputation in the town's wider community and predetermined reaction to changes in technology and work organisation when these affected their access (to cargo). Fiddling was often the key factor in appreciating many of the difficulties in industrial relations.'

Fiddling was not the anarchic behaviour of a lawless rabble, but was subject to rules. People never just grabbed what they could from whomsoever they could. There were always rules that governed limits and amounts, rules about who could be fiddled and who not; and rules about who could be incorporated and who must be excluded. Following Henry (1978) and Ditton (1977), Mars (1982) provided a

**Table 2.5** *Fiddling and* blat: differences and similarities

| Differences | Similarities |
|---|---|
| 1 A regular economic activity, aimed at material gain | 1 Normally forced by hard (working or living) conditions and thus legitimised by necessity |
| 2 Does not imply reciprocity, no non-material favours involved | 2 The 'covert reward system', social satisfaction from 'beating the system' |
| 3 No personal basis in relationships | 3 Misrecognition |

neat and helpful means of understanding the motives, opportunities and consequences of fiddling in different occupations. Mars' main emphasis was on the study of occupations and on the hidden benefits normally obtainable in them – the 'covert reward systems'. The rewards that derive from alternative economic activity are distinct from official rewards, they are allocated outside the official system and do not appear in official returns. They often involve a higher degree of social satisfaction than is derived from the same activities carried out for formal rewards (Henry 1978). The economic component of this reward is often less than would be expected from official work, it is likely to involve an element of reciprocity – doing favours, swapping services – so that the high expense or scarcities or bureaucratic complexities inherent in obtaining official provision can be overcome by mutual cooperation. It may also be characterised by an exchange of obligation or increased prestige in return for economic benefit (Henry 1978; Mars 1982).

Fiddling can be, and usually is, a pleasurable departure from routine and an implicit challenge to authority. When a worker feels that he or she is beating the system, and is in control of his or her fate, the rewards are more than monetary. Another non-material reward enjoyed by fiddlers is status in the eyes of contacts and friends. By getting services or goods cheaply, a network member can demonstrate that he belongs to a group of people 'in the know' who have influence and the ability to get things done – a point well demonstrated by Henry (1978: 34). The flavour of violating the rules and 'beating the system' is thus not only a Soviet-type 'double-think' product. It is also confirmed by ethnographers of fiddling that there is nothing controversial in the morality of those involved in it – they sincerely misrecognise the 'fiddle' and view their ways as the only ones possible.

Many other comparative aspects still await their researcher, while I move on to the last aspect of the conceptualising of *blat* and undertake to show why such a pervasive phenomenon was left unanalysed.

### Misrecognition of *blat*

In this section I will argue that it is the misrecognised character of *blat* that accounts for its pervasiveness, on the one hand, and the lack of attention to it, on the other. A conceptual idea of 'misrecognition' first formulated by Pierre Bourdieu in his critique of economic or objectivist explanations of gift exchange, helps to clarify this point. According to Bourdieu's account, though objectivist explanations uncover the underlying structure of strictly-enforced equivalent exchange present in every act of voluntary gift-giving, they miss the fact that:

> gift exchange is one of the social games that cannot be played unless the players refuse to acknowledge the objective truth of the game, the very truth that objective analysis brings to light, and unless they are predisposed to contribute, with their efforts, their marks of care and attention, and their time, to the production of collective *misrecognition*. (Bourdieu 1990: 105)

In other words, if gift-givers openly acknowledge that they are involved in equivalent exchange, and that they expect something of equivalent value in return, this is no longer gift-giving. In the case of *blat*, misrecognition is not collective in the same sense. As in gift exchange, misrecognition of *blat* is normal for the participants, who often practise *blat* while recognising it as 'helping out'. From the perspective of an observer, the deal is recognised as *blat*. Perpetual switching of perspectives enables one to engage in *blat* practices and at the same time to distance oneself from them.

The complexity of the *blat* 'misrecognition game' cannot be fully grasped by Bourdieu's concept of misrecognition, where even being outside of the gift exchange transaction, a member of a community would admit that it is a gift that has been given. As not all individuals accept the internal rhetoric of *blat* relations, the misrecognition game is incomplete. The fact that people could question *blat* and recognise it indicates that this did not endanger the foundation of community –

that is, there was no universally shared sense of 'honour' involved in *blat*. Attitudes to *blat* varied a lot. The practical implications and strategies of misrecognition were dependent upon the situation itself (type of need, social context and outcome), personal dispositions, social background and occupation of the actor, as well as broader social and political contexts. To analyse these multiple possibilities the notion of 'misrecognition' has to be elaborated further. Misrecognition of *blat* should be understood as a phenomenon (with reference to different strategies of misrecognition) bound with a system of denial, a system of ambivalence and a system of power.

### Misrecognition as a system of denial

The system of denial is based on a contradiction between what one sees in other people as an observer and in oneself as a participant. Some respondents were quite straightforward, saying basically 'if *I* do it, it is not *blat*'. The negative character of the term '*blat*' facilitated its denial even if the fact of providing or receiving a favour was accepted: 'In my environment [nomenklatura] this word is a bit critical. If we do a favour, we do not call it *blat*; [34] 'I can't do anything by *blat*. If I do something, it is not by *blat*. [11] In this sense, *blat* is like 'gift-giving' where a 'gift' is recognised to be reciprocal, with a difference that in recognition of the reciprocal nature, 'gift' is deprived of its positive charge while '*blat*' retains its negative meaning. The negative character of the term introduces a new element in the misrecognition game: it can be recognised in the case of the other, and misrecognised in one's own case. *Blat* communities suppress the use of '*blat*' and prefer 'we are friends' terminology. They cannot stop outsiders, however, from noticing '*blat* ties'. Involvement in *blat* relations thus determines whether the case is presented in participant's, personal and subtle, terms or labelled bluntly as *blat*. In general, when one speaks of others *blat* is a kind of bad, whereas in one's own case it's never like *blat*.

Many people were inhibited from identifying things they did or were forced to do by *blat*, for it could have disturbed their self-perception as honest and respectable people, damaged their self-esteem or presented their personal relations in the wrong light. Once, when asked whether he happened to obtain things through personal contacts, a respondent, a worker, answered: 'It is not in my character' (31a) and was corrected by his wife:

To tell the truth, he did do it. As a valued specialist he got me a part-time job at his lab. I am not educated. But he told them directly: 'If you want me to work for you, my wife has to work here as well.' [*Addressing him*] You say this is nothing but influence, but still, one can say that you helped arrange it by *blat*. [31b]

In another interview it was a neighbour of the respondent who entered the conversation, reminding him of various occasions where she was used as a channel. The respondent, an academic (14), kept insisting that he never used *blat*, but eventually he was forced to accept that he did at least once – he employed her husband by *blat* as a favour to her. The pressure she put on him created a tension: he could not see what she wanted him to grasp in their relationship. He was convinced he had nothing to do with *blat*, and there was no alternative for me than to change the topic of conversation. Afterwards this woman felt offended: 'Can't he remember me giving him prescriptions for free medicines? And himself going to my butcher and all the delicatessen products I obtained for him? And the banquets at restaurants I arranged?' [7] In this case, the reason he denied his participation in *blat* was rather obvious. It was important for him to protect his image as a well-known academic who was not to be associated with such down-to-earth activities.

Some respondents claimed that there is something negative in *blat* that is incompatible with personal relations. Implying that *blat* is an equivalent exchange, motivated by expectation of return favour, people counterpoised *blat* relations to relations of friendship or kinship in which a return favour was considered unacceptable. In so doing, they again distanced themselves from *blat*: 'It is purely human relations. If I like a person I will do my best to help, if not – then no. This is not *blat*. In my understanding classical *blat* is calculative - when you ask somebody and that person assesses what he or she can get out of you.'[31a]

The 'classical *blat*' mentioned by the respondent is nothing more than a transaction in which a favour is exchanged for another favour. But it is the misrecognised cases – in which the motives of reciprocity are denied – which are absolutely crucial to the activity, for they establish the reciprocal ties and circulation of favours in the long run. Small favours, altruistically given and received as 'help' or 'friendly support' are inherent in *blat*. Another respondent expressing the same idea of warmth in relations seems to grasp the essence of *blat* more accurately: 'My connections are friendly attachments, no more than that. It is not that I want something in return when providing a pass to the theatre, but as I have no time my friend may arrange a hospital appointment for me.'[29a]

Given that under Soviet conditions the routine use of friends for extracting services was justified by the necessity 'to help' or 'to be helped', the difference between friendly and *blat* relations became blurred. Reciprocity in *blat* relations and the intersection of *blat* with friendship will be considered in more detail in chapter 5. Here we are concerned with the rhetoric of friendship or personal sympathy which serves as the strategy of misrecognition. The rhetoric of friendship implies care and attention devoted to maintaining personal relations. It requires a sincere disposition to provide all those marks of attention, friendly gestures and acts of kindness that are done properly, at the proper time, for the sake of the 'Other', thus providing a moral basis for *blat* practices (see p.155 on mediated networks and legitimacy of *blat*). Responses along the lines of: 'I could arrange things for my friends, for my wife, but never for myself' [33] allow for the existence of *blat* in exceptional cases, those in which it is absorbed (and disguised) by attention, care or bare necessity.

The ability to construct such 'exceptional' cases is elaborate. Consider the following confessions of an ex-party official:

> Well, of course, I could finish my work at 5-6 p.m. and go shopping. But who gains from this? You can call it *blat*, but if I work till 9 p.m. and I've got a family, certain commitments towards relatives and friends, I find it natural to ring somebody able to deal with my problem, that is, to buy something or to arrange necessary formalities. I know there will be a queue for hours if I go formally. To solve my problem I ring my contact and we decide whether I turn up somewhere or somebody comes to me to deliver the stuff. I always thought: what's better for people, whether I leave my working place for 2–3 hours to stay in a queue or give a ring to arrange an appointment, which takes 5 minutes? When I worked as a Deputy of the Local Soviet my electors used to ask me about privileges, a state car, etc. And I always replied: 'I can go by tram, no problem. But in 40 minutes in the car I manage to patrol the whole area – to see whether the snow has been removed from the roads or if they've been sanded. I could walk. It is even better. Calm. But I'll be arriving an hour later and leaving an hour earlier, which is no good for those who queue at my door.'[34]

Clearly, he would be better informed about 'the whole area' if he fought to get into the tram in the mornings as other people did, and passengers in the tram would report much more than was seen from the car window. But one had to misrecognise what one did in order to proceed with it. Some misrecognised *blat* relations as they had no self-interest in what they did for others, some were forced to construct self-legitimating narratives, as in the latter case. Much ingenuity and energy in disguising self-interest was devoted to the refusal to recognise *blat*.

The interviews showed that retrospectively people were able to consider their relations in terms of reciprocation, or to recognise the underlying cynicism of their 'help discourse' when relationships broke down and the other party refused to give a reciprocal favour or signs of indebtedness, gratitude, loyalty, etc. While actually practising *blat*, however, people cannot discursively admit that they seek a special good or service in exchange for something else, but rather grant or appeal for help and support. Otherwise, the one who controls a good or service in demand would be embarrassed to provide it. The discursive forms such as '*sochtyomsya*' (deriving from *schitat'sya* (to count), meaning both financial counting, of mutual favours and claims and also recognising significance with regard and appreciation) or '*Ya v dolgu ne ostanus*" (I won't stay in debt) still imply the continuity of the relationship rather than an immediate pay-off terminating it. The tactics and etiquette, the practical skills of making an offer without saying it, of promising a return without mentioning it, concealing the expectations if any, were shaped by the rules of this 'misrecognition game'.

### Misrecognition as a system of ambivalence

The reverse side of denial of one's own participation in *blat* was blaming others. Negative attitudes in relation to *blat* expressed in the interviews were always focused either on some particular groups (mainly 'cadres' and tradespeople), unworthy people or unjust cases: 'There is no *blat* in our circle. It is a prerogative of powerful people, directors, chief accountants, those who can turn decisions for their own benefits. At our level, it is not *blat*, it is minor,' said a housewife now a 'shuttle-trader'. [10] Talking about 'cadres' and administrators caused a great deal of resentment: '*Blat* is not simply a protection or recommendation in general, but a recommendation for a complete idiot, that is, a fully incompetent person. It is a promotion of someone incapable, with no faculties at all or inferior in comparison to the other candidate whose only problem is lack of *blat*,' said a former waiter, now in business. [8] 'It is disgusting when one supports somebody unworthy. It is not help, it is pushing him through.

Pushing despite all rules,' commented a worker. [31a] His wife went on blaming the high-ups: 'When we got robbed, everybody in the block began to install security metal doors. Our neighbour, the head of some personnel department, brought some soldiers and they made him a door in one day, clearly at public expense.' [31b] In all these cases, the fact of using public positions or resources for private goals was recognised and related to those in power.

Pushing one's own interests over those of others – as 'recognised' *blat* was often defined – gave the term '*blat*' its negative meaning. This was not only because of a zeal for justice or because of personal resentment by the deprived, but also because in Russian tradition, as well as in Soviet official ideology, a preoccupation with everyday life for its own sake was considered unpatriotic and subversive. Such negative attitudes were often a reaction of resentful people, unwilling to make, or incapable of making, contacts:

> We do not use *blat*, but can watch others regularly. There is a superstore downstairs with its back door right in front of our windows. We can see cars and people approaching and leaving with huge bags. It was especially bitter in 1991, the hardest time, when we had nothing to feed our children while they went off with full bags. It is clear who they were: either *blat*-people, or tradespeople, or swindlers. For us, it's all the same though,

remarked the same worker. [31a] The ambivalence of the attitudes towards *blat* was embedded in the ambivalence of the Soviet distribution system, in which the official ideology of equality came into contradiction with reality. This was acutely grasped by one respondent,

> I would not say people are negative. To be honest, *blat* causes bitterness only in those who do not use *blat*. But there is always a level, at which they do use it [misrecognising this]. It is not the negative attitude towards the phenomenon itself. The problem is caused by the dissociation of levels in obtaining particular material goods. And it is not at all clear whether *blat* is good or bad. [21]

Another respondent stressed the same point in speaking of relative deprivation as the main reason for blaming others: 'some people occupy better apartments, drive better cars, everything because of their acquaintances, while we work, work all our life and have nothing. What kind of attitude, then, do you expect us to have towards *blat*?' [31a] Such attitudes were normally coupled with strategies of stigmatising other occupational strata as *blat*-ridden:

people referred to their occupations as unrelated to *blat* while others were designed for it. *Blat* possibilities, for example, were available for top officials and tradespeople, not for engineers: 'Before I retired I was a military man and then an engineer. What could an engineer achieve? How could he possibly be helpful? I was a small man. *Blat* was all about Party and Soviet nomenclatura who always used the law for themselves while common folk never knew laws and always suffered.' [30]

The majority of the respondents readily identified medicine and trade as the occupations most productive of *blat*. [29a] Those engaged in medicine or trade themselves followed more sophisticated lines of distancing themselves from *blat*. Even recognising *blat* connections (as in Natalia's case, see p.105) and suggesting that their *blat* was warm and human, they avoided applying the word '*blat*' to themselves:

> I can see now that my *blat* was not the same *blat* as people mean, it can rather be related to the idea of a family doctor. I was always a family doctor, not only in my profession. There were no family doctors or psychologists those days. It was a heavy burden, but for this I had lots of privileges. There was a number of families where everything was solved through me. Not only health problems but everything – quarrels with husbands, troubles with daughters. I had to help with everything: tickets to Yalta, booking places in health resorts. My dedication was strong, and of course those people sought to express their gratitude. They treasured me. The word *blat* in this case I wouldn't apply. [7]

A tradeswoman in rejecting '*blat*' as appropriate word in the context provided another insight in the etiquette of *blat* exchanges:

> *Blat* sounds a bit vulgar. In my case, it is not *blat*, it is something else. I came to see a solicitor. She understood my problems, tried to help me. I was grateful for everything, even for the way she talked to me. Naturally I always wanted to please her: a present as a sign of gratitude, a New Year present, etc. She asked her contact at the insurance office to register my dacha. Normally they did not go to the countryside in winter but on her request they did me a favour. Of course, I made a present for that. When I came to that office to sign the documents there was an awfully long queue. They let me in at once, signed everything and did not even take money for that. Is that *blat*? No. Imagine another person who might come into the office, arguing with and swearing at her. There is a difference. I think my way is the way to deal with people. [23]

The strategies of misrecognition of those who felt less deprived often stemmed from considerations about the efficiency or rationality of acts which allegedly improved the formal procedure. Even though *blat* results in a breach of some formal procedure, it does not necessarily subvert the formal targets, able people can be supported and promoted. Moral approval of what was received or given through informal channels derived from the discourse of justice and merit. The latter did not exclude the former, but an emphasis on the one side and repression of the other is a typical strategy of misrecognition:

> It depends on how you look at it. How did I change my job? First I became friendly with the boss (we are neighbours in garage cooperative) and then he invited me. He invited me because he knew I was a qualified worker and worked hard. This was important, because it strengthened the situation morally both for him and for me. But for others it could have of course looked like *blat* . [31a]

Another worker commented on a similar situation:

> I don't consider as *blat* the fact that my aunt helped my wife to get a job of book-keeper. Accountancy was not her profession, but she was educated, had a diploma, she could count. She was in her place, worked well. Those who come in by *blat* do not work, they just receive money. [9]

Ambiguity in recognition of *blat* overlaps with mechanisms of social control exercised over a person who has got what he was not worthy of getting. A recommendation for an appropriate person was not included in the everyday meaning of *blat*. To get a job by *blat* meant that one was not suitable, did not deserve it and got it for a return favour: 'If a good-for-nothing man got promoted, the case qualified as *blat*,' an academic remarked. [37] Two stages are thus to be distinguished here. In the first, speaking objectively, a job is arranged by *blat*, but people decide whether it was *blat* or a support for a good specialist retrospectively, on the basis of their subsequent experiences. It also happened repeatedly that despite the generally negative first reaction to the term '*blat*' and all forms of misrecognition strategies, by the end of the interview people provided examples, jokes and autobiographical details showing a great deal of practical competence.

### Misrecognition as a system of power

In the case of *blat* there is no universally shared code of 'honour' as in gift-giving. Rather *blat* became a counter-ideology of the Soviet system which nobody was supposed to follow, but could practice according to the rules of the 'misrecognition game'. Millar (1988: 15) suggests that 'the Brezhnev regime contracted a deal with the Soviet population, especially with the urban population, tacitly agreeing to overlook an expansion throughout Soviet society of the quest for the individual's, but especially for the individual's household's, gain – as opposed to collectivist and traditional socialist aims', a so-called 'Little Deal'.[5] The metaphor of 'deal', however, is inappropriate, for the alliance of group (household, family, friends, acquaintances) and collective interests did not necessarily imply a compromise of beliefs. Nor can the question, 'how is it possible to be a good Communist and engage in *blat* practices?' be solved by the concept of 'double morality'. The Soviet system is often characterised as engendering a morality of its own, endowed with two ethical scales in everyday life: one of official ideology and one of human sets of values which governed relations between people. It is not the case, however, that one was generally adhered to and the other not, rather it was a complicated mixture which was intrinsic to being a Soviet citizen. In other words, the distinction is an analytical one; in practice people do not 'compromise', they follow the logic implied in concrete situations with reference to both scales of values. It would not be correct to say that personal relations were generally valued more than loyalty to the state, but somehow being a decent citizen and a Communist was not incompatible with rule-breaking.[6]

The metaphor of a 'deal' suggests that there was a 'tacit agreement' between the authorities and the population about the combination of

[5] The metaphor refers to Vera Dunham's analysis of the 'Big Deal' in the period from the end of the war to Stalin's death (Dunham 1976: 3–5). The Big Deal represented a dilution of the idealistic, egalitarian goals of Marxist socialism by means of a tacit accommodation in practice to the materialistic, self-regarding behaviour of the New Soviet middle class.

[6] Zinoviev remarked in *Homo Sovieticus* (p.63) that all his efforts to explain the essence of the Party and its position in Soviet society, what it meant to be a member, and the relationship between ideology and morality in Soviet society were a total failure in the West:

Everything would have been clear to them if I had said that I joined the CPSU for career reasons. But I never made a career and never tried to. Party membership did not hinder me in any way. On the contrary, it made life a bit more interesting. And there was no 'double-think' about it. In general, 'double-think' is an invention of Westerners who don't understand anything about the Soviet way of life or Soviet people. I'm a Communist not in the sense that I believe in Marxist fairy-tales (very few people in the Soviet Union believe in them), but in the sense that I was born, reared and educated in a Communist society and have all the essential characteristics of Soviet man. I mentioned casually that business people come in wearing ties and jackets, although it is hot outside. Why did they do this? For career reasons?

formal and informal criteria which legitimised *blat* within certain determined limits: *infrequent transactions conducted in modest volume, with discretion, normally in situations of urgent need and within a closed personal circle*. *Blat* was deemed illegitimate by both the system and the people. It annoyed the authorities because it violated the state system of distribution, and it irked the people because of the inequality behind the facade of equality. In effect, *blat* practices were not accepted, but connived at in this double denial. They received a 'negative' legitimacy from the combination of the strategies of mis-recognition, in other words, the 'overt disagreement' and denial of *blat* on both societal and individual level.

On the societal level, for ideological reasons, *blat* could not have been recognised by the state as an attribute of the Soviet system. Rather, *blat* was either left unnoticed (unmentioned in official dis-course) or subject to a limited, usually satirical, critique. It was criticised as an anti-Soviet phenomenon deriving from the moral perversion of some individuals (*'koe-kto u nas eshchyo poroi'*). Its origins were never related to the system itself; the shortcomings were always reported as *'otdel'nye'* (literally translated as 'separate' – meaning individual, unattached, non-systematic). Such incompatible-with-socialism phenomena were attacked in a sequence of critical campaigns in the press.[7] The critique of these phenomena was however doomed to fail in Soviet conditions, for it was limited and censored. Power institutions could not eliminate what in effect sup-ported them and what they were coupled with; yet, in terms of the rules of the 'misrecognition game', the critique was sincere. The inability to recognise that *blat* was rooted in the institutions of power led to a situation where the success of a campaign was judged by the detection and punishment of scapegoats while the phenomenon as such remained untouched. The words *'blat'* or 'connections' were excluded from official discourse thereby automatically withdrawing them from research and analysis; they were left to satirisation by *Krokodil*.

'Objects of critique: a report of *Krokodil* for 10 years' provides some data on such campaigns as early as 1932 (see table 2.6). Among the clientele of *Krokodil* we find a considerable number of 'obtainers' (*dostavala*) and 'procurers' (*prolaza*) (630). The number of criticisms on

[7] Campaigns against *semeistvennost'* (nepotism), *kumovstvo* (relationship of Godparents), *zemlyachestvo* (association of people of the same origins, places, background, experi-ence), etc. are pervasive in the periodical *Krokodil*, starting in the 1920s and throughout the 1930s in particular.

**Table 2.6** *Objects of critique: a report of Krokodil for ten years*

Numbers of critical publications about the following categories:

| Clientele of Krokodil | 1922 18 issues | 1923 48 issues | 1924 29 issues | 1925 48 issues | 1926 48 issues | 1927 48 issues | 1928 48 issues | 1929 48 issues | 1930 36 issues | 1931 36 issues & supp. | 1932 12 issues & supp. | Total criticisms for 10 years | No. of those under critique |
|---|---|---|---|---|---|---|---|---|---|---|---|---|---|
| Antisemites | – | 6 | 2 | 7 | 9 | 3 | 14 | 8 | 8 | 2 | – | 59 | 343 |
| Illiterate paperwasters | 13 | 78 | 52 | 133 | 166 | 128 | 80 | 113 | 56 | 38 | 26 | 883 | 3876 |
| Bureaucrats | 4 | 76 | 42 | 136 | 115 | 82 | 128 | 158 | 69 | 42 | 28 | 880 | 3554 |
| Bribetakers | – | – | – | – | 4 | 9 | 6 | 5 | 7 | 3 | 2 | 36 | 110 |
| Harm-makers | 1 | 47 | 17 | 25 | 41 | 57 | 99 | 26 | 14 | 2 | – | 329 | 1719 |
| Stupid-headed | 7 | 93 | 16 | 217 | 104 | 88 | 191 | 136 | 46 | 35 | 39 | 972 | 4069 |
| Chatterboxes | 8 | 28 | 14 | 19 | 30 | 42 | 108 | 64 | 26 | 27 | 14 | 380 | 1941 |
| **Obtainers–procurers** | 6 | 45 | 14 | 48 | 108 | 64 | 113 | 124 | 25 | 41 | 42 | 630 | 2138 |
| Lazy bones (*Oblomov*) | – | 9 | 8 | 8 | 13 | 6 | 10 | 54 | 32 | 6 | 9 | 155 | 531 |
| Opportunists | 6 | 29 | 9 | 42 | 57 | 17 | 43 | 66 | 24 | 17 | 2 | 372 | 2265 |
| Flatterers (*podkalimy*) | 4 | 17 | 4 | 23 | 57 | 26 | 21 | 29 | 14 | 8 | 2 | 205 | 540 |
| Absenteeists | – | – | – | – | 3 | 5 | 12 | 16 | 18 | 36 | 11 | 101 | 255 |
| Alcoholics | 7 | 38 | 34 | 36 | 54 | 62 | 54 | 56 | 28 | 3 | 3 | 375 | 5004 |
| Careerists (*rvachi*) | 3 | 12 | 2 | 18 | 28 | 21 | 25 | 30 | 32 | 29 | 12 | 212 | 532 |
| Soviet fools (*sovduraki*) | 9 | 136 | 23 | 211 | 87 | 15 | 15 | 83 | 10 | 8 | 6 | 603 | 2980 |
| Hooligans | – | – | – | – | 6 | 8 | 4 | 3 | 2 | 2 | 1 | 26 | 223 |
| Total | 76 | 673 | 285 | 1090 | 1057 | 773 | 1120 | 1352 | 583 | 569 | 308 | 7841 | 37137 |

*Source:* Adapted from *Krokodil* 1932, 15–16: 12.

these matters is lower than criticisms of Soviet bureaucracy – 'stupid-headed' (*golovotyapstvo*) (972), 'illiterate paperwasters' (*bezgramotnye bumagomaraki*) (883), bureaucrats (880), Soviet fools (*sovduraki*) (603) – but precedes alcoholics (375), and opportunists of all kinds (372).

The topic is equally widespread in the post-war *Krokodil* and ever since (see the cartoons throughout the volume). Despite all these campaigns, individuals sheltered themselves from 'noticing' their own involvement in *blat*, as indeed did the system. People used similar strategies: negating, criticising, laughing at *blat*. These strategies were sincere, for unless these criticisms were considered important, taken seriously and followed, it would not be possible to manipulate them for personal advantage. On the other hand, the logic of life took over: despite verbal disapproval and estrangement, people were forced to use connections. Personal excuses for the involvement with *blat* normally referred to the structural conditions, such as shortages, inefficiency of institutions and bureaucratic procedures, etc. whereas at the societal level shortcomings of the system were explained by inefficiency of some 'immoral' individuals. Here are a few examples of people's excuses:

(1) *Common sense*

> One has to follow common sense to survive. If one needs something, one takes it. There is nothing that can be done about it. This is the logic of life. We can denounce such practice but this does not prevent it from existing. It would not be possible to survive in the Soviet system if there was no *blat*. People are not ascetic, people are meant to live. [37]
>
> Once at a party meeting in 1968 the communists raised the problem of closed distribution systems. They spoke about the discrediting of the ideas of communism and socialism, about equality and human rights common for everybody irrespective of degrees and titles. Next day the most active ones were summoned to the secretary of the local party organisation: 'Do you want Akademgorodok to collapse? The best scientists will leave. (In fact, some of them did leave that year. It was a very severe winter.) We've got to support scientists somehow. After the revolution there was a special decree of Lenin providing superior rations for scientists. Since then the Party gave an incentive to scientists. It was just a necessity.' They couldn't help accepting this as many other necessities of the system. [33]

(2) *Untrustworthy institutions*

When your television set goes wrong, you cannot trust a service shop: higher prices and unreliable service. They might replace some spare parts from your TV for older ones. You must wait for service. If you have a friend or contact, the problem is sorted out fast and efficiently and then you just have a meal or drink together. [31]

(3) *Shortage*

Shortage of goods and low wages result in people losing their independence. It is important to give people an opportunity to earn and to solve their problems with their money. But this was never the case. No amount of money could have bought the goods and services you wanted. As everything was in short supply, one strongly depended on contacts to live. [27]

(4) *Scarcity*

To work properly for this money is ridiculous. 'They pretend they pay, and we pretend we work.' We cannot live reasonably for what we are paid. We've got to compensate either by privileged access to cheap goods, by fiddling the system or by exchanging favours. [8]

(5) *Exceptional cases*

Exceptional people do not make a secret of the fact that they have to solve the problems of the others. When asked about his fame in his TV show, Ryazanov[8] replied that fame is a burden but also helps a lot and gave examples of how he was continuously used by his friends for arranging flats, telephones, obtaining medicines, etc. [26]

Some circumstances are exceptional. It always happens with sportsmen and artistic people. They come today and have to be abroad tomorrow. Everyone in my place would help. They go with a mission. And they are sympathetic people. Of course, I did my best, helping them with their passports. [25]

(6) *Social conventions*

You wouldn't treat a guest with what was bought in a shop, it had to be something obtained. When you visited someone and got treated with something special, you did not ask where he obtained this, you were pleased. [33]

You can't help helping people out, it is just a norm. [36]

These practices did not form any conscious compromise or discur-

---

[8] Ryazanov is a film director of enormous popularity in Russia for his comedies 'Beware cars!', 'The Irony of Fate', 'Garage' and many others.

sive agreement. Rather, they implied a niche of practices exercised in misrecognised form. The objective necessity of re-distribution and rule-breaking for the system to function and for the people to survive thus resulted in a specific form of 'negative' legitimacy. Such legitimacy resulted from both criticism and, in misrecognised form, performance of *blat* and other ambiguous practices of the Soviet system. Some of these elements are grasped in six paradoxes of socialism noted in the well-known anecdote current in Soviet society:

> No unemployment but nobody works.
> Nobody works but productivity increases.
> Productivity increases but the shops are empty.
> The shops are empty but fridges are full.
> Fridges are full but nobody is satisfied.
> Nobody is satisfied but all vote unanimously.[9]

Therefore, roots of *blat* can be found in the nature of its legitimacy, negative legitimacy, ensuing from the 'misrecognition game' on the societal level. This also explains why the role of *blat* in the Soviet system was understated and unexplored. In the terminology of Bourdieu (1990: 234), *blat* would be contained in the game of

> twofold objective truth, a double game played with truth, through which the group (and individual), the source of objectivity, in a sense lies to itself, by producing a truth whose sole function and meaning are to deny a truth known and recognised by all, a lie that would deceive no one, were not everyone determined to deceive himself.

[9] *Istoriya SSSR v Anekdotakh: 1917-1991*. Riga: Everest, 1991, p.188.

# 3    The Soviet order: a view from within

A concentration camp was not a political prison or exile. It was a Noah's ark with both goods and bads on board, in fact with more bads than goods. A struggle for survival here took specific forms. 1. *Blat* was flourishing. A folk saying "'I'll buy everything,'' said Gold. "I'll gain everything,'' responded *Blat'* was more than true. 2.*Tufta* [*pripiski*, falsification of sheets – A.L.] – managers of all levels falsified data in their reports about work and productivity. 3. *Stukachestvo* – denouncing and informing managers – and *ssuchivanie s nachal'stvom* (allying with authorities) – offering information and other clientilist services in order to establish *blat* relations and obtain favours from the camp authorities.

> From the 1918–34 memoirs of N.P. Antsiferov, a historian and
> survivor of concentration camps at Belomor Channel Construction
> Site and Solovki (*Zvezda*, 1989, 4: 154)

## Everyday subversion

If this study were historical its perspective would probably be close to the works of so-called 'new cohort' of social historians.[1] Their works are distinctive for two reasons. First, they approach the Soviet regime as *historians* rather than political scientists – that is, they explore the available documentary evidence free from the preconceptions of the 'totalitarian state' model. Second, they are *social* historians, which means that they seek to understand the historical process in terms of social divisions, conflicts and alliances, rather than in terms of regime actions imposed upon an undifferentiated and essentially passive 'people'. In so doing the 'new cohort' offers a new understanding of the regime as well. Contrary to the historians who consider the forms

[1] In a summary of the *Russian Review* debate Andrle includes Fitzpatrick, Getty, Rittersporn, Manning and Thurston into the 'new cohort' as opposed, for example, to historians such as Lewin and Cohen and Sovietologists such as Fainsod, Schapiro and others (Andrle in Lampert and Rittersporn 1992).

in which society related to government as the only significant type of social relation, the social historians focus not on the actions of the state, but the dynamic of relationships between different social strata and classes; social distinctions and their significance for the lives of individuals; the ways in which individuals could improve their status and protect themselves; the various aspects and repercussions of social mobility; and the ways in which some features of social hierarchy could persist or emerge in spite of, rather than because of, the actions of the regime. They assume a perspective 'from below', similar to the perspective taken in the present study.

Fitzpatrick, the leading figure of the 'new cohort', considers social history as a field involving not particular sets of events, the lives and decisions of particular individuals, but the rather less tangible, though undoubtedly important, realities of social life that shape the experiences and actions of large sets of anonymous individuals. Discovering these realities in historical documents requires interpretative and conceptual work, rather than establishing what particular people did at specific points of time and space. *Blat* seems to be such kind of reality that routinely shapes everyday experiences of people, even if not all of them are involved in it directly. These practices, however, would probably be impossible to trace in historical documents, unless *blat* is properly conceptualised. Not only because it is a routine and rather discursive practice, pervasive in day-to-day socialising, but also because it has to do with personal consumption, which is available only in historical documents in its irregular forms: expressed either as its celebrated achievements, as in the case of *Stakhanovtsy* (see p.93), or its criminal implications, such as violations of state distribution principles, facts of bribery, other workplace crimes, cases in comrades' courts, etc. Fortunately for this study, *blat* persisted throughout the Soviet period and has only recently started to undergo basic changes.

The origins of *blat*, as shown in chapter 1, are to be found in the Stalinist era. This is another point of connection with the studies of the social historians. Their works, sometimes criticised for their lack of moral judgements of Stalinism, were meant to show that the terror did not overwhelm social life – it coexisted with it, that the terror was a result of collective process rather than Stalin's caprice. The contribution of social historians, often referred to as revisionists, to the 'totalitarian paradigm' in the analysis of the Stalinist era renewed debates about the subversion of the Soviet system.

The diagnosis of the Soviet system's tendency to subvert itself was given by Trotsky as early as 1936. He was disillusioned with the

Soviet regime, in particular the contradiction between the egalitarian, ascetic socialist ideals associated with the Bolshevik Revolution and the emergence in the 1930s of a privileged new elite whose values would have been labelled 'bourgeois' a decade earlier. Trotsky spoke of a 'betrayal' of revolution by the bureaucracy; and the thrust of Milovan Djilas' later description of the 'New Class' (Djilas 1957) and its privileges was on the same lines. Outside the Marxist camp, the émigré sociologist Nicholas Timasheff (1946) wrote of a 'great retreat' from revolutionary values which occurred in the 1930s, and Vera Dunham (1976) characterised the culture of the Stalinist period as a triumph of 'middle-class values'.

Fitzpatrick has argued that the origins of 'great retreat' lay in the rise of new elite generated in the late 1920s when higher education was thrown open to the children of workers and peasants. Born of Stalin's revolution from above, the new elite supposedly repudiated further revolutionary mobilisation in favour of stability and the revival of familiar patterns. Explaining that the new Soviet elite supported the regime precisely because the regime created it, she sought, in effect, to make Trotsky's assertion that the subversion of Soviet system had a 'social basis' in the bureaucracy less pejorative (Fitzpatrick 1992: 216–52). The pervasiveness of *blat* among ordinary people indicates a further development of the social basis of such subversion: oriented towards the same 'middle-class values', many people used their informal contacts to acquire commodities available to bureaucracy or elites through their privileges. The humble origins of the new elite and bureaucracy only facilitated the diffusion of *blat* all over society, both under Stalin's regime and afterwards.

A similar understanding of the Soviet system was developed by Lewin (1985). Also taking up the Trotskyite framework, Lewin focused on the formation and character of the Soviet bureaucracy as a key to explaining the revolution's demise under Stalin (1985: 286–314). Lewin employed the term 'the Soviet system' to describe a situation where the state bureaucratised the society and yet the social patterns of the village reasserted themselves within this statism (Lampert and Rittersporn 1992: 1–24). The statistics of the 'ruralisation of the cities' (Lewin 1985: 209, 220–3) is telling. The population census that was carried out in December 1926 found 26 million (18 per cent of the total) living in towns and 121 million (82 per cent) living in the countryside. According to the census of January 1939, the total population amounted to 171 million: 33 per cent living in towns and 67 per cent in the countryside. Almost half of the town dwellers in

1939 were recent (post-1926) arrivals from the peasant countryside. Eighteen million peasants had moved to the cities within the six years 1929–35; the peak year for migration was 1931, when more than 4 million countryman arrived in the towns as fresh immigrants, while another 7 million peasants moved around the country on temporary labouring contracts. During the first five-year plan alone, the cities grew by 44 per cent, that is as much as they had done over the preceding 30 years (Andrle 1988: 32). It is possible to argue that such a rapid process of the ruralisation of the cities, in which the features of communal life merged into processes of formation of the new elite and introduction of a hierarchical system of distribution, gave an additional impulse to redistribution 'by *blat*'.

Another step in pursuing the 'subversion' thesis was taken by Kotkin (1995) in his detailed study of Magnitogorsk ('Magnetic Mountain City', an industrial Stalinist project). He argued that the kinds of lives that the urban inhabitants came to lead and the identities they formed involved frequent circumvention of, and resourceful, albeit localised, resistance to the terms of daily life that developed within the crusade of building socialism. One resists without necessarily rejecting, by assessing, making tolerable and, in some cases, even turning to one's own advantage the situation with which one is confronted. Rather than an extension of Communist party control over more and more areas of life, therefore, it is possible to see – without denying the coercive force of the Communist project – a two-way struggle, however unequal the terms, over the drawing of lines of authority, a struggle that involved continuous, if usually indirect, challenges to the perceived rules. Kotkin regards as resistance many actions normally seen as passive or 'deviant', of which *blat* is but one example. In the USSR, he argues, power was not localised in the central state apparatus, even when there seemed to be no separation between the spheres of 'state' and 'society'. Rather, its power rested on the characteristics and behaviour of the people (Kotkin 1995: 23). In these terms, *blat* practices were unintentionally made possible by the state, and thus can be considered not only as a 'deviant' outcome of the centralised system of control but also as creating 'characteristics and behaviour of people' indispensable for the functioning of the system. I try to show how the practices, functional for the Soviet system in economic and practical terms, can also be subversive in terms of ideology and morality. One might make an analogy with adultery, which can be seen sometimes as contributing to the stability of the institution of marriage, but also as subverting it.

Let us present some 'from below' views on how *blat* practices were made possible by the state and then turn to the analysis of socio-economic conditions facilitating *blat*.

### Three principles of Soviet order

*The principle of suspended punishment*

The Soviet bureaucracy was often viewed as if the distinction between the state and 'civil society', state affairs and private affairs, became entirely blurred. In totalitarian vision of the Soviet regime (Arendt 1951; Brzezinski and Friedrich 1956; and others), bureaucracy was claimed to envelop almost everything – every economic transaction qualified as a matter of concern to the party and the state. This was perhaps true in principle. In practice, there was a degree of freedom in many spheres, such as those of culture, religion, family life and others. Achieving such freedom, however, was predicated upon following the unwritten rules and a subtle understanding of what was possible and what was not, and to what extent one could pursue one's interests. Such environment can be seen as uncertain, as in the description of the similar order of things in Poland made by Wedel (1986: 14):

> Nothing is certain here. Today you can buy a mineral water; tomorrow you can't. Today the censorship committee lets you rehearse your play, but tomorrow it will decide not to let you perform it. Today the passport office says I need this particular form to leave the country; the next day it is the wrong form. It is an odd feeling to be living in a country where there is no final word; no one knows for sure what is going on.

The availability of unwritten codes alongside the written ones, and the usual practice for authorities to switch to the written code only 'where necessary' created certain freedom and flexibility. On the other hand such leniency could be restricted at every moment. This arrangement is based on the idea of suspended punishment. As Zinoviev (1974: 326) described it:

> it's a typical way of keeping social individuals in a state of submission. And don't think that it's been invented deliberately. It happened on its own, and it's more preventive than punitive: it's an attempt to create in man's subconscious a psychological background that tells him that his very existence is unauthorised and even illegal.

The mechanism of suspended punishment was meant to keep everyone under self-control: 'if one doesn't comply, they charge with control, pressure, extra requirements.' [14] The popular version of the idea of suspended punishment was expressed in an anecdote about a person who happened to be sentenced to five-year imprisonment. He was not guilty and did not understand what he was accused of and it was explained to him that if he were guilty indeed he would be sentenced to 10 years.

Blat is a 'survival kit' reducing uncertainty in conditions of shortage, exigency and perpetual emergency, in which formal criteria and formal rights are insufficient to operate. Although everybody was under the threat of 'five-year imprisonment', the actual punishment was exercised according to one's status and could be reduced considerably, if there were connections. Alongside all other kinds of privileges to be considered in more detail below, every bureaucratic position, for example, was endowed with some allowance for a personal excuse (beznakazannost'). People used to say, 'one person was sentenced for taking a nail while the other smuggled by lorries'. Party membership provided an exemption: a party organisation could take responsibility (vzyat' na poruki) and punish through party channels (po partiinoi linii): 'In war time, arriving five minutes late at the workplace took 20 per cent off your wage; if repeated – one year of compulsory labour. But this general instruction never applied equally to everybody.' [30] Different status in the face of the law was, perhaps, one of the most subverting aspects of the system, for it violated the idea of social justice and undermined people's belief in legality.

Formally the laws were passed by parliament, but in practice the relevant party organisation decided what the law had to stipulate. Moreover, there was a vast number of state regulations that did not even formally have the rank of law: they remained as government or ministerial orders, or, most common of all, simply the personal rulings of a particular member of the bureaucracy. For the bureaucracy itself decided the kind of legal shape it wished to give to its various rulings:

> We have equal rights for both an army general and a collective farmer. The law is supposed to be the same for everyone. But there is a proverb: 'The law is like a sheep, it walks the way it faces' (Zakon chto dyshlo, kuda povernul, tuda i vyshlo), and so it happens in practice: the one with connections is punished by reprimand, the one without – by the Criminal Code.' [30]

Another respondent added bitterly: '*Blat* is everywhere, it used to be, it is and it will be. As a response to the lack of formal rights. When the law protects human rights, there will be no need for *blat*.' [23]

### The exception principle

Not every rule in the society could be broken by *blat*. Opportunities for circumvention were implicit in those restrictions which applied differently to groups and individuals. *Blat* was embedded in rules of a particular kind, rules which were both accepted and avoided. Any system of privileges or closed distribution system will provide an example:

> After the war, the front-line soldiers could enter an institute without competition. You could pass exams and get enrolled. If you did not pass, they could consider your case (*poiti navstrechu*), to give you another chance, that is, to organise re-examination. This opportunity, however, was not provided to everyone equally. It was more likely if there was someone pushing you or asking for you. [30]

In a way, the system counteracted its own centralisation. The decisions made by the centre or at the higher levels of the organisational hierarchy could not take into account all the nuances and specialties of lower, subordinate units. Some departure from the general line had to be allowed. Once introduced, however, the 'exception principle' showed a tendency to multiply. The 'exception principle' opened a variety of loopholes by which people could push for their interests. This factor stimulated a certain 'individualism' (advancing one's own case and disregarding others) that became a matter of practice rather than personal morals. In such a mundane example as buying meat in the local state butcher store, or apples at the market, an informal talk with a meat-seller and explanation that these products are purchased especially for someone in hospital could improve the ratio of lean cuts of pork and fat. Describing informal practices in Poland, Wedel remarked that in situations like these lies come out almost automatically. She notes that one does not always lie blatantly or tell the uncomfortable truth. People have learned to mix the two into credible stories to resolve bureaucratic problems or to talk their way out of trouble (Wedel 1986: 17). These lies should be perceived as practices of creating exceptional cases, rather than dishonesty, as an ability not only to live with the contradictions of their society, but also to manipulate them creatively (see cartoon 6).

*A parent's example.*

РОДИТЕЛЬСКИЙ ПРИМЕР

Рис. Е. ГОРОХОВА

— За то, что ты солгал, гадкий мальчишка, сиди дома и не смей никуда выходить! А если мне будут звонить из министерства, скажи, что я ещё не вернулся из командировки! Маме же передай, что я ушёл на совещание в министерство! Понял!!

**Cartoon 6**

You naughty boy, telling lies like that. You're grounded! Don't you dare go out anywhere. And if I get a call from the ministry, tell them I'm not back from the business trip yet. And tell mummy I've gone to a meeting at the ministry. Have you got that?

(Krokodil 1952, 23: 12)

### The principle of krugovaya poruka[2] (collective guarantee)

In formal terms the power of the bureaucracy could be considered as permeating the whole of society and influencing every citizen: an account was kept of every resident and employee by the party branches, mass organisations, state apparatus and police authorities of each locality and place of work; every adult carried an identification document which was stamped with one's place of birth, place of residence and family status. A change in any of these was registered in one's ID, which one was obliged to present at the behest of any authority. In reality, there existed semi-legitimate mechanisms for avoiding such forms of registration or manipulating them as, for example, fake marriages and divorces to get a residence permit, to qualify for a bigger apartment, or to become exempt from army service. Even in the harshest times, among the most deprived groups of population the ways of circumventing the formal regulations were known and used:

> My parents were collective farmers. The collective farm was more like peasant serfdom then [late 1930s–1940s]. Everyone had a collective farm work-book (*knizhka trudodnei*) but not passports which were necessary to travel. We had paper rights only. But this was only one side of the story. The other one was that men could leave the collective farm by entering military service. From there one could be forwarded to a high school and thus received an opportunity to stay in a city. Women could escape to relatives in the cities to do babysitting or to clean houses and then look for other opportunities. A person could also escape if he or she had a good connection in the administration. [30]

The dependence on every tick or record paradoxically created an appropriate environment for the flourishing of *blat*:

> If one is independent, he can function without regard to your occupation, relatives or acquaintances. He considers your case and decides objectively what to do about it. But in reality one always has to think who will back up in case he finds himself in a difficult situation. Perhaps you may be of use one day, or your relatives, and a system of mutual dependence is thus created. [30]

[2] *Krugovaya poruka* is not directly translatable into English. Literally it derives from *krug* (a peasant community) which provides collective responsibility or guarantee, that is, mutual support and control within a circle of people, in which everybody is dependent upon the other.

The same patterns of collective guarantee characterised communal life in tsarist Russia. The reverse side of such psychological and material support to a member of community has always been the moral pressure and circular control of deviants from the established code. In this respect, the Soviet ideology of equality and social homogeneity, continuously reproduced in communist up-bringing, established 'intolerance towards a neighbour's success and well-being. This did not make them think of what is to be done to earn more but rather how to harm the neighbour'. [25] The community provided joint help for needy members of the community but restricted individual achievements. This partly explains the nostalgia experienced by many today and their urge to return to the 'communist' values. An old anecdote recently became popular again: 'The person prayed for God to hear him and finally got heard: "I'll give you anything, but mind: your neighbour will get twice as much." He thought and asked for one eye to go blind.' [22] It was ideologically correct: people were not supposed to enjoy advantages over others.

Some people resisted entering such a system of mutual dependence but in the end regretted it:

> I was brought up with principles. I can't tell you how many opportunities I missed. When I was a peoples' deputy I could arrange a telephone line for myself, to solve an apartment problem. I had proper connections, knew those people who were engaged in all this. And the fact that I did not use them made me even less respected. But those days I understood everything literally, believed in every slogan in the newspapers, in Komsomol and Party ideals. But the nomenclatura people I met did not pay me any respect for that. They respected those who made them feel powerful and helpful. My friends told me 'You must be abnormal. Can't you just tell somebody you have a problem, they will sort it out for you somehow, you've been waiting long enough for a flat.' And I felt I couldn't. Not because I was honest, just silly. I simply didn't know the rules of the game. [26]

In a situation where demand greatly exceeded supply, formal criteria were not sufficient for distributing resources. A person in charge of distribution, having to choose between two applicants equally deserving of some scarce good or service, would normally grant them to the one with whom he had some personal or even remote tie. The ramification of *blat* networks was thus facilitated by the establishment of mutual dependencies and obligations within formal institutions. Trying to meet others' interests in expectation of future concessions for oneself, all engaged in practices of subversion of bureaucratic rules. Classically defined as rational and impersonal and known as particularly oppressive and inflexible under the Soviet regime, the bureaucratic system in fact became personalised.

## The personalisation of the Soviet bureaucratic system

The personalisation of the bureaucratic system was related both to Russian culture and to Soviet-type conditions. The analysis of personalisation can go back the 'Slavophiles–Westernisers' discussion of the 1840s regarding the state of Russian national development in relation to the rest of Europe (Kireevsky 1911: 23). In rejecting rationality as the only principle of cognition and as principle of social order, Slavophiles counter-poised the principle of community and *sobornost'* (a spiritual community, from *sobor*, which refers both to cathedral and to a gathering) to formal laws. Their concept of *sobornost'* implied a specific constitution of the social world based on consent (like singing which is not conducted but harmonised) beyond all formal laws and guarantees. Despite the differences in their perspectives, however, both Slavophiles and Westernisers related their views to national character with regard to a moral spirit, deep-rooted archetypes and value systems which determine etiquette and social idioms governing interpersonal relations. In her study of Russian national character, Kasianova (1994) notes that Russians are not only confused about the distribution of functions between institutions, modes of their interaction and subordination, but often refuse to recognise the very principle of their functioning: as long as we can we try to 'manage' without them, solving problems by our own 'means'. When we do not succeed after all, we break into the first, more or less suitable, organisation and immediately begin claiming a decision of our problem, with no papers and without involving other organisations and preliminary procedures, if possible. If this does not succeed, we express our indignation, criticise the organisation for bureaucratism and procrastination and demand to be treated 'humanely' (*po-chelovecheski*). Just to prove that formal relations are absolutely excluded in our consciousness from the sphere of 'human' (Kasianova 1994: 71–2). In *Zadachi Rossii* (*Thoughts on Russian Soul*, 1956) Weindle remarked that Russians always were inclined to look for a human in the official and, if they did not find it, would relapse into despair (Weindle 1956: 122) or critique of bureaucratism.

The role of personalisation in the functioning of formal institutions was equally emphasised in the interviews: 'The Russian mentality is oriented towards personalising one's contacts – not only retrospectively, but also today. As a rule, formal contacts in Russia are either based on personal relations or supported by them. Formalities never meant more than personal relations. It is a country which is *governed by mores rather than laws*.' [21] Another respondent admitted that most of her connections were formed on the basis of relations at work: 'For us, Soviets, our work is our life. We live by work. And my work mates were friends, everything was lived out together. It is all changing now. For me it's inconceivable.' [13] Personal contacts were crucial in dealing with bureaucracies:

> People react positively if you go to see them, once, twice, ring regularly. They see your commitment, and try to help. To organise conferences, meetings, symposiums I had to contact administrators in the hotels, resorts, local authorities, etc. All the same people every year; of course, we became friends. We always celebrate holidays together and drink together even when there are no occasions, you know. And then, if business goes well, we want to see more of each other. Our socialising is feasts of course. This is normal. [13]

This partly explains why people did not always 'become automatons as soon as they were placed behind the desk', as suggested by Hertzfeld (1992). Hertzfeld argued that in terms of bureaucracy, the totalitarian state and democratic regimes were the same in their idiom of representation, in their indifference. Indifference was predicated upon one's discovery or decision that the other did not 'belong' (see p.121). *Blat* was a form of proof of one's belonging. The personalising of formal contacts ensured a positive decision. On the other hand, when a positive decision was taken, the bureaucracy became personalised. The significant factor determining the indifference of the Soviet bureaucracy (or the lack of it) was a tacit aiming at a return favour, whatever it might be: 'I am grateful for every bit of attention. If I see that it is not just a "workplace" here, but a person who is interested to help and does a good job after all, I want to encourage her or him. I offer theatre tickets, the easiest for me.' [29]

The personalisation had both good and bad aspects – or rather, it was a structural fault which could be of benefit to some individuals: 'If you go to the local post-office to collect your pension for years, you'll get know the person in charge. She knows some aged people as well and they are served fast, without ID and waiting in the queue, in parallel with those who are waiting.' [33] Similarly, everyone in his or her workplace could treat the other favourably, thus creating a

personal resource to engage in *blat* exchanges. There was no equality
in what one could get through personal channels, but there was an
equality in that everyone enjoyed what his or her personal contacts
provided (see pp.113 and 121 for details).

Another implication of personalisation was that people tried to
avoid bureaucracies and formal channels, if possible. The informal
ways of dealing with the system were perceived as most natural,
simple and efficient. There was no trust in the formal channels of
information or reliance on generally provided level of services. One
had to be advised or recommended to be sure of doing the right thing:

> The state primordially is an opposition to a Russian person as
> somewhat inimical, and moral restrictions do not thus spread to it: as
> an enemy, it can be cheated and robbed. Promises, given to a state,
> are not obligatory. We can struggle with it in different ways except
> the most obvious strategy: to win one should know the enemy. But
> we *do not want* to know our state. (Kasianova 1994: 72)

Rather, people rely on informal contacts, support and solidarity.

Stalin seems to have understood the danger of personalisation of
bureaucracies. In some interpretations the attack on personalisation is
considered as the main target of the party purges (Rittersporn 1991).
The problem of cadres was a well known concern of Stalin, particularly when the central power could not monitor regional situations
due to the autonomous power of local authorities. The fact that a
leader could arrive for his new appointment with his own team
including sometimes dozens of people contributed to a certain independence of local authorities from the central power. This could not
satisfy the authorities which had to have reliable information and
keep everything under central control. The flourishing of informal
relations required periodical purges that temporarily solved the
problem, but in a while life took over again and brought the necessity
for new purges. Another overall purge was ready to be launched just
before Stalin's death: the system had to be driven back to centralised
control. Everything that happened after Stalin was by and large the
result of informal connections developed in Stalin's time. In effect, *blat*
and other forms of informal practices turned out more stable than any
formal system, partly because of the advantages of informality (micro-
scale, continuity of personal relationships), partly as reaction to
insecurity in politics and to economic scarcity.

The personalisation of the bureaucracy, or informal connections
within formal structures, became a significant factor in keeping the
command economy afloat. Personal contacts supported business ties

and maintained economic cooperation in times of hardship. Plans could not normally be fulfilled by formal means. As remarked by Mikhail Yarikov, famous for his sarcastic observations: 'in the fourth year of a five-year plan, *blat* is decisive in fulfilling the plan.'[3] Enterprises either negotiated the planned targets or had to engage in informal efforts to obtain extra resources. The system of relationships with suppliers, mutual trust and support between partners were the practical necessity for the functioning of socialist production.

In the 1950s, as Berliner pointed out, *blat* had industrial connotations, mostly to do with the process of distribution and procurement of supplies, materials, equipment, etc. The distinction between the use of *blat* for personal consumption and for smoothing the work of the enterprise was emphasised in his interview testimony: 'Sometimes this sort of activity was done for the sake of the enterprise and sometimes for the one's pocket. But in fact we were often compelled to do illegal things or [accept] informal requirements not for our own benefit but simply so that enterprise could function' (1957: 197). Berliner concluded that the primary use of informal connections in production was in obtaining necessary commodities from other enterprises without the proper authorisation for doing so. These informal social relations were responsible for the processes required to keep the formal institutions operating. Berliner argued that Soviet industry would fail to work without informal mechanisms, without 'tolkachi' (pushers) providing many needs not delivered by the command economy, without networks of informal relations among Soviet industrial managers. These informal mechanisms usually carried an affective element, which could be used to counter-balance the formal demands of the organisation, to render life within it more acceptable and more meaningful. Importantly, such mechanisms could reduce the feeling of individuals that they were alienated and dominated by forces beyond themselves. They also had some instrumental functions, in rendering an unpredictable situation more predictable and in providing for mutual support against surprise upsets (inquiries from outside or competition from inside).

The practical indispensability of *blat* was caused by shortcomings of the command economy and all-pervasive shortages. The methods whereby the system handled the conditions of shortage (systems of

---

[3] '*V chetvyortom zavershayushchem blat yavlyaetsya reshayushchim.*' Mikhail Yarikov, deputy resident in China, became one of the announced enemies of the people. Quoted from P. and A. Sudoplatov, *Special Tasks: The Memoirs of an Unwanted Witness – A Soviet Spymaster*, Little, Brown & Co., 1990: 61.

privileges and closed distribution) not only generated the informal ways of obtaining goods and services but also provided a kind of moral justification for using them: people were given a chance to sustain their private life and interests in the face of structural constraints. As a result, the very economic and social functions of *blat* also served to damage commitments to the Soviet ideological tenets and thus had a subverting impact for the system in general. To prove this argument I shall consider in more detail how the conditions of shortage were dealt with by both the authorities and the people.

### Conditions of shortage

I shall start with the analysis of shortage of goods and services, which was commonly regarded as the fundamental reason for pervasiveness of *blat* in the interviews: 'Shortage is the foundation of *blat*. In Soviet society everything was in short supply, that is why *blat* was pervasive: if something was in short supply it could be obtained by *blat*.' [28] Shortage should be considered in two ways: as the methods of the state to ration resources, goods or services, on the one hand, and people's efforts in circumventing the rationing through personal methods of redistribution, on the other. The problem of shortage was recognised by Soviet economic science as early as the 1920s (Kristman 1925; Novozhilov 1926). Later on, however, for decades people only talked about shortage (as well as about *blat*) in the family, perhaps when queueing up, but shortage did not figure as a topic of scholarly research. Economists avoided investigating shortage and other, similarly 'delicate' questions for ideological reasons: socialism was declared to be a system satisfying all desires of mankind. All of its laws, by definition, were supposed to have positive outcomes. Consequently, unfavourable, harmful phenomena, which caused human suffering or economic loss, were merely passing inconveniences, resulting from negligence or ineffective work on the part of individuals.

In the economic analysis of the Soviet system Grossman and others[4] conclude that shortage accounts for a large part of informal activities in Soviet economic system. In this, the informal economy is a component that is not only structural in nature, it is also indispensable to the functioning of the economy. It enables economic agents to acquire resources they need to achieve their production targets, but

---

[4] See Grossman (1992).

which they have not been allocated through regular channels because of their unavailability. Without the informal economy, the agent would have to use resources of inferior quality, otherwise plan fulfilment would become impossible. This function of the informal economy also creates a vicious circle: by subtracting resources from the formal economy (in particular, through stealing and mismanaging of state property), it continuously reproduces shortage. Informal activities open up numerous opportunities for gain and personal enrichment for managers and many workers in state enterprises and cooperatives, as well as for private individuals. At the same time they increase the supply of goods and services available to customers. In brief, informal activities create a strong network of vested interests committed to the informal economy's continued existence and create informal property rights (legally unsanctioned and even illegal, yet in reality effective, control over assets for private profit or other forms of access to future streams of informal (illegal) income and consequent wealth (Grossman 1977). Shortage is a direct cause of the growth of informal activities in which some products are exchanged for other goods and services lacking in shops. According to Kornai, the informal economy acts as a means for adapting to shortage, insofar as it provides economic agents with an opportunity to find a way around it, supplementing a whole series of other adaptation mechanisms available to the economy (e.g. queueing up, substitution of resources and goods in shortage by disposable ones, decrease of production targets, worsening of quality). Shortage therefore acts as a magnetic force, drawing as many resources as possible into the economy (Kornai 1980). In the command, non-monetary economy these possibilities are created by the use of one's workplace (access to state property and decision-making), engaging in exchange of favours and establishing personal contacts.

Even though Kornai mentioned connections and personal methods of redistribution in his analysis of the schemes of the allocation of resources in the economy of shortage (auction,[5] rationing, and

[5] The auction scheme is based on price mechanisms. It divides all claimants into two groups, those who receive the product and those who are excluded from receiving it. The sole criterion in the auction scheme is the demand price. It operates in a pure form only if the following two conditions are met. First, the buyers have been ranked strictly according to their demand price. Second, the actual price is set precisely at the level at which supply is entirely allocated to those willing to pay this price. The ranking by demand price does not necessarily correspond to a ranking by wealth or income. There may be poorer families for whom it is highly important to place their child in a kindergarten and who thus offer a relatively high price at the cost of their expenditure on other items; conversely, there may be more well-to-do families willing

queueing), it was not his aim to consider their social implications. In social terms, shortage meant that one had to have a circle of contacts, in some way connected to someone with an access to the distribution system. As one respondent put it:

> within a personal circle it was possible to exchange favours of both material and non-material kind. Everything depended on people having certain positions in the economic and state structure, positions that gave privileged access to the distributed goods and services. Not necessarily official positions: everyone in one's workplace could be useful in number of small things. If, for example, you had an acquaintance who was a shop assistant, she would keep things for you; take care of their quality (meat would be boneless); let you know what was available at the store and inform you when something special was going to appear on the shelf. Goods in short supply, etc. Also, *blat* had to do with the distribution of apartments and the construction of garages and dachas. In such more substantial matters one had to have contacts in local authorities or organisations. [22]

According to Kornai, the very term 'rationing' means allocation according to non-price criteria. The selection criteria frequently employed in practice are the following: (1) urgent need; (2) merit; (3) family background (colour, religion, nationality, the occupation of parents); (4) social status; (5) political conduct; (6) personal links of kinship and friendship with the allocator; (7) return of favours done to allocator; and (8) corruption. Criteria (2), (3), (4) and (5) are much more open to question than criterion (1). There is no society in which these criteria of selection do not operate at all in the allocation of goods. The differences between various systems consist in (a) whether the criteria operate openly or covertly, through informal mechanisms; (b) whether rationing is done by administrative authority or by the producer; (c) how widely rationing schemes based on these criteria are applied; (d) how the particular criteria are specified in practice. How criteria (2), (3), (4) and (5) are used in a rationing system is an important indicator of the nature of the socio-economic system. The use of criteria (6), (7) and (8) is openly condemned by any publicly declared and generally accepted moral rule; it is usually forbidden by law, too. Nevertheless, there is no system free of such abuses. The

---

to pay only a small amount. It seems certain, however, that there is a close positive correlation between the wealth and income of the family and the demand price offered. It is precisely this property of the scheme which provokes opposition by those who feel that this principle of allocation is unacceptable politically and morally.

issues are only how rarely or how frequently the criteria are applied and whether in important or essential decisions.

My analysis of *blat* provides an empirical description of the functioning channels of (7) and (8) in Kornai's classification and their role in circumventing the rationing schemes in the Soviet distribution system. The task is difficult since, as has been already mentioned, the selection criteria were not openly declared and, even if they were open, the actual selection process could deviate from the principles stated. In fact, it could not even deviate but still be influenced by *blat*. Consider the situation where one flat was to be allocated to one of eight top candidates in the eight privileged queues for housing. Any resource allocated through administrative rationing had to be claimed on a formal basis. People receiving this resource with the help or support of the allocator still have to have all relevant documents. The only difference was that their documents were picked from the pile of applications. It was also a matter of being attached to the privileged queue: for veterans, for single mothers, for people working in conditions of extra risk, etc.:

> When I moved into my flat I needed a telephone line to be connected. I arranged all the formalities, collected all the documents: a certificate that I am a single mother, a certificate that my child is often ill and I need to ring to the hospital in emergencies. And then I asked my good friend working at the telephone station to go to the head of the station with my documents. [3]

The same applied to the appointments for jobs, etc. In the final analysis, any rationing system affected the distribution of income. It gave preferences to some members of society over others. Rationing thus carried out a redistribution which overrode the distribution of money incomes. The effects of this redistribution were crystallised in the system of privileges which was in turn affected and deformed by the use of connections.

Rationing also implies queueing, which Kornai considers as a specific scheme of allocation of resources. He distinguishes three main types of queueing: (1) physical queueing (those waiting to be served queue up in the literal sense of the word in front of the person making the good or service available); (2) queueing by numbers (having obtained a serial number, the claimant may leave and return when it is his or her turn); (3) allocation by order of arrival (there may never be two claimants simultaneously present at the supply point, thus no physical queue can form; as consumers arrive, each of them receives as much of the product as one wants, until it is sold out). It is common in these three types that the order of arrival at the supply point (or equivalently the order of putting up a claim) operates as the only selection criterion. The order of arrival may be strictly random. But some people have more time for queueing than others. Also, much depends on the information available to the buyer: if the product arrives at the supply point at irregular intervals, then the supplier can help somebody by telling him when to come for the product. In this case the queueing scheme only apparently operates; in reality rationing (and *blat*) is taking place: the allocator has decided on the basis of his own selection criteria who should be at the head of the queue.

In everyday life queueing implied a whole range of techniques (reserving a place in a queue for somebody, ringing friends and acquaintances, buying goods for somebody else) which are not my concern here. Rather, *blat* was a way of circumventing queueing, for which it was usually hated by those who queued up. The justification of those using *blat* instead of queueing can be exemplified by Zinoviev's view on queues (1974: 283):

> In fact there's a very deep meaning in queues. For example, you take your shoes to be repaired. It's only a five minute job. But you spend at least a half an hour in the queue. You hand over the shoes. You get a ticket which says they'll take a week. Oh, you want them sooner, do you? Very well, put 'urgent'. And they tell you it'll take one day, or two or three. It makes no difference. The main thing is that they've given you a precise date. If you're inexperienced at this sort of thing, you go back on the appointed day, you stand in the queue and they tell you they're not ready, come back tomorrow. You don't go tomorrow but the day after. You queue up again and they tell you there's a delay at the factory, come back tomorrow. If you are experienced, you don't come back on the appointed day but several days later. You queue up, and they tell you they are not ready, come back tomorrow. You think: What the devil is all this mystery? It's really a mystery. In such situation one can't avoid the standard procedures of deception, queueing, insults and exasperation. You must always be in a state of confusion, anger, and ready for all sorts of unpleasantness. There is sense in all this. You must regard everything you get without difficulty as a gift of fate, a triumph, a blessing, and you should think yourself happy if you eventually manage to achieve what you have reckoned to achieve without effort. From this comes your attempts to reduce to a minimum your number of formal contacts with people on whom you depend for anything, i.e. it leads in the final analysis to a self-imposed restriction of demand. From here too comes the habit of grabbing everything that comes to hand, i.e. a lack of control of consumption which depends on external circumstances. On the other

hand people are forced to waste time on no purpose, time which they could otherwise turn to good account, for such purposes as thinking about their life, about art, or generally about themselves and their self-improvement. Bear in mind that when people spend their time in queues getting upset about the details of day-to-day life, their personalities are degraded. It isn't while standing in queues that great discoveries are made. It isn't while standing in queues that a sense of honour and human dignity grows stronger.

From this perspective, *blat* may seem quite an honourable activity.

Another distinction, drawn by Kornai in relation to shortage, has an important implications for *blat*. There is a 'vertical shortage', that is, a resource, good, or service allocated by administrative rationing, which appears in the vertical relationship between the allocator and the claimant. And there is 'horizontal shortage', appearing in the horizontal relationship between seller and the buyer, in which a resource, good or service is sold by the supplier to the customer for money. The resources of 'vertical shortage' (flats, telephone, dacha, car, etc.) are normally more valuable and desired. They are supposed to be distributed according to some known criteria, so that people are generally much more resentful towards *blat* occurring in this respect. *Blat* strategies in circumventing the rationing of 'horizontal' shortage are generally more accepted and practised. In relation to the latter, a phrase of the beloved comic actor of Soviet times, Raikin, concluding a monologue on shortage became proverbial: 'Let everything be available, but something special be lacking!'

In a situation of redistribution of scarce resources in small social worlds *blat* can be seen as a working model of survival. In rural collectives, it served the basic needs of a teacher of a rural school or a disabled or aged person incapable of producing enough in their households and allotments and thus dependent on a centralised supply. State shops in rural areas very often contained no more than ten items, normally uneatable preserves from a local factory and no basic products for everyday consumption. The only way to obtain food (which was still a problem after the administrative ration of 2 kilo of buckwheat a year, etc.) was to network in the small community. Managers or shop assistants, keeping a share for someone ('under the counter') in fact provided some real help for those unable to participate in queueing. It might be argued, however, that it was not the scarcity and shortage by themselves that generated *blat*; rather *blat* practices originated in the peculiar combination of the economy of shortage and the system of state privileges and closed distribution.

## The ideology of equality and the practice of differentiation

To understand the principles of Soviet rationing, one needs to analyse the genesis of Stalinist politics of distribution.[6] The rationing system was introduced from the very conception of the regime as an emergency measure against scarcity, starvation and extreme shortages of food supplies. Designed to satisfy immediate needs, the rationing system became linked to a worker's productive output and was supposed to guarantee supplies for the working class 'vanguard'. In the first half of the 1930s, the 10 per cent highest-paid industrial workers were earning more than three times as much as the 10 per cent lowest-paid ones. It was emphasised as an achievement of the system that the best was provided for the working class, and additional efforts were made to supply central industrial regions while peasants and declassified groups had to shoulder the burdens of this policy. Hierarchical principles of distribution were also introduced within the working class itself. According to their performance workers were allocated different rations. Shock-workers (*udarniki*) shopped at special stores, had cheaper and better food, received extra supplies and additional tokens for boots and clothes when they exceeded their plan tasks. For skilled workers material incentives increasingly displaced moral incentives.[7]

By 1929 the token system had been introduced in all urban settlements of the Soviet Union. Starting with bread tokens, rationing was extended to the other products in short supply (sugar, meat, butter, tea, etc.), and by the summer of 1931 to all other consumer

[6] Considering the origins of the socialist distribution system, we rely on the archive data published by Osokina (1993).

[7] Privileges became an instrument of the 'anti-levelling' policies of stimulating high work performance during the winter of 1935–6, when the excesses of the Stakhanovite movement reached their heights and factory trade unions boasted in press of the special care they lavished on their best-performing workers. The decree of the party committee of the mine 'Central-Irmino' of 31 August 1935 (the record was performed overnight on 30–31 August) said:

> To give him [Stakhanov] a bonus at a rate of a monthly wage . . . To allocate a flat to comrade Stakhanov till 3 September, to connect a telephone line . . . At the expense of the mine to furnish the flat with all necessities and . . . to allocate a family place at a resort for comrade Stakhanov. To reserve from 1 September two honorary seats in the club for Stakhanov and his wife to attend all movies, theatre performances and other events. (Pravda, 26 July 1987)

The speech of a Stakhanovite worker Vinogradova at the All-Union Meeting of Stakhanovites of Military Construction Sites (December 1935) contained the following: 'Since July I bought a good bed – paid 280 roubles [*applause*], bought a winter coat – paid 400 roubles [*applause*], paid 180 roubles for a summer outfit, 180 – for a watch [*applause*], 165 roubles – for a autumn coat [*applause*]' (quoted from V. Volkov, 'Kontseptsiya kul'turnosti', in *Sotsiologicheskii zhurnal*, 1–2, 1996).

goods. Trade was replaced by distribution through closed distribution systems (*zakrytye raspredeliteli*), the closed workers' cooperatives (*zakrytye rabochie kooperativy*) and the ORS (departments of workers' supply, *otdely rabochego snabzheniya*). Rations were differentiated into four categories: industrial workers on the special list, such as miners and workers in heavy industry; workers in other industries were attached to List I; other employees were attached to List II and III, according to their professions, thus constituting the other two categories (see table 3.1).

The dynamic of centralised rationing reflected political fluctuations and campaigns in relation to different groups in the population throughout the Soviet period, such as the formation of the working-class elite in the 1930s, the intellectual and artistic elite in the 1960s. It was used not only as stimulus but also served as sanction against groups and individuals. Naturally, those who were expelled or marginalised tried to conquer the system by *blat*.

Rationing policy gave members of the party-state apparatus an exceptionally privileged position. Monthly rations in the closed distribution system for nomenclatura in 1931 were as follows: 5kg of meat and sausages, 5kg of fish, 0.5kg of caviar, 5 items of canned food, 1kg of cheese, 30l of milk, 10 eggs, 1.5kg of sugar and 1.5kg of dry fruits. Apart from that their ration included clothes (2 coats for different seasons, raincoat, suit, trousers, manufacture, shirts, under-wear), as well as soap and boots. In comparison with the workers' rations at the same period of time (table 3.1) the nomenclatura enjoyed more variety (dairy products, sausages, caviar, canned food) and higher rations.

Closed distribution resulted in frequent abuses: arbitrary increases in the number of closed distribution organisations, expansion of the attached personnel, giving out foodstuffs on written (*po zapiskam*) and oral (*po zvonku*) commands of the nomenclatura, redistribution of goods within the closed distribution organisation, using the closed distribution system for serving meetings, official gatherings and conferences (Osokina 1993: 65).

> I first heard the word '*blat*' at the beginning of the 1930s when my father brought a box of sweets, nicely wrapped sweets, simple but really delicious. It was a famine those days. He bought them of course, but he bought them by *blat*, through an acquaintance working at the factory. My father was a chief engineer of the big construction site, privileged in many ways, but I think, he also used *blat* quite a lot. Another case that I remembered occurred in 1946. It

**Table 3.1.** *Monthly rations$^a$ of foodstuffs in the closed distribution system, 1931*

| | Special list (miners, heavy industry) | | | List I (other industrial workers) | | | List II (qualified employees) | | | List III (other employees) | | |
|---|---|---|---|---|---|---|---|---|---|---|---|---|
| | 1 | 2 | 3 | 1 | 2 | 3 | 1 | 2 | 3 | 1 | 2 | 3 |
| Bread | 0.8 | 0.4 | 0.4 | 0.8 | 0.4 | 0.4 | 0.8 | 0.4 | 0.4 | 0.75 | 0.35 | 0.35 |
| Flour | 1 | 1 | 0.5 | 1 | – | 0.5 | – | – | – | 1 | – | – |
| Grain | 3 | 1.5 | 1.5 | 2.5 | 1.5 | 1.5 | 1.5 | 0.85 | 0.85 | 1 | 0.5 | 0.5 |
| Meat | 4.4 | 2.2 | 2.2 | 2.6 | 1.3 | 1.3 | 1 | 1 | 1 | – | – | – |
| Fish | 2.5 | 2 | 2 | 2 | 1.4 | 1.4 | 2 | 1 | 1 | – | – | – |
| Butter | 0.4 | – | 0.4 | 0.2 | – | 0.2 | – | – | – | – | – | – |
| Sugar | 1.5 | 1.5 | 1.5 | 1.5 | 1.5 | 1.5 | 1 | 1 | 1 | 0.8 | 0.8 | 0.8 |
| Tea | 0.3 | 0.3 | 0.3 | 0.25 | 0.25 | 0.25 | 0.1 | 0.05 | 0.05 | 0.1 | 0.05 | 0.05 |
| Eggs | 10 | – | 10 | – | – | – | – | – | – | – | – | – |

$^a$ Rations are given in kg, except for eggs, per person per month. The subdivision in every list is norms (1) for workers, (2) for members of workers' families, (3) for children.

was a post-war famine, well before the abandonment of the rationing system. We youngsters wanted to celebrate the 1st of May, but we had no bread tokens. There was a door next to the bread shop entrance, to which I was occasionally sent by my father. I used to go and say 'From Victor Bogdanovich' and they sold a loaf of brown bread without tokens. And this time I went on my own risk. Asked for it, paid and went off straight to my friends. [33]

Special commissions and campaigns were organised to eliminate such abuses, but there was no way to stop these processes. The redistribution of goods took place socially, outside the sphere of production, and was often determined by personal relations. It was the result of the pressure put on those who had access to these closed distribution systems by those who did not have it.

Dunham emphasised the role of the Second World War in the potential conflict between the people and the regime. The people knew who had won the war, and how. Defeat was averted by mass exertion. So when, now in the name of peace, Stalin continued to make harsh demands of the citizens, these were resisted as they had not been before or during the war. In early post-war years this challenge was met with a policy of stepped-up coercion and intimidation: terror and the proliferation of concentration camps proved effective tools of control. Yet it is unlikely that these alone explain how the system managed to maintain itself. Dunham argues that policies of mediation, of concession, of internal alliances, of conflict resolutions came to be adopted. One such major alliance during the period from the end of the war to Stalin's death was called the 'Big Deal' (Dunham 1976:3–5). The Big Deal represented a dilution of the idealistic, egalitarian goals of Marxist socialism by means of a tacit accommodation in practice to the materialistic, self-regarding behaviour of the New Soviet middle class. It resulted from two seemingly contradictory processes: one impeded modernisation, the other worked in its favour. The wartime fatigue of the people, the devastation of the country and the strain on the economy had seriously disrupted the pre-war economic pace of development. The leadership had been forced again to put a premium on skill, on productivity, on performance, instead of on political adroitness and ideological orthodoxy, and the need for a new legion of productive engineers, organisers, administrators, and managers became pressing (Dunham 1976).

This seemed to proliferate the privileges of the nomenclatura, including not only access to goods in short supply, but also very cheap meals in specialised canteens. The apparat were provided with institutionally owned apartments (*sluzhebnaya kvartira*) and sometimes dachas. Functionaries received medical treatment in hospitals that were better equipped and less crowded than those available to others; they spent vacations in closed places better supplied than the usual holiday centre; and so on. These special services could even be provided in several grades: a higher-ranking functionary was treated in an even better hospital, shopped in even better stocked stores, used a chauffeur-driven, institutionally owned car, had a personal vacation home, etc. Many of these material privileges were also available to the functionary's family, and often to the serving personnel. Once introduced, the system of privileges was never eliminated.

High rates of growth and a general rise in material standard of living of the bulk of the Soviet population during the early years of Khrushchev's rule created a strong sense of optimism.[8] In contrast to Stalin's policies, egalitarianism was taken seriously by Khrushchev, or so it would appear. Wage differentials for managerial staff and skilled workers were reduced, and the urban–rural gap narrowed too (Nove 1982: 347–9). These changes were masked in the early years by the general rise in material well-being. Everyone, or almost everyone, was experiencing real income increases, and the reduction in differentials did not appear to be at anyone's expense (Millar 1988: 4):

> It was commonly known that the party and the army elites, artistic and scientific intelligentsia had a housekeeper and a cook. This came to an end in the late 1950s when the wage differential, which used to be 20–30 times between top and lowest wages, was reduced so that it became insufficient to employ servants. Even though the quantitative difference was reduced, professional privileges developed. [37]

A conspicuous example of professional privilege was the creation of one of the largest and advanced scientific complexes in the world, in the middle of the Siberian forest, 20 miles from Novosibirsk (Carlitts and Hall 1994: 41–57). In 1957, advised by a leading Russian mathematician, Lavrentiev, Khrushchev decided on the foundation of Akademgorodok (Academy town), which grew up into a complex of 30 research institutes, the University and infrastructure. One of the

---

[8] Consider, for example, Khrushchev's prediction: 'In the coming 10 years all Soviet people will be able to obtain consumer goods in sufficiency, and in the following 10 years consumer demand will be met in full', *Documents of the 22nd Congress of the CPSU*, vol. 2, *Report on the Programme of the Communist Party of the Soviet Union*, 17 October 1961 (New York: Cross-currents Press, 1961: 85).

boldest experiments creating a new town as an instrument of techno-economic development,[9] Akademgorodok also represented a perfect example of the hierarchical distribution system which endured in Brezhnev's times and after.

Housing in Akademgorodok was extremely stratified both geographically and qualitatively:

(1) There were high-quality residential cottages with attached land for gardens and allotments for academicians and distinguished professors. Member-correspondents[10] lived in semi-detached cottages. These cottages were located in the forest, not far but apart from the blocks of apartments, traffic, shopping areas, etc.

(2) The 'upper zone', formed by apartment buildings of reasonable quality was for middle-level scientists. Doctors of sciences occupied better apartments than candidates. Their apartments were much more spacious, comfortable and better located. These blocks were called 'doctors' houses' and their style was closer to Stalinist architecture. The rest lived in extremely small flats called '*khrushchevka*', although it was still quite prestigious to have a '*khrushchevka*' in the centre of the Akademgorodok.

(3) Flats in more modern blocks (4 flats on the floor, 9 floors, 6 blocks in one monstrous square) were better designed but poorly located. Their location was called the 'lower zone' or 'dormitory area', for they were distant from cultural centres and were crowded only after working hours.

Until 1992 every resident of Akademgorodok was attached to the food distribution system, differentiated according to status. Those in

---

[9] This accorded well with Khrushchev's vision of developing Siberia and the Far East, to take advantage of their untapped wealth in natural resources and to populate and colonise that entire half of the Soviet territory that remained sparsely inhabited. Besides, this pioneer spirit, in the view of Khrushchev and his advisers, would help shake up the bureaucratised Soviet academic institutions, giving the opportunity for rapid advancement to a new generation of scientists whose creativity was hampered by established senior academicians in the main science centres of Moscow and Leningrad. The chance to move to a new area, to start new research institutes with greater autonomy and considerable resources, proved appealing to a number of bright scientists frustrated by bureaucracy. It proved equally attractive to other scientists, young or less young, who happened to be ideologically liberal or of Jewish ancestry, and so found themselves blocked for promotion. A liberal atmosphere and a pioneer spirit prevailed. The 'Integral Club', mainly attended by physicists, was known for passionate discussions and the intensive social life of '*shestidesyatniki*' (derived from the 1960s, the generation of Khrushchev's 'thaw'). The university tolerated dissident activity, such as the only public demonstration against the Soviet invasion of Czechoslovakia in 1968 (Carlitts and Hall 1994: 47).

[10] The academic gradations in Russia are: academician, member-correspondent, doctor of sciences and candidate of sciences.

the upper stratum of academics could order things to be delivered to their doors, while the lower ones had to queue to collect their rations. The range of goods varied a lot: the supply for academicians used to include clothes and consumer durables, while for a common resident of the Akademgorodok it included 2kg of meat and 10 eggs a week with occasional extras (wine, instant coffee, canned tomatoes, tinned fish, fruits) for public holidays. The distribution of tokens for food-stuffs in irregular supply (like butter, sausages and tea) operated efficiently through this system. Prices were cheap and availability was guaranteed.

In the beginning, goods and foodstuffs for this special distribution system were supplied directly from Moscow, but even later, when goods were less plentiful, residents of the Akademgorodok were considered privileged by the industrial working-class population of Novosibirsk. This created a great hostility on the part of the local authority (the Novosibirsk Soviet), which always saw Akademgor-odok as an artificial implant that siphoned off Moscow funds for the gratification of a useless intelligentsia. It responded in predictably petty ways, for instance by allocating less water than the town needed. In turn, the Academy of Science took charge of as many practical needs as it could, bypassing the local authorities, thus fomenting the hostility (Carlitts and Hall 1994: 45). For example, the health care service for top academics was, and still is, in direct contact with Moscow medical centres: it was much better equipped, not crowded, friendly, willing to see the patient at home. The list of those attached to this special clinic was renewed annually and had to be endorsed by the Presidium of the Siberian Branch of the Academy of Sciences. The list included the following categories: (1) academicians and members of their families (including grandchildren under 18); (2) member-correspondents and members of their families; (3) doctors and members of their families staying with them; (4) candidates in leading positions (chief of the laboratory, scientific secretary of a research institute); (5) candidates with diseases cotracted in the work-place or in their profession; (6) pro-rectors of the University, (7) holders of the titles 'Hero of the Soviet Union' and 'Hero of Socialist Labour' and other prestigious awards; (8) top academics, non-members of the Siberian Branch but resident in Akademgorodok; (9) the head and the chief engineer of *Sibacademstroi*, the construction enterprise (the monopolist construction firm in Akademgorodok); (10) heads of the departments of the Presidium of the Siberian Branch; (11) the disabled who worked for the Siberian Branch. Before 1990 it also included personal pensioners, directors of schools, the local party organisation (*raikom*) and KGB bosses.[11]

Such privileges were also available to those who did not belong to the list but had executive or serving functions within distribution systems. For example, drivers delivering foodstuffs to the cottages were able to obtain everything. Special medical services were available to the clinic personnel in general and doctors in particular. Not entitled formally, the latter were normally supervised by their colleagues on informal basis. They used to have privileges in 'housing' and 'telephone' queues. In situations of conflict they could be protected by their powerful patients. Doctors[12] were stratified by their patients' status: doctors for academics, doctors for member-correspondents, doctors for doctors, etc. This resulted from the 'free choice' of patients, who recommended their doctors to their friends. Staff could also use the facilities and serve their own relatives and friends. To be served in a closed distribution system one either had to be formally entitled (which did not exclude *blat* as a possible way of attachment to the list) or to have personal contacts with someone working in it.

It should be mentioned that closed distribution systems are closed particularly in terms of information. Whereas privileges are common knowledge, there is no open information about criteria for entitlement, services and rations. Despite *glasnost'*, access to such information is still difficult to get. Osokina, the author of a book on hierarchies of distribution (1993), mentions the difficulties of obtaining information necessary for the book in the allegedly open historical archives, and explains the ways of dealing with such difficulties. The data on the health care services were also provided 'by acquaintance'. The analogous data on food special distribution system were not allowed to be given out from the archives personally by the President of the Siberian Branch of Russian Academy of Sciences and I was forced to find an informant among the former staff of the *ORS*. Getting access to closed information implied the same mechanisms and strategies as in obtaining a thing or a service. It was perhaps more difficult, as it was not so routine as obtaining food or medical treatment.

[11] In 1994 the number of the attached was 3,434, including 39 academics and 121 members of their families; 44 member-correspondents and 145 members of their families; 763 doctors of science and 1,723 members of their families; 259 candidates; 18 bosses without scientific degree; 61 widows of academics and member-correspondents; 261 others (titles and awards).

[12] Most doctors in Russia are women, and the occupational rating of the profession is lower than in the West.

Further development of privileges and consumerism became Brezhnev's contribution to socialism. It brought about an increased freedom to 'wheel and deal' at the micro-level of Soviet society, whereas at the macro-level managerial discretion was restrained and overt political dissent was persecuted and generally repressed. One aspect of such situation was tacit rationing of what was meant to be equally accessible to every citizen. Even though people were used to inequalities and considered privileges, especially related to personal achievements, as legitimate, there was a great deal of resentment towards restrictions on personal characteristics which did not depend upon people's attainments – for example, family background, place of birth or nationality. One respondent mentioned that 'the central universities had quotas for different republics and national minorities. Using his informal contacts, our Minister of Education could get more places for Buryats'. [24] I was told that in some places there were tacit restrictions for Soviet Germans and Jews entering universities or particular faculties. There were restrictions for children of dissidents, for the Chechens exiled to Kazakhstan and other minorities. [29a] Some universities and high schools even had a special reputation for such tacit rationing and were known as 'not to be approached without *blat*'.

Connections were necessary to avoid the restrictions for travel abroad. It was a common practice everywhere that groups for tours abroad were formed according to some implicit principles that people knew from experience: (a) a worker, (b) a peasant, (c) a certain percentage of women, (d) party members and candidates, (e) a Komsomol member, (f) a supervisor (normally a KGB man), (g) a leader of the group (a boss of the party or state apparatus) and (h) a couple of *blat* people (a lover of the leader or a relative of some VIP): 'It should be said that in the period of the "cold war" the (a)–(c) people were also special, so-called "nomenclatura-workers" who went abroad regularly and knew what to say and how to behave. Some others went occasionally, but the selection was severe. Interestingly enough, we were liked abroad more then.' [26]

'Party membership' was itself a privilege. Apart from material privileges supplied to the party-state nomenclatura, it was generally true that every party member was more privileged than a non-member. Party members were more privileged in at least three senses: first, as already mentioned, in relation to the law; second, in access to resources; third, in career opportunities:

> It was common knowledge that unless one was a party member, he
> or she couldn't be appointed for a leading position. Party member-
> ship was like an extra diploma to qualify for further career opportu-
> nities. I wanted to enter the party, not only because it was necessary
> for a career, but also because I believed in communist ideas of those
> days. But I realised that I couldn't get there, because membership
> was also rationed. Workers were in demand while I belonged to the
> intelligentsia and had to wait about ten years in the queue. [13]

Party membership was not normally referred to as obtained by *blat*,
even if recommendations were given by acquaintances and other
breaches of formal procedure took place. This was partly because of
the nature of the 'by *blat*' language games which used to be applied to
the mundane, not the political. Partly, because the procedure was
collective and public. Partly, because challenges to, in this case
collective, misrecognition game in which trust and piety was routinely
granted to the Communist party were more severely punished. For
common people the privilege of jumping the party membership
queue occurred rarely. Some people, however, were forced to join the
party without any queue as a condition of occupying leading positions. In fact, party membership became a practical condition for
entering any leading post, and there were only a few exceptional
people who could flout this tacit convention.[13]

Despite the practice of differentiation in every sphere of the Soviet
life, the ideology persistently referred to equality and self-sacrifice as
necessary conditions for achieving the goals and tasks of socialism. It
could be said retrospectively that people's beliefs in a radiant and
happy future were exploited, but it was also true that such values
gave people a spirit to survive and resulted in real achievements.
People often commented on their experiences as dedicated to the
grand mission. Yet at the same time these ideas became muddied by
the exigencies of day-to-day life. The expectation of a bright future to
come all too often turned into a parasitic attitude towards the state
supposed to provide free or cheap services and take care of every
member of the society.

On the family level, the practice of self-sacrifice in favour of future
generations became reoriented towards one's own children. The
Communist slogan 'All the best – to our children!' turned into
practices of nepotism by parents and parasitism by children (*izhdi-*

---

[13] These people were known and particularly respected. One of them was an academician Budker, who headed the Institute of Nuclear Physics in Akademgodorok for
more than twenty years. He was a friend of Sakharov and continued this relationship
throughout Sakharov's exile and disfavour.

*venchestvo*). Parents were meant to help, to support, to take care of grandchildren, often at the expense of their own personal lives or interests. It was a very common practice that children (especially sons) got married and brought their spouses into their parents' flat, because there were no places for young families to rent and usually no money to support themselves. Parents were thus forced to apply for improvement of their housing conditions, and the most influential were given a room in a communal flat. It was called 'being given a room "for exchange"'. In other words, one received an opportunity to exchange one's own flat and this room for a bigger apartment, but it went without saying that the young family moved into that room to stay separately. The most powerful parents could arrange a separate flat. One of my respondents, a daughter of the party apparatchik, reported about her brother:

> My parents did everything for him. He got married in April, and as early as the end of May (!) father arranged him a flat. He bought them a car in a year, then constructed a garage. They supported me financially and bought all my best clothes, but this was minor. I wanted to be independent, did not ask for anything, left home for the University in another city. Foolish! If I stayed, I could have had a flat as well, I suppose. [11]

Interestingly enough, receiving things and services 'for free' at the expense of the state and settling problems for a child became as common and legitimate as obtaining commodities in short supply and thus provided even more incentives for *blat*. Consequently, *blat* was quite fundamental to the day-to-day working of Soviet society. *Blat* stood in a paradoxical relation to the Soviet social and economic order. Quite literally, the system could not have functioned without it: *blat* was the prime way of getting things done in a non-market society in which money counted for rather little. At the same time as it was the condition for continuation of the Soviet order, *blat* also subverted it. It ran counter to official ideology and meant that centralised control of economic life was routinely undermined and placed in question. We shall consider the workings of personal networks in Soviet society in more detail in chapter 4.

# 4    The use of personal networks


Do not have 100 roubles, do have 100 friends.          (A folk saying)

*Blat* has both intimate and institutional dimensions, so access by *blat* to goods and services is a matter of personal qualities and occupational opportunity. The role of personal and occupational ties in the allocation of resources has been studied extensively within the framework of network analysis (see, for example, Wellman and Berkowitz 1988). Network analysis is concerned with how to locate people in occupational, educational or personal networks, how to estimate who and what they know, the resources to which they have access and the social constraints affecting their behaviour. But our interest in this chapter will be a more focused one: to consider the impact of personal and occupational factors in the formation of *blat* networks.

It has already been mentioned that *blat* networks are not strictly speaking personal networks. Personal networks – defined from the standpoint of focal individuals – can be conceived as a set of nodes (kin, neighbours, friends and colleagues) and ties (intimate/non-intimate, routine/non-routine, active/non-active).

Those who research personal networks usually interview a large sample of respondents and inquire into the composition, relational patterns and contents of their networks. The content of such networks includes emotional aid, companionships, household aid, lend/give items, housing search aid and job information. *Blat* networks overlap with personal networks but also imply occupational access to public resources. On the one hand, they can be narrower than personal networks, for not all intimate or routine ties are used for the purposes of gaining resources. On the other hand, *blat* networks can be wider than personal networks, for they also include non-intimate, non-routine ties – ties which are not necessarily active. These ties can be impersonal, that is, mediated by members of a personal network.

They can also be non-active, actualised only when a need arises. Despite all the difficulties in definition, it is possible to discuss the types of nodes and ties constitutive of *blat* networks.

As the topic was delicate, the quality of the data depended significantly on the willingness of people to disclose their networks and the access to resources, often public, that these networks yielded. The interviews were particularly telling when people were pleased about their connections or nostalgic about 'mutual help' and human relationships in Soviet times. I shall begin by describing one of the most elaborate life histories, because it allows insight into the construction and maintenance of *blat* networks. It also indicates how the institutional and everyday contexts which made *blat* both possible and necessary are disappearing with the winding-down of Soviet society.

### Natalia's story

Natalia is a retired doctor with a good reputation in her field. Needless to say I could approach her only by introduction. She was a strong character, confident and optimistic, looking much younger than her age. I came to her place in the evening and we sat in her kitchen till very late, talking, having tea and supper which she cooked for me without even interrupting the interview. Some would call her a *blatmeister*. As she put it herself:

'Everybody in the clinic considered me the essential "*blat*" person. They told me directly, "there is nobody who has more connections than you." They used to say, "She can do everything" (*ona mozhet vsyo*). All 650 people. I just laughed. Why me? There were other doctors, but they did not care so much. I always called the patient after an appointment, and asked how they were. People came to see me, not to see others. They were grateful, they knew my birthday and something special always arrived on it.'

I asked questions occasionally to change the direction of the interview or to focus it on particular details but generally it was a self-contained story.

'I had a lot of privileges through our Party organisation even though I was not a Party member. For example, at work people preferred not to bother me. I had a hobby, I liked to travel abroad. I used to go every year or so. Some people were not given permission but I always had it. This caused many rumours, "Where does she get the money?" It was difficult to obtain permission to travel abroad.

One had to struggle for the right to go. One had to take on some party burden which party members did not want to carry themselves – anything to make the party unit approve the application to travel which was then directed to the local party organisation (*raikom*). I was responsible for press subscriptions for seventeen years. All "*Soyuzpe-chat*"[1] were my patients. Subscriptions were rationed but in fact it was me who controlled distribution. Our clinic was always in favour because of me.

Once the party unit did not want to approve my application, but there was a telephone call from *raikom* and thereafter the party unit ceased to bother me. After that people decided the City boss must be my relative or acquaintance. In fact, one man, a senior police detective, was chasing me at that time and he ensured that I was not troubled. His rank meant a lot. For example, people always underwent a test before a tour which I never did even though I went abroad seventeen times. It was a known fact. I did not bribe anybody but I took care of many things. All the secretaries knew that they could come to see me any time. If personal troubles occurred they could come to talk to me at the end of my surgery hours. If they were unhappy they could even come to my place. These relations were not about money, they were very warm. In my understanding this was not *blat*.

Of course a contact in *raikom* had much influence. Once I called a secretary, "Oh, what shall I do? I've got everything ready and signed but where shall I go?" She said: "Don't worry. There is someone who used to head one of the offices here who is now booking places for tours abroad." I went to him "from her" as it were that time. And in general, coming "not from the street" but "from somebody" was prevalent.'

Q: And why was it so important to be introduced?

'Because there were always shortages in the days when prices were acceptable. Many could afford tours but it was not easy to book them. Those who were engaged in trade had no chance to go at all. I knew one shop assistant who I sympathised with (apart from anything else because her husband had deserted her, left her with a small daughter). She was wealthy but I felt sorry for her. I always tried to help her. In order to arrange for her visit to India, not to speak of the West, just to India, I had to go to someone in the City Council and vouch for her, only then was she approved. But this was not easy for tradespeople were treated like those who smuggled currency, possession of which

---

[1] *Soyuzpechat'* is an All-Union organisation concerned with the distribution of periodical press.

was a serious crime. After some time (in my sixth or seventh tour) I realised why they let me go so easily. It turned out that my father was in the NKVD troops. That's why they let me go to the capitalist countries, to France in 1974, to Japan, to the round-Europe tour. This caused much envy, especially from those who did not get a permit.

People were longing for tours. Imagine there were no tours to Japan for five years. And then suddenly there were 35 places. How could you be sure to get one? Only if someone influential was representing you. My people used to say, "OK, we helped you, but you helped us to help you." There had to be a doctor in every tourist group. It rarely happened though that I was the only doctor in a group but my occupation helped to get me a place. I never paid for such help.'

Q: You were saying that the importance of introductions was predicated upon shortages so that only people who came 'from Ivan Ivanovich' could get what they wanted. But it must also have been important that those who provided an actual favour, could expect one in return. Wasn't that another stimulus?

'That would depend on Ivan Ivanovich's position. If the Chief Doctor sent someone to me, I would not accept even a small present. I would say, "Thank you, excuse me. This must be for Ivan Ivanovich. I've done it for him." Often someone introduced turned into my friend after a while. One has to observe carefully what, where and how.'

Q: How did you know 'what, where and how'? How is it possible to know when and whom to ask and whether to bring a present or not?

'It was very silly indeed when you happened to have a proper contact but just did not realise it. A problem was urgent but you did not recognise you had the solution to hand. Or you made much ado when it was not needed. For example, on one occasion I thought my son was not automatically exempt from army service and started pulling all the strings I could. When I contacted someone at a senior level, do you understand me, senior level, he said, "there was no need to fuss, he's been exempt since he was fifteen."

Then there was another question, to transfer him from a part-time to a full-time course at the University. I tried to do this through official channels. What an example of formal procedure. A file of documents certifying that he couldn't study in the evenings because of poor sight, and that his evening work coincided with his part-time course, his references and grades, everything was sent to the Ministry of Education of the Russian Federation. It was a clear-cut case but it got rejected. When I got hold of a contact I was told, "You can send anything there for five years and more, but you won't get it processed until the file is 'ticked.' There is a tacit agreement with the University." So I became desperate for that tick. I asked everybody I could think of but in vain. There was a woman, the vice-dean of some faculty, whom I knew from my tours. She had asked whether she could come to see me in the hospital, and I had said, "Of course, what you are talking about?" It was long ago. But now that I felt I couldn't do much, I went to her. I asked directly whether she was friendly with anybody and she said "Him and him . . ." One of them was the right man. I had seen him ten times or so. I went again with introduction and he said, "Oh, you are from her . . ., why didn't you say at once?" The documents were ticked, sent off again and the question was solved positively. The idea is simple: from many equals the one who is known gets chosen. It is likely that some bribery occurred but I never bribed anybody. I paid with my warmth, attention and care. It was also important to find proper words, to have a way with people. Perhaps, I was a psychologist of a kind, but I also had experience. For I had to make everything happen myself.

Life was harsh. I did not even have a residence permit in the beginning. I got it by chance. I worked at a birth clinic then. At 8.30 a.m. all personnel got together to change their robes, and I asked jokingly once what was the full name of the City Council so I could write to them. Everyone laughed but afterwards someone came and told me. She knew because her sister worked there. That's how I got temporary registration. Nobody listened to me before: my husband had left me, I had a child and wanted to get registered temporarily at my father's place. The sister of that doctor introduced me to her chief.'

Q: Is it possible to repay such things?

'Her sister never came back to me for anything. I do not remember now whether I brought her champagne or not. Perhaps I did. Do you understand me, the favour was sometimes quite significant, a box of chocolates would be just a symbolic appreciation. It was not a repayment. I could repay kindness in my profession, talk with people and pay attention to them that was still inadequate.'

Q: You have a light character, cheerful, open. This must be very helpful.

'Yes, I was jolly, artistic, energetic. Everything was happening around me in the tours. People who went on those tours were elites in their fields. The head of the group was normally someone from the regional Party committee (*obkom*), and 4–5 people were from the KGB.

These contacts lasted, you made friends on such tours. I was not a party official but I watched state parades from government boxes. I did not pay or anything.'

Q: Is there any specific language or style for making contacts?

'I was told many times that I talk well. People felt that I had weight. It was a confident tone that made people do things for me. My professional experience as a chief, the ability to talk to people gave me a lot. There was a funny case again, in N town. We queued in front of a restaurant while locals were let in without any queueing. I went to the manager and required the "book for complaints" and she said to me, "You? Why didn't you approach me before? You would have had a table long ago."

Another thing which I think is important is not to reject or despise people, never to make a fuss or to toady, never to chatter or boast, but to remain discrete and to be nice to people. To give you an example. For ten years some VIPs in N town were my good friends. Of course, they would not visit me if they came here, not those friends. But every time I arrived there I was met by a "Volga-31" with dark windows. I could choose where to stay. Return air tickets (a particular problem during the summer season), when I decided to go, were delivered to the hotel.'

Q: How come?

'Because of one accidental meeting but also because of my character. I went into the Head Doctor's office once and saw a respectable looking man asking about a drivers' medical examination. "The Chief is busy," I said, "let me tell you all about it." We went out of the office and I explained everything, told him my surgery hours and generally helped him. We became friends and it lasted. Once I told him I did not have enough money to go abroad for a holiday. He persuaded me to go to N town introducing me to his friend who was director of a pioneer-camp there. I did not want to be surrounded by youths but it was cheap and organised. So I went and hardly saw the director. Only in fact twice, once to greet him and once to thank him. I told him that I had not expected it to be so nice, for I was used to going on holiday abroad. We have been friends for ten years now. He became a party boss in the meantime. It was not that I went every year, but I could ring any time and say "Oh, you know, I am exhausted. I would love 10 days off. What do you think? How much is one day in a resort?" I could go on my own or with my husband or send my son there. I never paid extra, nothing at all. But one thing was sacred: New Year greetings. I started it and he appreciated it very much.'

Q: Wasn't it your female charm?

'Oh, no. Not at all. New Year treats, something for the table, that's all! It did not matter whether I went that year or not. I sent something special even if I could not have it myself.'

Q: What do you mean by 'arranging' things?

'Well, if you are arranging a banquet in a restaurant, you need theatre. It is essential to talk to people, to explain, to inspire. Such a big man, such an occasion! The person who is paying has also to be prepared: instructed what to say, given a French perfume to give to the manager, taught to kiss her hand.

Lots of time is spent on the phone. You do things all the time. You may have your supper and think: some go to sleep early so I have to make three calls before 9 p.m., two calls after, two long distance calls after 10 p.m. (cheap rate). It is important to keep busy. Sometimes I did not react to a first request, waiting for confirmation of need. Otherwise, you do something and they say afterwards: "Thank you, I don't need it yet." It is necessary to conserve effort.

The reason that I was treated well in the clinic and my patients were taken first for operations, I think, was that I never admitted that I did not need what I requested (even though it happens in my profession that patients change their mind and do not show up for the operation). I could sometimes lie tactfully, but never rejected a favour. It is important to help also those who are not useful people. I especially feel pity for women and try to help them. I knew a single mother in my block and gave her food and things. I did not believe in God but still thought it was important to do good deeds.'

Q: Do you know anybody more energetic than yourself?

'Yes, I've got one college mate. She is a genius of organisation. Funerals, ceremonials. She dresses perfectly, all outfits go to a second-hand shop (komissionka) at top prices. "My" second-hand shop, of course, but all the same. She helped everybody but did not hesitate to press for reciprocal favours. She was not occupied by housework as her mother did it for her. She got people clothes, got furniture or whatever.'

Q: What for? Was it for profit?

'No profit whatsoever. It was natural for her, just a talent for fixing. All my friends were like that, lively and cheerful.'

Q: Who was closest to you?

'I had eleven friends, all women, who were my very best friends and there were people who helped me in times of hardship (they were lower in social status and never came to my birthday parties but if they asked for a favour I strained every nerve to provide it).'

Q: What are they?

'Not doctors. Friends from various situations. One had an operation. She was first introduced as the friend of another doctor and then attended me every half year for tests. She found my weak spot. I was a theatre fan and she brought me tickets for all the premieres. I paid for it, it cost nothing in those days but, of course, I remembered her. This went on for three or four years until she helped me in a crisis when I was robbed of a large sum of money. Later, I would say, I did her many favours. She used my contacts quite actively (booking tours and holidays, medical certificates, etc.). I introduced (*svodila*) her to people. Some people charged for that, but not I. I introduced people with no profit for myself. You need a ticket, go to Polina and pay as appropriate. She needed tickets all the time for her husband. I could not get them for her every time, so I introduced her to Polina. Polina must have got something from that.'

Q: Are you still in touch with your friends and acquaintances?

'Relations are changing now. I have a neighbour with whom I used to get together all the time. Now we do not eat together any more. My husband did some plumbing for him recently and he invited us for a cup of hot chocolate. That's all! Life used to be more social. Perhaps it is my age. But generally speaking I notice that people have tended to reduce their contacts to family, to go for dinners only with relatives even if it was not the case before. Things used to be easier. I can't imagine that I would go somewhere and not be offered a bottle of wine. Most improbable! Now it is a cup of coffee. Soon you won't be offered even that!

Those who have became wealthy have dropped out of my circle. And I also prefer not to contact them so as not to feel poor and miserable. I never was prosperous. I only indulged myself when I was on holiday. Shoes were borrowed for the duration of my holiday and taken back to the shop afterwards. If I bought a dress, I put it on a couple of times and then sold it, that was the way to be (*tak i krutilas'*). My birthday is in the same month as the director of that shoe shop. I do not need shoes nowadays but this does not mean I have cut her off. I sent her a very good present this year, but I can't just drop by for a cup of tea or something, it doesn't even spring to mind. Every time I go to see her I try to look respectable. I am on formal terms with her (*na 'Vy'*). Recently, however, nobody but her helped me out again.'

Q: Have you ever broken any relationship?

'Rarely, but I regret that now. Sometimes I was not fair. I was angry with one woman who came for an appointment and offered a saucepan set which she claimed was worth 140 rubles plus 20 rubles extra in cash. I could not stand it. If she said 160, I was not going to argue about the price. Later I decided she was right, not me, she was honest. I was unfair towards her. It was explained to me later that shop assistants pay extra themselves. If they sell you something at its price, they must pay the difference. So they limit their favours.'

Q: How did you know when to limit your requests?

'From practice. I always felt it, but there were, of course, objective limits. I had good contacts in many health resorts. I could stay in hotels as long as I wanted. Once I went to stay in a hotel with my son who stupidly did not have his passport on him. Even though I had been introduced the manager demanded that his passport be provided. When the passport was conveyed through a train conductor and brought to her, she sighed explaining that she was not sure till the very last minute that he was my son. The hotel was plagued by gigolos and "sugar-mummies" and even though I was introduced she had to check.'

Q: Did everyone use *blat*?

'Party bosses did not need to fuss, they had everything without *blat*. Everybody else needed it. Just remember what life was like. Everything had to be "obtained": furniture, books, subscriptions, wallpaper, tiles, cosmetics, underwear. Everything was prohibited, rationed and censored.

I even arranged schools for children. My college mate asked me to arrange a place for her child in an elite school (she helped me once with my flat documents). That school was nearby. Chatting with my neighbour I happened to ask about our common acquaintance who turned out to be friendly with the vice-principal of that school. Wow! I said, she's a good girl and her father is a worker who will put things right in the school, windows or whatever. Nobody paid, rather mutual interests were served (*poshli drug drugu navstrechu*).

Of course those close to the nomenclatura, their mistresses, for example, could also have many things: apartments in the city centre, telephones; rumours overlooked and forgotten. I happen to recall an example. It is kind of funny now, but at the time was all too serious. Minor troubles could turn into big problems. When I was in India, I went to a shop on my own. It was about closing time and I hailed a velo-cart (*ricksha*). Well, I did not even hail it actually, they begged for a minor sum for the round trip and I agreed. The trouble was that using a ricksha was considered exploitation of slave labour and I was to be discussed and publicly accused at a formal group gathering. I shared my room with a doctor who was having a relationship with the head of the group. He did not mention the incident in the report. That was important, for I would not have been able to go abroad again if he had done so. That's for sure. One learnt from such experiences and acquired a practical sense: for example, of how to make an offer without overtly making it.'

Q: Did money play a role in such relations?

'I never had enough money in fact. When I needed something I had to borrow money. It could happen that I borrowed money and did not give them back, but that was minor. When I needed a fridge I had to ask twice, then she called and said "Come and take it, and I'll give you money if you don't have any now." I do not remember how I returned the debt.

It was a hard time for me, I was always out of fashion. At that time they had already started taking 10 rubles above the price of a dress. But my acquaintance, a shop assistant, could not charge me 10 rubles extra. How could she come to see me after that? A state price was only for the closest circle, in which I was not included. So, it was easier for her not to offer me dresses at all. I never paid extra, I had no money. Food was another matter. I went to familiar place (*k svoim*) and "ordered" stuff. Goods in short supply were available to me but I had to count kopecks.'

Despite all these problems Natalia complained in the end that nowadays her status has declined, her occupation is not so much in demand: 'Many private surgeries have appeared. If someone needs to save money, I can still arrange operations more cheaply. But now money, money, money is everywhere,' she concluded sadly.

### Personal ties and dispositions for networking

Natalia's case is one of those where lack of direct access to goods was compensated for by talent in creating a *blat* network. Certain individuals could make themselves as powerful as those who held high formal positions just by developing refined skills of negotiating and acquiring an ability to form a large social network that could serve as a form of wealth or as a resource-base in itself. *Blat* was often related to the character of the person in question: to some it came naturally, some had to exert themselves to build it, some never used the opportunities they had. Every member of a *blat* network can be described in terms of one of the following categories. The first was formed by those who seemed naturally endowed with this kind of talent (for example, Natalia). Most people belonged to a second category – competent players of the misrecognition game. They used their relationships only if need itself legitimised the request (if people of this category tried to be strategic in *blat*, this often had a negative effect on their personal relationships). The third category were those who had a capacity to engage in *blat* but did not wish to because they considered it distasteful and demeaning (if they did, they militantly denied it). Let us consider these three categories in more detail.

The first category consisted of the '*blatmeisters*'. *Blatmeisters* engaged in fixing those daily problems of others would match the function of 'brokers' in network analysis. A broker linking two networks (circles) often takes a share of resources passing through that position. Using his or her contacts as a resource, a broker can prevent the formation of direct links. Brokers, by virtue of their structural location, cannot be full members of any one circle. Often their very marginality means that they are not fully trusted because no one circle can exercise effective social control over them.

An example of the pervasiveness and importance of connections was documented in the Soviet film, *The Blond Around the Corner* (1985). The heroine, an important person in a Moscow supermarket, presented her acquaintances to her fiancee by whispering what services the friend was able to provide – tickets to shows, resorts on the Black Sea, airline and railway tickets, and so on. She was so convinced of her power that she asked a prominent scholar, one of her private clients, what food (caviar, perhaps) the members of the Nobel prize committee would need in order to encourage them to vote for her husband, who in her opinion had made a sensational discovery. The most remarkable trait of this influential woman was her deep conviction that these private exchanges of goods and services were the most natural thing in a socialist society (Shlapentokh 1989: 210–11). Another image of the blatmeister was represented in a satiric comedy *Ty – mne, ya – tebe* (You help me, I help you). The film depicted twin brothers: one was an honest fishing inspector struggling against theft of state property in a provincial town while the other – a charming individual of the same appearance – served in a prestigious sauna in Moscow and was very popular among his VIP customers. The plot derived from the fact that the latter substituted for his ill brother at his workplace. He created a great deal of trouble in the area but obtained a new boat and equipment for the fishing inspection, organised an article about his brother in the local press and arranged the construction of a garage

for him. He also insisted on his brother's moving up in the apartment
allocation queue (where his brother had not even been registered due
to his principles), made everybody cheerful in his brother's family
and sorted out his brother's strained relations with the director of a
local enterprise polluting the river. He used the names of his customers and acquaintance with them in order to achieve his targets. His
life style was lavish: a flat in Moscow, an antique-type telephone,
imported goods, stereo music, caviar and sturgeon, the best places at
the theatre, tours abroad, prestigious resorts and contacts with well
known people. His cheerful energy, good will and humour appeared
attractive despite the obvious moral of the film: while *blat* was not
illegal itself, in the final analysis it was connected with illegal
activities. When the hero arrived back in Moscow he was offered
caviar as many times before. This time, however, he realised it was
obtained illegally. The film revealed the roots of *blat*: it was indirectly
related to criminal activities and a system of privileges. After the hero
realised where the caviar he used to obtain came from, he turned
against his *blat* 'friends' and his VIP customers.

The exaggerated image of the *blatmeister* in the film in fact represented a very human character – warm, perhaps simple-hearted and
not quite aware of what he was doing, but by no means calculative or
egoistic. In reality, such characters who solved problems and arranged
things for others formed a stratum called 'useful people' (*nuzhnye
lyudi*), who were in demand when something was needed. They were
people with lots of contacts, not necessarily pleasant to everyone, but
as was mentioned by Natalia, energetic, jolly and cheerful – a
demeanour that allowed them to acquire new contacts as well as to
sustain *blat* networks. As a rule, *blat* networks originated in long-term
relationships and consisted of regular access to each other's resources
rather than just favour-for-favour exchanges. Needs were also generated by these networks, for they would throw up unexpected channels
by which resources could be obtained. There was no clear-cut quanti-
fication of reciprocity within such networks, there was a more
intuitive sense of mutual obligations supported by eagerness to
belong to the system and fear of being excluded from it. Trust enabled
the admission of need from the critical to the minor – say, two lemons
to be sent to a hospital. In these networks many problems were solved
by phone: a call to a trade organisation to find out whether lemons
were available in the city at all, where they were distributed, who
would introduce one to the distributor and finally how the lemons
would be picked up. *Blatmeisters* had the most widespread needs

because they also sought to satisfy the needs of others and therefore the most intensive use of contacts.

The second category of people misrecognised *blat* in their relationships and often conceived it in terms of mutual help. They valued relationships in themselves and did not think of them in terms of costs and benefits. They did, however, take advantage of relationships when such possibilities arose. Potentially they were able to make use of their relatives and friends but they tried to only when moved to do so by an urgent need. Such needs normally arose at the major stages in the life cycle. Needs connected with biological cycle – pregnancy, birth of a child, a serious illness of a member of the family, funerals – were of great importance and most often figured as an excuse for using *blat* contacts. The major social stages of the life cycle stimulated *blat* as well: starting school (as education was free and formally all schools were the same, to obtain a place in the best one was a matter of *blat*), entering high school or university, getting exemption from military service, searching for a job, etc. One should also note that needs are context-bound. They can be defined only in the context of individual circumstances and personal preferences as well as the level of general provision of services and the Soviet cultural context. It is this contextualised concept of need that allows us to grasp the idea of *blat* networks. People were forced to face such problems by the basic exigencies of life. The more desperate the situation was, the more likely that the whole family and all friends would be involved in the search for necessary contacts.

The third category was formed by the minority of people sometimes called 'true Soviet citizens' who not only declared that they did not use *blat* but did not in fact use it. Even if they were not happy with a standard of living offered by the system, they accepted it. They found it moral to queue and hated those who avoided queueing. They helped others but did not like to be helped. This attitude led to lower expectations, thus producing individuals with a peculiar perception of independence: to survive the system without the softening effects of *blat*. They protected themselves from bureaucracy by the passive decision to stand aside from it as much as possible. One respondent explained:

> It is immoral to go and arrange something at the expense of the others. I have been waiting for the telephone to be connected for 21 years. And I am still waiting. This is all because I did not go there and did not complain. If I had complained, I would have got it long ago because I am the holder of the Order of Labour honour.

I have no phone because I have no *blat* and don't want to have it. [31]

These people of high morality were acutely described by Zinoviev as adaptable *Homo Sovieticus*, who did not mind queueing, lowering their needs and 'keeping their heads down' (Zinoviev 1974: 326). It would not have occurred to them in the Soviet Wonderland, where public esteem has never been on the side of efficiency or initiative, that waiting for 21 years might not be meritorious.

Among those who claimed they did not use *blat* connections (51 per cent of the population in 1992 according to VTSIOM data, see Introduction, p.81) we should distinguish those who would accept the opposite when reminded about 'help' given or received in emergency cases and those for whom *blat* efforts were redundant, for they were partners or relatives of *blat*-users (for example, Egor Ivanovich, see p.137). Because for a *blat*-user personal needs are often identified with the needs of the family, other members of the latter can be sincere in saying that they were personally not involved with *blat*.

There were individuals, sometimes called 'truth-lovers' (*pravdo-lyubtsy*), who expended energy in opposing *blat* and who did not fall in the above three categories. They struggled 'for principles' either publicly or by writing complaints. But normally the consequences were limited, for the overall struggle against *blat* also implied struggle against privileges and therefore against the socialist distribution system and the state.

### Types of needs and *blat* networks

*Blat* is not easily subject to network analysis. This is not only because people are forgetful or unwilling to reveal their needs and networks. Data on *blat* networks are difficult to collect for a number of reasons. First, *blat* connections intersect with personal networks so there is scope for the 'misrecognition' of *blat* networks (even though the criterion for distinguishing *blat* from 'mutual aid' seems obvious for an outsider – if one helps not from one's own pocket this is considered as *blat* by others – in conditions of pervasive use of state property people see it differently). Second, except for *blatmeisters*, the *blat* networks of ordinary people are largely potential and actualised only when an urgent need arises. Third, *blat* networks include not only immediate contacts but also people who one knows only indirectly by recommendation. Let us construct a model of a *blat* network for Natalia's case (see figure 4.1). The contacts are presented in the top

**Figure 4.1** *Natalia's blat network*

| Contacts: | Family | Neighbours | Colleagues | Friends | Friends of friends | Useful people | VIPs |
|---|---|---|---|---|---|---|---|
| **Regular needs** | | | | | | | |
| Foodstuffs | | | | | | X | |
| Clothes | | | | X | | | |
| Household | | | | X | | X | |
| Housework | | | | | | X | |
| Hobby | | X | | X | | X | |
| **Periodical needs** | | | | | | | |
| Holidays | | | | | | X | X |
| Health resorts | | | | | | | X |
| Travel tickets | | | | X | | | |
| **Life cycle needs** | | | | | | | |
| Birth clinic | | | X | | | | |
| Kindergarten, school | | X | | | X | X | X |
| Military service | | | | | | X | |
| High school | | | | | | X | X |
| Job | | | | | | | |
| Flat | | | X | | | | X |
| Hospital | | | | | X | | |
| Funeral | | | | X | X | | |
| **Needs of others** | X | X | X | X | | – | – |

row, where the personal contacts Natalia named in the interview, such as family, friends, useful people, etc. are ordered from the more routine and frequent to the less routine contacts. The same logic underlies the classification of Natalia's needs: more routine and frequent needs are presented as 'regular needs'; less routine as 'periodic'; needs which arise rarely, at particular life stages, are classified as 'life cycle needs'. 'Needs of others' include similar types of needs which Natalia can satisfy by using the whole range of her contacts. By being an intermediary she is capable of keeping such a ramified *blat* network.

In a network model of somebody whose needs are satisfied through Natalia, she may figure as a neighbour or a friend, but her needs would not be necessarily included in the line 'needs of others'. In this case, that somebody is a customer of Natalia's *blat* network. There would be some other significant 'others' in his or her network though, for he or she may also appeal to Natalia to satisfy needs of his or her family, best friends, etc. Dealing with the 'needs of others' is therefore an important aspect of *blat* networks. It is both characteristic of *blatmeisters*, indicative of mediated contacts and constitutive of the 'misrecognition' of *blat*.

It is possible to imagine ex-Soviet citizens fitting their personal experiences into such a scheme retrospectively and in so doing, perhaps, recognising their own engagement with *blat* and estimating the extent to which their needs were developed and their connections used.

### The gender dimension in networking

*Blat* networks can also be examined in terms of gender. What was most noteworthy about this line of inquiry was that my questions relating to gender often puzzled interviewees. When asked about gender differences in creating *blat* networks, respondents, whether women or men, were vague or tentative in their answers. For most of the people I interviewed gender was not a salient category in considerations of *blat* ties.

Although there was no general consensus as to whether *blat* was practised more often by men or women, gender distinctions did affect the focus of people's *blat* efforts. 'Tolkach' was a classical male hero while women tended to use *blat* for 'smaller' things. There was a Soviet joke, however: women decide on 'small' things, like where to go for vacation, whether to buy a car, men on 'big' things like whether the USSR should get out of the war in Afghanistan. 'Small' things also included buying foodstuffs that were not readily available in stores through friends, or trying to enter their child in a nursery with a good reputation. More complicated tasks, such as obtaining a job, acquiring construction materials, or obtaining official permission for a dacha or an allotment, were usually left to men to handle. Division of tasks, however, was not the same in every family. Rather, there had to be at least one person in a family, even if extended, who could take care of the needs of other members. This person, whether a man or a woman, assumed this role because of his or her occupational position, social talent or type of character. If a man could not play this role for one or other reason, however, his wife or mother were most probably forced into it.

It follows from the above that divorced women were generally more involved with *blat* practices than were married women. Most of the *blatmeisters* I met were single or divorced women forced to deal with the outer world to maintain their well-being. Their extra-familial status allowed them to flirt and involve in relationships facilitating *blat* exchanges. It also allowed them to spend more time for socialising with clients and acquaintances, both at work and at home. Their homes and kitchens could serve as a base of *blat* communities, whose various needs, including the most intimate, were arranged to be satisfied.[2] The high rate of divorce and lower rate of remarriage for women meant that it was not unusual for women to face the harsh condition of bringing up children on their own.

Traditionally, married women in Russia have carried more responsibility for maintaining the household than men, a tendency which only got worse as a result of the socialist movement for the 'social liberation of women' and the post-war legacy of a relative shortage of males. In any case women engaged in *blat* practices if their husbands were not in a position to supply necessities. Women were more conscious of family image and thus more involved in obtaining prestige objects. They were also more demanding for consumer goods, such as fashionable clothes or consumer durables. In the 1970s possession of imported living-room furniture was a common aspiration of many women in the Soviet Union (as were American jeans for teenagers). Much effort was made to entertain and be hospitable. All the best things were given to a guest: new sheets and the best food, both difficult to obtain were saved especially for guests. Also women were

[2] I am not yet ready to present sufficient evidence of the importance of sexual practices for *blat*. Some indications are in the text but this subject requires an extra research.

generally more attentive to the obligations, debts, warmth and reciprocities involved in interpersonal relationships. All these daily concerns were borne by women and this stimulated them to network (see cartoon 7).

Further evidence indicating that women were more involved in *blat* lies in statistics on the structural aspects of women's employment in Russia. Statistics show that while men were engaged in engineering and working-class occupations it was mostly women who were engaged in trade and services. This tended to draw women into *blat* networks. Shlapentokh (1989: 80) pointed out that the increasing role of consumerism in Soviet life has dramatically increased the popularity of occupations in which one could obtain access to consumer goods and services. Apart from salary, occupations in commerce and services provided the possibility to exchange one scarce good or service for another, which led to a dramatic rise in their attractiveness. After being openly disdained by youth in the early 1960s (these occupations were rated lowest in popularity, even behind that of agricultural work), these occupations became really popular. Shubkin's data show that the attractiveness of sales-related occupations for women rose by 81 per cent in the 1970s (Shlapentokh 1989: 81). Institutes of Trade were commonly known as most difficult to enter because of *blatbit* (*blat* competition) – a competition of 'pull', in which those with the strongest network got what they desired (Klugman 1989: 100). It would be wrong to conclude, however, that the occupation or a particular access to resources necessarily led to engagement in *blat*.

### Horizontal and vertical ties: 'people of the circle' and 'useful people'

It is important to distinguish 'horizontal' and 'vertical' *blat* networks: horizontal networks were composed of people of similar status, known as 'people of the circle' ('*svoi lyudi*'). Vertical networks were composed of people of different social strata interested in each other's connections and linked by kin, personal contacts or, most often, intermediaries known as 'useful people' ('*nuzhnye lyudi*', see p.115). Relations within circles were grounded in shared practices at work or in leisure. It was explained to me that people of the circle had similar standards of values, scales of needs and scope for satisfying them. They were united by their business activities or social lives (close

— Соглашайся, Иван-Царевич, на фиктивный брак,
а я тебе импортный гарнитур хоть со дна достану!

Рисунок М. БИТНОГО

### Cartoon 7
Prince Ivan, if you'll agree to a fictitious marriage I can sort you out
with an imported three-piece suite in no time flat!

(*Krokodil* 1980, 7: cover)

relatives, friends, sport partners, etc.): 'You are either one of them, sitting at the same table, going fishing and hunting with them, going out to sauna or dacha (for which you've got to be male and occupy the position not lower than vice-rector of the University), or you must be useful to them, obtaining something necessary.' [28] This is not to say that people of the circle were not useful to each other, they were indeed. But the logic of mutual use within the circle was different:

> Even today, if you are in the circle, everything happens by itself. When you are involved with business, you see other businessmen solving problems for themselves and you join in. We go to a certain sauna, to the known doctors and dentists. Tickets, voyages. You don't even have to ask. You always get advice where to go and whom to address. There are four tourist firms, for example, but you go to the one you were recommended. They all are the same, perhaps, but if you come with an introduction, you will be waited on and treated better. We belong to a circle where everyone is well connected. Talk a bit and one may discover areas of mutual opportunity. You may have to pay anyway, but you won't be treated as someone 'from the street' and you will know where to go. No need to go rushing around. All the information we need we have between us. This month furniture will be available in such and such place, if you need a bath with hydra-massage – you will hear all about it in a week: where, when and how much, and they will even reserve it for you. [22]

These contacts differed from those which, he said, were most important for his work:

> banks, personal contacts in Moscow for obtaining recommendations and providing up-to-date information on custom law, people in local customs offices and in the Committee of Standardisation for obtaining certificates for legitimate trade rapidly. These contacts are needed to get better conditions throughout my contracts. If one is not pushy, things don't get done. Nobody will talk about consignment, deferment of payments, etc. And that's right. [22]

He referred to his work contacts as useful contacts which could overlap with his circle, but need not do so. Generally speaking circles were closed. One needed an introduction to enter them. When I had to refurbish my flat, my grandmother, a retired dentist, asked her former patient, a retired painter, to help me. I was lucky to make this contact ('nuzhnyi chelovek') because the painter was able to fix up much of the flat. Varvara, the painter, was married to an electrician (and plumber as a second profession) and had a neighbour who could obtain some paint and wallpaper glue. Her advice was always sound: 'Go to the construction site behind such and such kindergarten and ask them for a pack of cement for 10,000.' Her sister worked in the emergency service and guaranteed us another plumber if Varvara's husband got into hard drinking that week. Varvara was not a *blatmeister* and felt terribly uneasy about other areas, such as education and the sport club of her granddaughter. Within her area of competence she could handle everything through her contacts and was certain that it was cheaper, faster, better and more reliable. This was a widespread state of affairs in large cities, where *blatmeisters* linked those who had different contributions to make. No wonder *blatmeisters* were often middle-class people able to deal with both upper and lower social strata.

Transactions within circles differed from contacts with useful people. Whereas within circles *blat* relations were routine and regular and almost indistinguishable from the continuity of information exchange, interactions with useful people were more instrumental and intermittent. In the latter case questions of reciprocity were more explicit: 'If one has no *blat* connections of a vertical type the only way of penetrating different social circles is by payment, if possible, or by mutual favours. But normally people have either a relative or a friend in a different circle, so that they can be introduced without having to make explicit repayment.' [26] In fact, opportunity for *blat* arose throughout a person's life: through family, education, army service and occupation (see p.171 on establishing *blat* contacts). In these arenas one unintentionally acquired contacts that were horizontal but which might be useful for reaching vertically different social strata. Having elaborate personal and useful contacts, one could reach 'vertical' targets through horizontal contacts. The mechanism was simple: one asked a person whom one could talk to frankly, she or he did the same with someone else and so on, until someone who could solve the problem was found. One tradeswoman emphasised that all her friends occupied different positions: 'If they all had the same social status, I couldn't have got things I wanted.' [40]

In conditions of shortage, networks provided access to desired goods or any other resources. Shlapentokh (1989: 174) noted that Soviet people provided each other with considerable assistance in 'beating the system'. Friends played a vital role in procuring necessary goods, for they constantly bought each other food, clothing, shoes or other items when the chance arose, i.e. when these items appeared in stores. Even more important was the assistance of friends who had access to restricted stores or cafeterias. It was considered perfectly ethical for people to ask their more privileged friends to bring food or clothes from places that were generally inaccessible to them:

> Friends were extraordinarily active in providing assistance in everyday life. They helped each other to find jobs, place children in good schools or colleges, get into hospitals or health resorts. The importance of friends was directly proportional to the unavailability of goods and services, and was inversely proportional to the importance of money in obtaining hard-to-find items.

The family also played a central role in developing *blat* networks. Not only immediate but also extended kin networks were main channels for redistributing goods and services. Members of families tended to trust each other completely in these activities and served as important connections in assisting each other in obtaining what they needed. According to Shlapentokh, the family has become a symbol of the institutions opposing the state. Paradoxically, the official recognition and support of the family as a positive social value made it possible for individuals to turn this support to their own advantage. For example, university students were expected to repay the state for their education by accepting work assignments, often in far-flung regions of the country. Yet by appealing to the official support of the family as an institution, some graduates were able to avoid such assignments, arguing that severe familial disruptions would result (see cartoon 8).

### Occupational ties: positions as resources

Given asymmetrical ties with 'useful people' on the one hand and bounded networks of 'people of the circle' on the other, resources were redistributed by *blat* neither evenly nor randomly within Soviet society. The boundaries between social circles, and the patterns of ties within and between them, structured resource flows. Because of their structural locations, individuals and groups differed greatly in their access to the resources rationed within the state distribution system. Incumbency in a structural position was itself a scarce resource because it determined access to other resources. First, occupations supplied formal privileges. Second, and particularly important in the command economy, where monetary rewards were not the main criteria of social differentiation, many people profited from their positions as 'gatekeepers'. A gatekeeper controlling access to an organisation's leader or resources often gained favours, flattery, influence, use of the

*The graduation.*

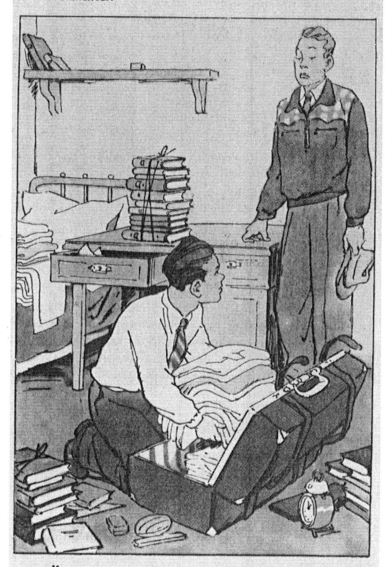

**Cartoon 8**
– How are you planning to start the independent life?
– I've got Daddy, Mummy, Grandad and Auntie running around sorting out permission for me to stay in Moscow.

organisational resources, and pleasure from exercising control. Occupational positions thus provided access to different kinds of resources
– material resources as well as contacts, time and information – which
could be involved in informal exchanges.[3]

From both perspectives, 'cadres' were seen as the most adept *blat*
practitioners. The fact that cadres had at their disposal decision-
making and resource-allocation powers made them frequent recipi-
ents of *blat* overtures. Another important resource which cadres could
handle better than others was information. Even if they could not
solve a problem directly they knew how to approach it. This was a
professional skill of Party and Soviet officials, which only experienced
*blatmeisters* could compete with. The professional skills of cadres were
applicable to 'any problem that had to be solved. There was always
somebody to contact. And this could be done without interrupting
their work greatly by using the telephone or sending other people on
their behalf.' [24] One top official commented that he was able to do
something in every case or at least to give advice:

> Depending on the problem, I can suggest a mechanism to deal with
> it. I am not one who can arrange anything. But every particular
> problem implies a mechanism for its solution which I do know. I can
> only give advice or help with information. Then, if the situation
> requires promptness and efficiency I can ring and request an
> appointment for the person in need. If there is a dead-end situation, I
> can also ring somebody and ask for their help. [34]

The respondents often drew attention to disparities between different levels at which *blat* was practised. A distinction was drawn
between *blat* channels for extra food or other goods in short supply,
which could be sold to the customer for money and where *blat*
provided just an opportunity to buy (the so-called 'horizontal'
shortage), and *blat* coupled with 'vertical' shortage, that is rewards
allocated by administrative rationing. Whereas in the first case *blat* is
really an informal system for bartering and redistributing food and a
few necessities of life, in the second, *blat* determines or promotes one's

[3] A survey of teenagers, carried out by *Literaturnaya Gazeta* and the journal *Sotsiologi-
cheskie Issledovaniya* (Sociological Research) in Moscow, Leningrad, Ashkhabad and
Erevan in 1987, cast light on the perceptions of Soviet young people about occupations. These teenagers were asked which professions bring the highest income in
Soviet society. They listed black marketeering first; military jobs second; automobile
servicing, bottle recycling, and jobs in remote areas of the country (Siberia oil–gas
complexes) third. Pilots, actors, and college professors were last on the list, preceded
by hairdressers, salesgirls, prostitutes and taxi-drivers. Thus occupations are openly
seen in terms either of privileges or of the access to resources that they provide (Y.
Shchekochikhin, 'Pered Zerkalom', *Literaturnaya Gazeta*, 2 September 1987: 13).

social and economic position, provides jobs and privileges. The latter led to a great deal of resentment towards cadres on the part of common people, which was mentioned on pp.63–4 in the discussion of mis-recognition strategies. It was a conviction that cadres did not need *blat* as much as others because they were provided with everything by the state distribution system officially. If, given those privileges, they used their positions for gaining profit or granting favours, their activities would be classified as corruption, protection or nepotism.

Opinions differed on whether intellectuals as a group had fewer *blat* connections than other occupational groups. One scientist suggested that 'the humanities were more subject to *blat* than sciences because humanitarian education was designed for Party cadres. Historical faculties and Komsomol were the most efficient channels for re-cruiting nomenclatura'. [14] It went without saying that the nomencla-tura formed that stratum where *blat* naturally resided. Certainly, most 'technical intelligentsia', including scientists and engineers, claimed so, as well as those who were identified with intellectuals in everyday life, including primary and secondary school teachers, doctors, uni-versity lecturers and professors, artists and musicians. The image of intellectuals is that they are normally too proper or too timid to engage in *blat* dealings. However, all *blatmeisters* I met happened to be educated people, and many intellectuals themselves argued that there was no difference between them and other social groups in their capacity for *blat*. Some respondents pointed to specific areas where intellectuals often have to resort to *blat*: for example, getting their children into good schools and enabling them to go abroad, getting a manuscript published, etc. (see cartoon 9):

> The academic sphere does not exclude *blat* nor does show business or any other field of activity. *Blat* was a significant factor in elections to the Academy. Of course, there were smart candidates who would do well in any case but the distribution of votes for the rest was in fact the old system of obligations and trust. Personal acquaintance played a great role. [13]

To grasp in which spheres *blat* ties were most applicable one has to think about the 'utility' of occupations for informal exchanges and the kinds of access they provided:

> Clearly, being an engineer was not useful while being a doctor or high school teacher was very useful indeed as most people need education and everybody needs medical care. It is also understand-able how a shop assistant, travel or theatre ticket seller could be

*Also a possibility.*

**Cartoon 9**
– My daddy says he'll buy me a motorbike when I grow up.
– My daddy says he'll get me a doctorate!                    (*Krokodil* 1952, 19:7)

used. They were universally in demand and thus formed a specifically *blat* strata [29a]

Service personnel such as shop clerks, restaurant workers, or ticket sellers had an advantage, for they controlled the goods and services which the public sought to buy from them. The power they exercised over the public (implying the 'monopoly of the seller over the buyer', Kornai 1980, and 'surly treatment of customers', Yang, 1994) partly compensated for the poor working conditions, hard work, and contempt in which their profession was often held. It was explained to me that such disparagement was caused by the profit-seeking intentions that come with their favours. Their favours could imply extra payment. If not, they tended to be based on strict calculation and explicit reciprocity, which went beyond the social conventions of the misrecognition game and thus undermined the legitimacy of their *blat* offerings. This is not to say that all shop clerks were like this, but those who were not were exceptions who only proved the rule. One respondent commented on her mother's position:

> She has been in the trade for 30 years and still has no apartment, no car, no dacha. She hid from her friends, did not answer the phone. It was normal to have a *blat* network but she was always ashamed of obtaining anything. Only her relatives and the closest friends could receive her favours. She could of course get a pair of boots for me and for my brother's wife, but she never bought things for resale. She chose a shop which had no direct telephone line and finally was left alone. Even now when everything is commercialised she does not like to ask or to be asked. [3]

Thus *blat* ties within primary networks (family, closest friends) were more commonly accepted than were connections used for profit or explicit exchange. It was not the illegal use of one's profession that caused a sense of resentment towards tradespeople and cadres. Rather, they were resented for their selfish and profit-seeking interests in interaction with those who did not belong to their personal networks. On the other hand, pointing at tradespeople as *blat* scapegoats deceived nobody: everyone recognised having used their favours.

The general argument against tradespeople was that they produced nothing but had everything. In this sense, the stratum which produced services was less vulnerable even though they were also considered as necessarily involved with *blat*. In respect of access to resources, we can separate services connected with processing of

*These matters were criticised in Soviet satire, but often in a sympathetic
way. The following cartoon inverts a well-known episode from Russian
folklore: the marriage of a tsar's daughter to Emelya who was not of princely
origin but had a spell to obtain everything. In the fairy tale the tsar could
not bear his daughter marrying a commoner while nowadays his comment
would be reversed.*

**Cartoon 10**
'No Nobleman! You'll marry the Cook!'                    (*Krokodil* 1980, 9: 4)

material resources directly (i.e. cooks, see cartoon 10), waiters, tailors), known for fiddling and pilfering, and secondary services, connected with repair, cleaning and do-it-yourself work. The resources of the former were similar to the ones of industrial workers. In his analysis of working class of the 1930s Andrle[4] (1988: 54) noted:

> Even an ordinary worker was in position of privileged access to something; for example, by being entitled to sturdy work-boots, or by virtue of handling scarce tools and materials, which formed a basis for his ability to promise reciprocity when claiming favours. By all accounts, success in obtaining valued goods by 'pulling strings' (*po blatu*) could make a lot of difference between living in serious want and living bearably well for many workers.

Workers did not occupy positions that gave them formal decision-making powers and direct control over allocating social resources, but they always managed to use material resources they were able to acquire to engage in *blat* transactions. Such occupations produced a specific ethic resulting in a pervasive phenomenon known as '*nesuny*' (carriers). To bring something from the workplace became a norm and even a matter of pride if something was given to a friend in trouble or need. The workers whom I interviewed kept mentioning this kind of help. 'I brought a water-repellent spray for my neighbour from my

---

[4] Vladimir Andrle also provides some evidence of workers' devotion to the wheelings and dealings of *blat* and suggests a difference of attitudes between old and new workers. He also mentions two specific features of workers' *blat* networks of that period. First, the network had a vertical dimension which was perhaps natural in the context of the high social mobility in which it was common for a worker to enter the higher realms of officialdom within a short period of time. Second, the networks cut across the agencies of state repression in the ordinary life styles of the period, with some examples of the use of personal contacts in the party and the secret police. I will quote one of them, for it also shows that people who tried to stay away from *blat* were misguided in their morals and subject to malevolent victimisation and social isolation. This example came from somebody who was a factory clerk rather than a shopfloor worker:

> The place where I worked in 1939 had an official car. The driver of this car was quote a s.o.b. We tried to talk to him so we could use the car during the day to go to the town and perhaps do some shopping or just to have a sip of vodka. But this bastard was so devoted to duty that we couldn't do anything with him, so we tried to fix him up for good. Yeah, we fixed him. One day we saw through the window that he was standing in line in front of the shop where butter was being distributed. Immediately, we reported him to the Trade Union Committee and the Trade Union Committee brought his case to RKK (factory disputes commission). The RKK decided to fire him. Brother, what joy was among us. The Director wanted to keep him but he had to fire him because of the 'breach of the law concerning labour discipline'. You know, all the workers laughed because everybody was in the line waiting for butter. The next day, there was a new driver, the guy with whom we had had previous contacts, and who was *blatnoi* [a person who takes part in *blat*]. (Andrle 1988: 56–7)

This is also an example of the 'principle of suspended punishment' in operation.

work. He simply complained that there were holes in his bathroom and I brought it to him, it went from my heart. This was a very expensive and professional spray, one could not obtain such a thing in shops.' [9] Another worker with metal-soldering skills told me with some satisfaction and amusement how he occasionally absconded with metal scraps from his factory, and borrowed factory tools to produce things for his friends. Of course all enterprises tried to limit such practices, but even when security was tightened such things happened. Simis (1982) described how a large wooden part for his boat was carried past guards and inspectors. He just explained to his acquaintance with whom he had dealings before: 'I have to have it, my friend. I need it this badly,' making the usual Russian gesture indicating a matter of life and death: 'slitting' his throat with the edge of the hand. Construction workers were also said to be good *blat* contacts because they had access to building materials such as bricks, cement and other things for refurbishment, which they could smuggle out of construction sites for their friends. These people felt very comfortable about smuggling things or fiddling (it was collective, i.e. partly their property after all!) for their friends but hated the idea of tradespeople or cadres doing the same.

Those who provided secondary services, such as car or television repairs, were also in great demand. The resource to which they provided access was their own skill or diligence. Acquaintance with a service technician meant receiving additional attention and extra quality of service and avoiding queues. In fact, this was also character-istic of services such as services of doctors, hairdressers, etc. The latter professions were specifically known to be *blat*-ridden, since they provided 'personal' services, thus building personal reciprocal deals.

Even the most insignificant clerk was able to enter *blat* networks by providing small symbolic favours. For example, in the archives or libraries, clerks were able to set aside necessary materials or books which were rare or in great public demand. Those who established a personal contact were given priority over other readers. Everybody had to find a way to enter into *blat* connections and thus either compensate for their relatively low occupational status or construct a symbolic value for their profession:

> In the society we lived in everyone was forced to use their workplace (I do not take into account a minority of 'saintly' people who did not need or want anything) for extra, even if only symbolic, benefits. The whole system was based on an unwritten law that forced compro-mise in entering into the informal networks that ensured mutual

support and understanding. For example, there was no explicit prohibition against non-Komsomol members entering High Schools and Universities. It was not a written rule but everyone knew that one had to be a Komsomol member to pass. I always had a problem with the parents of those 3–5 pupils who were not Komsomol members. It was not that they had different beliefs or were against Komsomol, Party or the idea of communism, they simply did not bother to follow the procedures (to learn the Komsomol Code, to attend Komsomol gatherings, to read newspapers), they were just lazy. Their parents had to find all sorts of ways to approach me. Their mothers told me: 'You are stepping on the throat of my child, you are building a barrier against his entry into higher education, why can't you recommend him for Komsomol membership?' [26]

*Blat* networks were an important feature of urban life, but this does not mean that they did not exist in the countryside. It can be said that *blat* ties permeated personal networks and existed along with them everywhere. Occupational ties in relation to *blat* were almost the same as in cities but in rural settlements people seemed to be more subject to social control. Cadres were given more respect in the countryside. People appreciated that the most important aspect of their work for maintaining, running and developing rural enterprises was the delicate yet difficult task of 'establishing good connections' with Party officials and local government. One chairman of a collective farm remarked that 'every chairman was only temporarily not jailed', meaning that there was always something to be caught for. Good connections in this situation could guarantee that the chairman was informed about investigative commissions in advance and was supported if there were attendant difficulties. Also, a rural enterprise had to rely on regional party and government organisations for a host of things: raw materials, electricity, labour transfers, transportation, distribution of products as well as negotiations concerning proper collective plan tasks. Since I spent most of my time in urban areas, most examples of *blat* in this study have been drawn from urban settings. The examples of *blat* in rural areas which I came across in the interviews were not, however, different in their occupational aspects:

> My mother worked as head of a Soviet farm buttery. She could sell really good meat and at much cheaper prices, or other foodstuffs in short supply. For example, when there was a shortage of butter she could obtain some. Naturally, she had good connections, and worked hand in glove (*dusha v dushu zhila*) with shop assistants from the clothes store. My father worked in construction all his life, and construction materials were always in demand. When he retired and

became a gas-supplier, he could offer a bigger gas cylinder in exchange for a small one. And city gasmen gave him more of the bigger cylinders because his wife would sell good meat to them. He also obtained fuel for his car by *blat*. He knew the tanker drivers and received an unlimited supply from them, normally for a bottle of vodka or 'moonshine'. He also paid, of course, but they did not offer this to everyone, only those whom they trusted. For him it was cheaper and free of queueing. Another example: a meat store-keeper in the village was a good acquaintance from long ago. Every year when she went on holiday she left him in charge. She trusted he was not going to cheat, whereas he was happy to help and to have this opportunity to buy meat for all his family. My father also helped my brother with dacha construction. You know how expensive it became. And he hardly spent any money. Contacts, old contacts. They allocated him cut wood for free or for a few kopecks. And he gave them fresh eggs or dung. [19]

In rural areas, the word *blat* was known as much as in the cities but perhaps less used. I did not interview people from rural areas specifically on *blat*, but analysed the oral histories of peasants collected by the team of researchers leaded by Teodor Shanin in their massive study of rural communities in seven regions of Russia. According to Evgeny Kovalev and Ilya Schteinberg,[5] in rural settlements it is more relevant to talk about patronage and support networks (if not theft) rather than *blat*. Some respondents, however, used the term and talked about *blat* a lot. The fact that they engaged in informal exchanges or provided favours did not disturb them at all even in cases marginal with theft. It was clearly a social arrangement, in which networks served to certify a social community. The way they explained their relationships was a traditional one: 'that's how we do things in the country.' It was simply their way of maintaining small group solidarity in the face of social and economic adversity.

Before I move on and analyse *blat* as a type of exchange with its norms of reciprocity and ethics let me offer a life history of a rural *blatmeister* Maria Ivanovna.[6] She was described as a tall and good-looking, strong and skilful woman. Born in 1916 she spent all her life in the countryside, in Tambov area. Her formal working record (quite ordinary) looked like this:

1934–8 – cleaner in a local savings bank
1938–49 – work in a *kolkhoz*

---

[5] I. Schteinberg, *Kuda Idet Rossiya?*, vol. 3 (Moscow: Aspect Press, 1996).
[6] Quoted from Y. Kovalev (ed.), *Golosa krestyan: sel'skaya Rossiia XX veka v krest'yanskikh memuarakh* (Moscow: Aspect Press, 1996: 107–10, 116, 126).

1949–56 – cleaner in local veterinary hospital
1956–65 – stayed at home, brought up a daughter Natasha
1965–7 – assistant of chef in a *sovkhoz* buttery
1967–70 – imprisonment
1970–4 – chef of a *sovkhoz* buttery.

Between these lines, however, there is a lot of interest for us:

'In 1935 after I got married I became a cleaner in a savings bank. Worked there till 1939 when the chairman of *kolkhoz* threatened to ban my cow from *kolkhoz* pastures if I did not work in the kolkhoz. So I had to.

. . . I worked in the *kolkhoz* then. The way it happened was, all spring you'd go and work hard there . . . But when pay day comes, they give you 100–150 g of grain per working day – it came to 1.5–2 poods (24–32 kg) – nothing to take home! I nicked more from the *kolkhoz* than I earned. We worked hard for nothing. So we had to take grain or whatever from the fields. It was the only way to get by. The chairman was "*svoi*", he just warned us not to take too much. He used to say: "Hey, babes, you'd better be cautious, so that I wouldn't account for you." But apart from that he turned a blind eye.

Then Polanin [head of veterinary hospital, a neighbour] offered me a job. I got friendly with his wife first. You know how it is – we used to go to the shop to buy bread together, we chatted a lot, then visited each other. When they went to see their parents I looked after their household, the cattle, etc. Polanin even gave his horse to Egor Ivanovich [husband], nobody else but him. He trusted Egor Ivanovich to treat the horse honestly. The job at the hospital was easy – from 9 to 2 only. They paid 360 roubles a month and I could run my own allotment the rest of the time.

. . . I only became better off when I took a job in a buttery. You can't live on a salary, you know. A buttery was a very "advantageous" (*dobychnoe*) place. Valentina, a controller of drivers from Kotovsk really helped me out then (*zdorovo vyruchala*).

There was no order in the *sovkhoz* then. Drivers brought meat but there was nobody there to weigh it. They brought one carcass for the buttery but registered it for 30–40 kg less than it was. For a bottle of vodka (*za magarych*). A bottle was cheap then. The deal was good for their hangover and good for me – I took some meat myself and gave some to the controller. She was only too glad to accept. Or I made cutlets from this meat and sold them secretly: drivers were always at the controller's hand and she also had a connection with a shop assistant in Znamenka [another village]. That lass helped to sell them.

Once I received 6 carcasses for the buttery, and the driver gave me the seventh for a litre of vodka. At once I was off to tell Val'ka (the controller). She called a driver, we slung the meat in the truck and sent it off to Kotovsk. Only then I could relax. You know, there always could be a commission from Znamenka or some other inspection. Lots of trouble then. Well, that's how I bought 60 kg of meat for 10 roubles – 1 litre of vodka (whoever had access to vodka could obtain or buy anything in the village!).

I never stole meat from the workers, though. There were 250 customers at my buttery and they all liked me and greeted me nicely, even when I left the job. They wouldn't have done that if they felt I was cheating them. I didn't need to cheat them anyway, there were other ways: if meat was registered for a little less than it really weighed, I could have the difference. Also, there were leftovers I could use. My husband was not the grasping type (*nedobychnoi*), so I didn't take much. He didn't even like meat. If I brought 3–4 cutlets home from the buttery, he'd eat one and that was it. I'd take the rest back. If he'd been a grasping person we would have bought a car, etc. But he couldn't make deals (*dela obdelyvat'*). He was a communist and didn't get involved in all this. He just wondered and warned me occasionally: "Oh, Marusya, watch your step . . . you'll get caught out."

I liked crockery and bought a lot. There were shortages of plates, etc. I had to buy them by *blat*. He always grumbled at me. So I stopped telling him. Bought something and stashed it away. When my daughters got married and came to see me, they took all the best plates. They saw them and said: "Wow, mum, can we have these?" Of course, they could. That was the idea. Nowadays, when they come and I offer something, they only laugh. They have everything now . . . Natashka said she took a set of 200 plates recently. It was delivered for the buttery but turned out to be so beautiful . . . So she bought it, cheap. Well, she is a chef in the buttery . . .

We helped our daughters out a lot. Egor Ivanovich arranged a job at a telephone station for Zina after her graduation. There were no jobs around that time. We arranged Natasha's wedding. According to custom, the first day is supposed to be celebrated at the groom's place, the second at the bride's. That's how we planned it first. But then Nina Fyodorovna [the groom's mother] came and said: "Let's hold it at your place for 2 days so we don't have to move all the furniture in two houses." I was an idiot to agree. We decided to contribute 350 roubles each for the feast – 2.5 cases of wine, sausages, fish, grapes. Then I bought meat from an acquaintance who worked in a warehouse. Potatoes were our own, the first cucumbers, etc. from the allotment – it was in summer. Nina Fyodorovna said she had *blat* everywhere and volunteered to buy everything cheap. But it was not cheap after all, I could buy the same for that price.'

# 5    *Blat* as a form of exchange: between gift and commodity

*Ty – mne, ya – tebe* (I scratch your back, you scratch mine).

(A folk saying)

### *Blat* and reciprocity

An instruction from a recent American handbook for barter deals in the contemporary United States says:

> Do not ask for money. You are supposed to trade your skill in repairing the sink for eggs from someone else's chickens. Such behavior (asking for money instead) injures the noncommercial image of the exchange or cooperation and undermines people's faith in its integrity . . . Whether you join a barter club, swap with a cousin, or use a network, most of your trade will be part of an ongoing relationship. In effect, this is what separates bartering from cash sales. Since mixing business and friendship is a delicate matter at best, you may need some general guidelines. Remember you want to keep the door open for the next swap. Besides you may meet your barter partner at the pool, or be invited to the same party. (Matison and Mack 1984: 99, cited in Humphrey and Hughes-Jones 1992: 6)

There is no need to learn this skill in the former Soviet Union; it was known, practised and, in fact, so widespread that people sometimes preferred to reduce their obligations by means of monetary exchange:

> I would prefer to overpay, 'for a service' as it were, because you pay and feel free from obligations. But money was not what people needed, especially tradespeople. Everyone could repay with money but this did not count. If you were given a privilege to buy something in short supply paying its state price, it meant that you were supposed to provide some access to other things in return. I never paid extra money but occasionally helped someone, arranged bookings in hotels, passports for foreign trips. These exchanges were

139

inseparable from good relationships. I suppose one could actually arrange something formally, but the habit of using contacts was so strong that one always asks acquaintances first. It was a specific psychology, I always rang a friend to ask him to ring another friend about me, about appointments or whatever. First, because formal procedures were and still are inefficient, while we, Russians, are too disorganised to apply in time. Everything becomes urgent because we remember about it in the last minute, and in a hurry, we surely go by *blat*. Second, it was a form of socialising, if you want. Like at an oriental bazaar, where they do not put price labels because they do not want to be treated instrumentally. They want to be asked, to talk, to bargain. Not for the sake of price, price is not that important, they want to be treated socially. For them it is socialising and they hate arrogant people who pay and go. Even though sometimes this is just what you want: to pay and go. [13]

Reciprocity is based on gift-giving.[1] In his study of the islands of the western Pacific, the anthropologist Bronislaw Malinowski (1922) pointed to the existence of a circular system of exchange. Shell armlets travelled in one direction, shell bracelets in the other. As he observed, the exchange had no economic value, but it maintained social solidarities. In his classic work, *The Gift* (1925), Marcel Mauss argued that the obligations of giving, receiving and repaying are not to be understood simply in terms of rational calculation. Gift-giving is a form of non-immediate reciprocity where reward is neither discussed nor consciously calculated at the moment the offering is made. In the long run, however, one expects gifts to be reciprocated. This creates the contradiction between the intersubjective definition of a gift transaction, as a ritual act that is independent of all other acts, and the objective fact that it is one element in a succession of reciprocal transactions (Mauss 1957). Bourdieu (1979: 22) has further argued, as mentioned earlier, that this contradictory structure is a necessary feature of gift exchange, and that the defining characteristic of gift exchange is the temporal separation of gift and counter gift in an indefinite cycle of reciprocity. It is because of the separation of gift and return gift that the actors can deny that there is in fact an obligation to make a return. According to Bourdieu, the symbolic negation of

---

[1] Polanyi (1925) distinguished three basic systems of economic organisation [1925]: alongside the 'reciprocity' system, based on the gift, there is the 'market system', subject to the laws of classical economics and the 'redistribution' system. Whereas gifts are exchanged between equals, redistribution depends on a social hierarchy. Leaders (or patrons) like the Pathan *khans* distribute to their followers the goods they have taken from outsiders. The followers (or clients) are not expected to give the goods back at a later time, but to offer some other forms of 'counter-prestation' (Burke 1992: 70).

economic calculation in gift exchange serves the requirements of strategic interaction. He conceived the gift as a form of capital in which individuals invest in order to carry through their projects:

> Gift exchange is an exchange in and by which the agents strive to conceal the objective truth of the exchange, i.e. the calculation which guarantees the equivalence of the exchange. If 'fair exchange', the direct swapping of equivalent values, is the truth of gift exchange, gift exchange is a swapping which cannot acknowledge itself as such.

As discussed earlier, *blat* exchange is even more distant from direct swapping. Psychologically, culturally and practically direct exchanges were not possible. Rather, *blat* exchange can be characterised by a reciprocal dependence, which engenders regard for and trust in the other over the long-term. Gregory claims that such reciprocal dependence is characteristic of the 'gift' as opposed to the 'commodity',[2] but I would see it as equally present, in a different form, in *blat*. *Blat* is an intermediary form of exchange to be associated neither with 'the gift' nor with 'commodity exchange'. In gift exchange, inalienable objects of the same kind pass between people already bound together by social ties, whilst in commodity exchange, alienable objects of different kinds pass between people acting as free agents. Gift exchange underwrites social relations and is concerned with social reproduction; commodity exchange establishes relations between things and ensures reproduction of the latter (Gregory 1982). Although *blat* certainly does transfer alienable objects, it does so on the condition that social relationships already exist. 'The other' is not only functional but is regarded personally and in this sense becomes irreplaceable. The favours therefore bear, as it were, a non-alienable character. They are marked by the personal stamp of the donor. This can be best imagined as the occasional borrowing of one's access (*dostup*) but the access itself is never alienable. Just as in gift exchange, where debt cannot be returned by a different kind of gift, a received favour is never equivalent to that which the recipient can provide in return. The

---

[2] Whereas Gregory counterpoises gift and commodity as a binary pair, Sahlins (1972) places them at the opposite ends of a scale: from the positive altruism of what he confusingly calls 'generated reciprocity' to the 'unsociable extreme' of 'negative reciprocity'. According to Sahlins, reciprocity is

> not a single relation between incomings and outgoings, but a 'continuum', a 'spectrum', ranging from the pure gift . . . to barter and theft which are each an attempt to get something for nothing with impunity. In between are those balanced reciprocities in which social conventions stipulate returns of commensurate worth or utility within a finite and a narrow period.

See also Davis (1992).

original favour leaves a 'memory' even if an unlike return has been made. I prefer not to use the term 'debt', for *blat* favours are not so deeply rooted in codes of honour as an anthropological concept of 'debt' would imply. Even though gifts and *blat* are both non-monetary exchanges which derive from and create relationships, it is important to see the distinction. What differentiates them is the compulsion and 'contrived asymmetry' of the gift, as opposed to the relative freedom and balance of *blat*. The compulsion of the gift, as Marilyn Strathern emphasises, lies in forcing others to enter into debt.[3] It is here that the 'contrived asymmetry' lies: one has to accept a gift and thus a debt. *Blat* also does not entail the reciprocal independence of the transactors. Indeed, it takes place within a given community between people who interact on a regular basis. But as it happens upon request, *blat* is protected from imposed generosities, even though some implications of 'debt' or 'honour' may occur. The specific character of *blat* as an exchange of 'favours of access' falls into neither the category of gift nor commodity exchange. Embedded both in private relationships and access to the public resources, *blat* implies certain difficulties in the analysis of reciprocity.

Reciprocity in *blat* relations is created and preserved by a mutual sense of 'fairness' and trust, in which each side takes responsibility as the recipient both for his/her satisfaction and that of the other. People trusted each other because they knew one good turn deserved another and this was in their mutual interest. Because *blat* tends to be repetitive and often operated with known partners, and because of the absence of any sanctions outside the relationship, it is possible to speak of balance in *blat* relations. This is in spite of the fact that objects always had a different status in the micro-systems of each of the transactors and the two sides had to agree that their transaction was fair. 'Exchange rates' are subordinated to the social relations between actors (Sahlins 1972) and therefore there is no criterion by which a general value may be established.

To represent the reciprocal nature of *blat* exchanges in all their variety three basic perspectives, or regimes, of reciprocity should be

---

[3] As Parry (1986) has pointed out, there are important differences in the ideology of 'the gift' between its classic tribal home (Melanesia, Polynesia) and the regions of Asia dominated by world religions. In India the gift does not constrain a return, but is rather a religious transfer without return, embodying the sins of the donor, a surrogate for sacrifice. The gift is separated from other transactions of the complex economy precisely by its religious connotations. As Parry (1986: 48) rightly points out it is only in the Christian, not the Asian, world that the theory of pure utility has developed, making the things of this world antithetical to the person's true self.

distinguished: the regime of equivalence, the regime of affection and
the regime of status. I use the idea of 'regimes' for the analysis of
reciprocity to avoid the assumptions implied in the usage of the
terms 'kinship', 'friendship', 'acquaintance'. It was argued in previous chapters that *blat* relations cannot be identified with personal
relationships. Consequently, the reciprocity of the former should not
be considered in terms of the latter. In her analysis of the analogous
phenomenon in China Yang (1994) undertook to consider connections
providing a more elaborate classification of personal relationships:
family and kinship, neighbours and native-place ties, non-kin relations of equivalent status, and non-kin superior–subordinate relations. The criteria of status, degree of familiarity and type of personal
relations, combined in her classification, in my opinion are to be
separated. It would be erroneous to suppose that kin, friendship
networks or neighbourly relations do not imply any purposive or
calculative interaction, whereas networks of acquaintances imply
nothing but calculation of prospective contributions. Neighbours
may be closer than kin, friends can also be in superior–subordinate
relations, etc. The proposed classification of regimes does not necessarily correspond to types of relationships: friends may happen to
communicate in the regime of status, relatives in the regime of
equivalence and acquaintances in the regime of affection. It enables
us to distinguish transactions of different kinds within a given
relationship: *blat* transactions between friends can fall into different
regimes according to the type of situation, kind of favour, previous
transaction or state of relationship: 'They differ depending on characters involved, how people want to view the relationship themselves and, most of all, on the situation in which one helps or denies
assistance.' [31]

Apart from that, neither the actual character of relations (degree of
intimacy or mutual help), nor the fluctuations in their character
(cooling down of friendship, separation of spouses) are reflected in
general concepts of friendship or kinship.[4] The idea of switching

---

[4] Boltanski (1992) suggested the distinction of 'affective regime' and 'regime of justice',
which the same relationship may undergo. In the regime of justice the stress is laid on
the equivalencies, explicated to manage disputes. On the contrary, in the ordinary
course of common actions equivalencies are not subjected to deliberate reflection. In
the affective regime, persons actively cooperate in the process of shoving the
equivalencies aside in order to make the cumulation and calculation operations which
are required to blame and criticise difficult. This regime is described with the stress on
the present moment, and on a form of forgiveness which borders on forgetting. The
person who goes on shifting from one regime to another looks back over past events
in a disillusioned way: 'how was it possible to be such a fool; so naive of me. For the

regimes is crucial both to integrate the dynamic of personal relations and to grasp the self-regulating mechanisms and the character of sanctions in *blat* relations. By switching from one regime to another people react to the changes in personal relationships, control and stimulate each other to action. To distinguish different regimes within the same type of relationship is particularly important in monitoring the processes of social change in post-Soviet conditions.[5] Let us consider the ties of reciprocity in these three regimes in more detail.

### Regime of equivalence

The distinctive aspect of *blat* in the regime of equivalence is the expectation of the potential 'utility' of the other. It is taken into account alongside the actual favour, received or provided:

> For example, I needed to have a coat made, quickly and well. A friend of my friend agreed to help. Naturally, I always helped her to obtain fabric after that, arranged her a credit at our shop, never took extra money. I do not need her services often but I know I can always go and ask her, and she won't refuse. If I obtain goods in short supply for someone who is not my friend, one has to settle up immediately or in the short-term. But this is rare. I only get in contact with those who or whose contacts can be useful. For someone who is a good friend of my friend or important person or has good connections I would rather credit my favour, in case I need something from them afterwards. [40]

This statement of an experienced tradeswoman in her forties was supported by a young waiter, who did not have enough connections and spoke resentfully: 'One has to pay cash only when one has no possibilities or access to offer and has no proper contacts. If one is a

last twenty years I have been making [all these favours] . . . Now, I realize.' But this experience of the moment of truth is not more real than the other. The regime in which one makes calculations is no more true, no more real, than the regime in which people inhibit their calculation abilities, he argues. It is the [change] in the perception of the world stemming from a quick shift from one regime to another which gives the illusion of a glaring truth (Boltanski, 'The sociology of critical capacity', lecture at IAS, Princeton, March 1992; see also Boltanski (1990).
5 The dynamics of trust will be considered in chapter 6. The study is indebted to the distinction between trust based on belief, characteristic of the 'pre-modern', and 'modern' trust based on mutual self-interest and functional interdependence, introduced by Luhmann (1979, 1988). The analysis of the transformation of *blat* in post-Soviet conditions can be seen as a testing ground for the role of trust and offers a particularly instructive insight into both the necessity and the difficulty of generating social cooperation based on trust.

son of someone important, everything will be free for sure. People credit him with favours to repay to his father or to be able to ask for a credit themselves.' [8]

*Blat* relations in the regime of equivalence were most widespread among those involved with trade and services, medicine, those who dealt with a great number of customers, patients, etc. They thus developed a certain cynicism. Customers also happened to cultivate a relationship when they needed a service. This did not necessarily result in a long-term personal or intimate relationship. Rather relationships came to terms of 'mutual utility' (*vzaimopoleznost'*), often euphemised as 'mutual help' (*vzaimopomoshch'*). But even then, relationships were more important than immediate repayment. Even those running a private practice did not sound profit-seeking:

> People do contact me about repair services. They could go to the repair shop, but my service is known for its guaranteed quality. I make it cheaper for good contacts because I value their assistance in delivering new customers and creating a good reputation for my service. I never serve an outsider, I want clients to be recommended and reliable, so that we always keep in touch afterwards, just in case. [38]

A dentist put it even more directly:

> I do dentistry and never make money out of it. But I make my contacts, I know that my patients will help me, if I need something. I keep these contacts but this does not mean that a long-term relationship cannot be developed from them. If my request gets refused the relationship breaks, but if the contact is good and reliable, we may become friends. [41]

The emphasis on mutual 'utility' is most marked in the regime of equivalence, but the actual balance of favours is not so important. Objects are not measured against one another. It is the relations between subjects, not objects, that are valued most and essential. In *blat*, the question of equivalency arises as a sanction in breaking (cooling down) relationships or switching to another regime. There is also no external criterion for the evaluation of exchange as the value of the object for a donor and recipient is often different. The objects exchanged are dissimilar. Therefore, the values which exchanged objects represent are indicative of the confrontation between ways of life, or, as Strathern (1992 : 169–88) puts it, of 'the regard in which the other is held'). The fact that *blat* relations are often mediated complicates the issue of balance even more:

> Mediation is not a favour to pay for. A box of chocolates, a bottle
> of cognac – maximum, but often not even that. I just introduced
> her to a proper contact. Who knows what will happen in life, what
> kind of help I may need. There might be a situation where I ask
> her to help or connect me to her friends. Everyone is good for
> something. [40]

> If I ask someone to help somebody else, I never get paid for this, I
> just reserve my right to ask in turn. [41]

The separation of favour from the return favour through an
intermediary whereby the return comes not from the person to whom
the original favour was given is another feature of reciprocity in *blat*
relations which will be considered in more detail on p.155. In every
situation, however, the parties know who is obliged to whom:

> In practice, one values the received favour to one's own standard
> and reacts correspondingly. If this satisfies the donor, the balance
> is maintained. On a psychological level, the parties are aware of
> their obligations. They feel their right to ask or obligation to repay.
> [41].

> The practical sense of obligation is simply a turn-taking. If I received
> a favour, I know it is my turn now. It is like in a board game, but the
> score is never equal. When I did something in return the score is
> closer to the balance, but not necessarily equal. I may be still obliged,
> and my partner will ask me again. If I accept his vision of the score I
> proceed with the game, if not, I quit. If my favour was significant, I'll
> be able to claim something else. And then, it is his turn to decide
> whether he proceeds with the game or not. It is impossible to
> calculate a precise score, but who is due is felt. You either feel it
> yourself, or they make you feel. [11]

*Blat* thus generates an in-built tendency to act fairly – that is, in a
way which will satisfy the other partner so that a return favour is
probable and the exchange may be repeated in the future. The
exchange is fully dependent on the interest which each side has in the
'other' and previous exchanges, which results in stability and reproduction of social relations.

If standards of value correspond, and expectations coincide with an
actual reaction (which may be expressed in gratitude or attention, not
necessarily a return favour), the relations become routine with no
need of probation within the regime of equivalence: 'The process of
establishing contacts takes time, not just one or two years, because
you must know the person well, to know his character and prefer-

ences, to know how to socialise, what to offer him and he must know what to expect from me.' [40]

Stable relationships based on achieved or *a priori* available standards of value, mutual sympathy and satisfaction, should be considered in the regime of affection.

### Regime of affection

While in the regime of equivalence *blat* is primarily an exchange implying a relationship, in the affective regime *blat* is focused on a relationship implying exchange. Participants are thus bound by the personal ties irrespective of whether they are involved in *blat* transactions or not:

> Between friends the requests can be unlimited, but at the same time, I will require from my friend to see why I can't help without taking offence. If I can't, I can't. He is supposed to believe that if I could I would do my best. It is mutual trust in each other. The relationship is based on the belief that we are friends and will do everything to maintain it. [12]

> The close friend will always understand if I can't do something. If I arrange tickets, they might not be the best places. He will understand that the best places I had to hand out to others for some reason. The level of trust is that I trust in him as in myself. We do not have to pretend or to impress each other. [29]

The availability to each other, an understanding of the other's 'standard of value', and willingness to help creates certainty that request will be fulfilled. *Blat* transactions presuppose an ability to understand the others' purposes and interpret the actions of others with regard to the self. Within an 'economy of favours', a set of normative obligations to provide assistance to others so that they can carry out their projects is considered as positive, and collapse of it provokes a sense of betrayal.

*Blat* relations in this regime are predicated upon belonging to a personal network – that is, a relatively closed social circle. It is one of the most common features of everyday life that individuals routinely construct, and are selectively recruited into, specialised social worlds or networks. These 'micro-universes' (Luckmann 1978: 285), such as kinship networks or company of friends, are the principal social contexts within which, and around which, ties to significant others are organised (Strathern 1981). Through these social networks, individuals gain not only opportunities for interaction but also access to resources. Moreover, the sense of belonging and feelings of affection disguise *blat* relations and thus contribute to their efficiency. Within circles the potential 'utility' is substituted for personal attitude:

> I will do a favour to a neighbour not because I want something in return, but because he is my neighbour. It is human relationship. He may, of course, do me a favour as well. He will look after my flat when I am not around. But it is not so important. What is important is that we are on informal terms. It is a relationship, rather than anything else. [9]

Aspects of equivalency are even less marked in this regime: 'One can't take money from a friend, we were just brought up like this. Even now that I run my private business I will see my friends in non-working hours and provide them any treatment for free.' Reciprocity must not, however, be underestimated:

> You can help a friend with pure motives, once, twice. But this cannot last on a regular basis. The system is still turn-taking. It does not matter what you can offer, nobody wants anything extraordinary, it can be just advice or information ('Sugar will be available in that shop at 6 p.m., go and get it' or 'I am going to queue for sausages, do you want half a kilo?'). It is important to be useful to the other, in other words, to care. [11]

> Between friends mutual help is natural, but it is mutuality of relationship, not mutuality of favours. Friends do not calculate, friends do things for each other anyway. [39]

Networks of friends are the most efficient and ramified:

> I have got many contacts who are, in fact, my friends: a car mechanic, all kinds of specialists in medicine, wives of my friends in trade, a dentist (used to be my client, now he has his garage opposite to mine and we often drink together), many friends are from the same plant I worked at long ago, some are in business now. One friend of mine goes to China on business. He brings me spare parts for my work and does not even take money. The spares are not, perhaps, expensive but they are indispensable for my work and he has to look for them on top of his own problems. None of these people are business contacts, even though we all help each other in many ways. We spend our leisure time together, go to sauna and for summer picnics. Our wives are friendly as well. This sauna, for example. It belongs to the plant where I worked. My friend was a master of our shop. Now he is elected a general director of the plant. He books the sauna and

we go there regularly. Our wives also go next day. For these friends I repair everything for free, with a quality as for myself. As they do for me. [38]

The moral obligations within such networks are particularly strong, reinforced by affective emotions:

For example, my friend helped me with moving to another place, he obtained a car somewhere, carried things, etc. Of course, I feel obliged and when he asks me to obtain a medicine or something, I'll strain all my nerves for that. If I can't do it myself, I'll ask my other friends, my wife's sister, who is a doctor, but obtain it. Friends, however, do not ask for things which I can't do. What I can I offer myself. [28a]

The rhetoric of friendship tends to conceal mutual obligations, as friendship is understood as the refusal to calculate:

I do lots of things for my friends but I wouldn't like them to feel obliged. I attended all the meetings of a building cooperative, when my friend could not do it himself and expected no obligation on his side. He is a godfather of my girls and does baby-sitting for me when I do my business trip. Why should I feel obliged? [10]

But in fact, if the balance in the relationship is broken, if one takes offence and feels that the code of friendship has been violated, the relationships are likely to slip into the regime of equivalence. If one does not repay appropriately, a number of sanctions can be applied: 'In some cases, I can even demand a repayment, it depends on the person and on the situation. To some people a hint would be enough, some need a straightforward reminder.' [41]

As was mentioned above, *blat* relations are self-regulating – that is, parties are forced to act fairly by the relationship itself. But in cases where someone is considered untrustworthy, sanctions can be inflicted. The cooling down of relationships is a signal for the person to realise it is his turn and to make his move. If this does not succeed, his reputation for untrustworthiness may spread, and relations break, especially if one lets the other down. An untrustworthy person loses his opportunities to be involved in the chains of relationships and thus falls out of the *blat* network. The specific of the affective regime, however, is that people may forgive violations of rules or sacrifice considerations of equivalence for the sake of the relationship itself. Within close and routine relationships people may forget their favours, and can be reminded of them. Sanctions are 'restitutive' – that is, do not necessarily terminate the relationship but, re-adjusting the balance, they involve restoration, the re-establishment of relationships. Relations become balanced in the continuous round of favours.

At the same time there is the 'reverse side' of these networks of assistance where the sense of common morality is substituted for by the morality of a selected circle of people. It is therefore important to trace both stabilising and 'corrupting' implications which *blat*, in fact, combines. Affective relations between those involved create a kind of solidarity on the basis of internal, or private, ethics of the circle. The public side of such inner solidarity is a group egoism, when one's own circle is considered superior to any other. Affective relations thus divide as well as unite people: 'I will help my sister or brother to get a job, not a stranger. A stranger may fit this job much better, but it does not bother me. I want to help my relative or friend.' [30] The relationship within this regime can be grasped by the metaphor of 'brotherhood'. 'Brothers' will share both good times and personal troubles because they have the desire and the obligation to help one another in times of need: 'If I have an access my friend or relative surely has it too.' [38] Actual kinship can play a significant role here, but at times 'the ethic of brotherhood' proves stronger than the bonds between husband and wife or child and parents.

### Regime of status

In Russia, people say 'someone has big connections, protection' and also say '*blat*' in such cases. It is important, however, to see the differences of this regime of reciprocity in comparison to the others. If in the 'affective regime' *blat* favours naturally follow from relationships, in the 'regime of status' they also convey messages about power, status and authority. In contrast to the other regimes, relations in the regime of status are not symmetrical. This regime comes into operation when one's 'status' is used to refrain or withdraw from engaging into reciprocal deals in affective or equivalent regimes, regardless of whether a favour is provided or not. The use of status can follow the pattern of patron–client relationships where the superiors are supposed to know the ways, to control them, and to take responsibility, while the subordinate is to be loyal and respectful. In the regime of status the balance is less contingent, as it is often the case that the value and character of favours are such that they cannot be repaid in principle:

> There are favours which cannot be paid off in principle. For example, to connect a telephone line or to provide an apartment. [15]

> Whatever one does for a person who helped with a flat and with telephone, it's never enough. [19]

Such favours are connected with the diversion of state property or redistribution which takes place in patron–client relationships and thus does not imply any equivalent exchange:

> When you deal with 'big men' (*bol'shimi lyud'mi*) they need nothing from you. It was not a relationship even, they just treated me as a 'small boy' with interesting ideas and honest eyes and helped me. It is clear that they see themselves as big bosses able to help the young, Komsomol, me as a representative of the International Festival Committee. Reciprocity between these people is not like *blat* exchange of goods in short supply. Their help is not in exchange for something else. I had nothing to repay with but they always helped. [32]

> It was often the case that I was given a favour but not the opportunity to repay. It happens with people who are not close contacts and who are powerful enough to solve your big problem easily. They help and forget about it, while I felt obliged and awkward because my gratitude would be irrelevant. Sometimes it is done to prevent another request, to keep one indebted or just to feel oneself powerful. [19]

Often bosses expect or pretend to expect nothing in return. One university administrator remembered that they employed the daughter of the deceased rector of university: 'It was done in his memory. She was not brilliant, not the best at the faculty, so we had to avoid the formal rules, by *blat*. And we are not going to have any return or gratitude for that.' [36] A favour could be paid off by loyalty, but in practice this may not be the case. Another example given by the same person related to his personal friend:

I had a good friend in Kuzbass in the regional party committee who used to help us a lot but has now lost all his power. His daughter submitted a dissertation which was no good. I helped her and she passed. It was altruistic on my side. She must have been aware that she passed by *blat* but I never had anything from her. I think when you enjoy doing favours, this is the return. [36]

> I help not because I expect something in return. My contacts are people who would not calculate the provided favours. If somebody asks for a favour I help because I respect this person, normally it is

someone whom I have known for a long time. Intuitively I know who is a right person to have a relationship with. I feel how respectable or responsible he is. There are mistakes, of course, but one realises them fairly quickly. [34]

Another example of non-reciprocal case was given by the organiser of Youth Festivals:

In spring 1991 I was organising an International Festival. Many foreign guests and other people had to be brought from Moscow to Novosibirsk. I needed a plane. I knew that Chkalov military plant had its own plane but to approach the director outright would have just spoiled everything. So I went to see the first secretary of the regional party committee. He knew us from the previous Festivals, we used to drink together and he liked the idea of Festivals. We wrote a letter to the director of the Chkalov enterprise from the regional Komsomol committee. The chief engineer of the plant was a good contact of Komsomol people, he said, 'we are all *svoi lyudi*'. The letter was signed by the secretary of regional party committee and that was it. Even though there was a phrase in the letter 'payment guaranteed', I know definitely that neither the regional Komsomol committee nor anybody else paid anything. Everything was done like that in those times. Connections were important. I did not have connections when I started, I never managed to get an appointment to see the mayor until the former secretary of the party organisation of our University, who was then a secretary of local party committee, took me to his place. But in time I acquired a lot of connections. I remember after Alexander King, the president of the Club of Rome, came to our Festival, people started contacting me. [32]

It also happens that the regime of status operates against a potential client. Playing out the duty and commitment to formal targets could be a preventive measure or protective device against *blat* overtures:

A person might think of himself as my friend and come to ask me about something. He is guided by the image of our friendship, while I am guided by the politics of my business. Whether one receives a favour from me depends on the person, kind of request, situation and the perspective I take in every particular situation. It used to be the case that moral obligations of friendship outweighed other obligations. Now it all changes because business interests have become dominant. [6]

### Blat gifts

The regime of equivalence and the regime of status can be distinguished from the affective regime by the presence of *blat* gifts.

*Blat* gifts are symbolic. They indicate that the favour was either too small or too significant to be repaid. In the first case, gifts were given for services which were supposed to be provided anyway, so that gift-giving was just an indication of 'personal touch'. In the second case, the favour was coupled with using one's power or influence in decision-making procedure, diversion of state property, roughly speaking, provided at the expense of state or collective pocket. In both cases gifts indicated the appreciation and gratitude of the recipient to the donor:

> It used to be very simple in Russia. The range was never really diverse. Gifts could range from a bottle of vodka or drinking together to a box of chocolates and greetings for festive days and holidays. Russian folk were modest and unpretentious. It used to be like that, and some are still the same. [21]

> Small gifts were signs of gratitude. They were not obligatory, but useful to create a benevolent attitude. [8]

> If you went abroad you normally brought souvenirs for those who helped with the documents, etc. [33]

For the most part, *blat* gifts were redundant transactions used for the construction of small social worlds. They did not imply help or redistribution of resources, as in gift-giving in conditions of scarcity within circles of friends or relatives. In intimate relationships birthday presents can be costly, friends know what the person needs, obtain it and share its cost. But gifts are not given for friendly favours:

> I never give presents or anything to friends, they are supposed to help anyway. If I need to go somewhere, I'd rather ring ten times asking them to drive me than go by bus. They will send me a car, will curse me but provide it. [3]

In professions where services can be converted into a personal favour, gifts are more specific and purposive, especially if given in the beginning:

> I had to transfer all the property into my name after the death of my husband. I was in despair and did not even know where to start. If my notary had not been so helpful, I would have lost everything. When I first went to see her, I gave her a present. She treated me informally, worked in her non-working hours, helped with her experience and contacts. We became friends. Giving her presents, I wanted to express my appreciation of her cordial attitude. [23]

> If one paid for my service [said a master of hi-tech] no presents were

needed, but they were given as a sign of gratitude. Nice chocolates were most often given to me. I do not drink and people knew this. My wife was given a French perfume for my services once. That person said: 'it has nothing to do with you, this is for the hostess.' [38]

Blat gifts could be French perfume or cosmetics for women and a good cognac for men. Flowers and chocolates did not count. The gift was symbolic, it was not a repayment, just a sign of thankfulness. At the same time, it was symbolic because French perfume and cognac were cheap but difficult to obtain. The cost of a present was not important, what counted was that it could not be bought:

To give such a present one needed to have other connections of which this present was a symbol. It used to be easy those days, everybody knew how to express one's gratitude, while now it is a real problem . . .

My mother was a known surgeon. She carried out about a thousand operations a year, brought medicines from abroad, took care of her patients with chronic diseases for years. She saved so many lives and, naturally, people were happy to provide her with everything they had themselves. She was a conscientious character, always embarrassed to accept gifts. Not to accept them was, however, also embarrassing. She ended up accepting self-made gifts (self-baked cakes, self-grown strawberries) and perfume. At that time the perfume sets 'Red Moscow', 'White Lilac' and 'Red Poppy' were popular to give. I remember in 1958 one woman left money in an envelope, my mother felt very cross and insulted then – sent me to return it. [13]

The embarrassment caused by giving a gift made people give them tactfully, on appropriate occasions: on high days and holidays, on one's birthday or as a treat for children; to bring flowers, boxes of chocolates for Women's Day or New Year:

I had many acquaintances and always engage in helping-out. Especially if someone needs money urgently. I ring around the city and solve the problem. This is just the way I am. I have nothing in terms of money, but my three daughters always get their 'Snickers'. Everybody knows they love them and learnt to bring them. [10]

Gift-giving was cultivated in institutions, especially in big cities:

It was impossible not to bring cigarettes or perfume to a secretary if I went to see someone important. These gifts were no measure of the favour provided, they were purely symbolic, just an entourage of *blat*. Secretaries and children of big bosses often became targets of such overtures. All this has been transformed now, however. First of all, there are no queues any more. If a firm needs a service regularly [service, not favour], they pay a 'salary' to the cashier who reserves tickets whenever they ring. It can be a normal rate of salary. If needs are not so regular, then again: gifts, chocolates, flowers, cigarettes; money can now be accepted as well. If we talk about more serious things, they also became calculable, because money became equivalent to 'possibility' which was never the case before. Those bureaucrats who used to work and could afford to work for credit became now much more explicit in their requests, expressing them in concrete sums of money. And not in a lump sum, but rather on a permanent basis. If we collaborate in business, he or she gets a commission, a percentage or 'salary'. [22]

Apart from gifts, sanctions have been revised as well. It used to be taking offence, or cooling down of relationships, while now they are becoming more violent and strict. Time becomes speeded up and waiting for compensation comes to be less possible.

### Etiquette of intermediaries

*Concealing the reciprocity of blat relations.*

In contrast to personal relations and simple barter, *blat* relations are not necessarily dyadic. *Blat* transactions can be circular: *A* provides a favour to *B*, *B* to *C*, *C* to *D*, and *D* to *A*, and the last chain might not have taken place. It was a circular indebtedness: 'If I helped people with my contacts, I knew they would pull strings for me (*pomogut svoimi svyazyami* ).' [30] What is important is that there should not be an immediate repayment: a factor which is the necessary condition of *blat* transactions. Reciprocity was to be masked by the delayed return. Mediated favours were even more efficient for avoiding practical and social constraints against immediate repayment. Under Soviet conditions, where monetary transactions were not fully functional, *blat* provided a specific system of 'promissory notes' (*spetsificheskaya sistema nematerial'nykh vekselei*) enabling the concealment of the exchange relationships:

> The mechanism supporting *blat* was psychological. If my best friend asked me something, I felt morally obliged and, in fact, preferred to compromise with my formal duties rather than break our relationship. He asked for someone to pass the exams, for example. I understood his fatherly instinct, I am a father myself, and I helped, even though I knew it was not fully legal. To do this I had to ask the

teacher of course, who valued the relationship with me, and wouldn't refuse for the same psychological reason. Thus I mediated the chain of relationship: my friend – his son – teacher – myself – my friend. All relations in this chain were hierarchical, except our friendship, but all of them were human relations, understanding each other's problems, helping each other without any payment. [36]

Psychologically, mediation was very important because 'it was terribly difficult to ask on behalf of oneself. It was much easier to ask for a friend, or for an institution, just to put in a word for somebody'. [36] It looked respectable when an intermediary asked to help somebody 'unselfishly', or when a donor helped an unknown person just for the sake of the relationship with the intermediary:

> If I rang about somebody, it was because I thought the person deserved it. I did it because I really wanted to help the person, not because I expected a return favour or anything. People could say that I did everything by *blat*, but for me it was not *blat*, it was help. [34]

Even when helped or helping 'unselfishly', a person entered this efficient (for the command economy) form of relationship called '*blat*' by outsiders. Apart from everything else, mediation in this case was an important mechanism of concealing reciprocity.

### Transference of influence

Many respondents remarked that in the formula 'I am from Ivan Ivanovich' the status of Ivan Ivanovich was of crucial importance. A client was perceived with respect to the status of the person who introduced or recommended him. The status of the intermediary was, as it were, transferred onto the recipient:

> If I get a call from my friend, or from a person whom I respect, I will do my best for someone whom I do not even meet. I do it for my friend rather than for the originator of request. The request will not necessarily be fulfilled, but at least I will do something about it,

said an intermediary, a high-up in the former nomenclatura. To be sure that the request would be fulfilled, one had to find an intermediary whose mediation would settle the deal. The intermediary had to have an adequate status either in personal terms, or in terms of position and influence. Sometimes one needed an intermediary who would be higher in status, sometimes the other way around: 'I can't ask someone who is expecting too much from me. It is just out of balance. I will find a person who would ask for me, but then I won't be obliged directly and won't have to repay so much,' remarked a respondent of high status. [36] Simply speaking, the contact must be appropriate to the request:

> There are cases that require serious connections and need to be approached from above, as it were, but there are things which are much easier to arrange from below. If somebody asks my boss for a small favour, he won't get involved in it. He will ask me to do it, reserving his right to ask for more significant favours. As an intermediary in this case, I won't get anything from my boss and from the originator of request. The latter will be grateful and obliged to the former, while the former won't be obliged or grateful to me. He is my boss and not supposed to repay. He can use my connections but I cannot use his. My relationship with my boss is non-symmetrical, but I can rely on his support and promotion if I am loyal and trustworthy. [12]

The repayment to the intermediary depended on personal relations between the parties and concrete situation. In case of advice or introduction an intermediary received nothing except for the advice and introduction when he or she was in need. And even the latter was not necessary. Some respondents, however, commented upon recent changes in this respect:

> In the West they pay a fee for mediation, while in Russia this was never the case. People were shy about money, especially with friends. Recently everything has changed radically. People have learned to calculate now. If I introduce one friend, businessman, to another and their business is successful, why can't I have a little something out of it? Now people offer and I do not refuse, even though to claim a cut is still kind of embarrassing. A recent example: business in present conditions is so complicated and corrupt that reliability and really good contacts are highly valued. I was just lucky that two close friends of mine (one is my foreign partner) were looking for each other. I introduced them to each other but not only that. They trusted each other, because I vouched for each of them to the other. They knew I had no decent flat, so they decided I could have a percentage from their contract. This is how I bought my flat. [6]

The form of mediation was itself very important because it conveyed a message about the degree of obligation the intermediary was ready to accept:

> I can give a telephone number of my contact and let somebody I know ring giving my name, for example, but the trick is that I have to ring myself. Because if I ring myself I enter the relationship, and

> the obligation I am taking is more straightforward. The person will
> do the same thing in the end in both cases, but it is important for him
> to do it for me and not for the one who is calling on my behalf

explained a respondent helping out somebody he did not know out of
trouble. [19] To be efficient, mediation had to be personal. But it could
also imply different degrees of trust and involvement:

> An intermediary can introduce me to other people with whom I will
> have further relations; alternatively, he can tell me how much or
> what is needed in return and obtain the thing for me without
> introducing me; or may represent me so that the person who helps
> will not even know that the favour is transferred to me. In the latter
> case, one must think twice before asking for somebody because he is
> taking responsibility for both parties. If one of them is not reliable,
> the intermediary runs a risk of losing the opportunity to ask again.
> [6]

With friends, mediation occurred more or less routinely. Friends
were always asked first, and if they could not help directly they
transferred the request so that help could be eventually provided by
some donor. In the latter case the recipient had to pay, or give some
present, but it was reliable and effective. Even with friends, however,
there were situations where one could not share one's *blat* connection
with another, that is, perform as an intermediary, easily:

> Normally, intermediaries are friends of whom I can be as sure as of
> myself. But some deals require intermediaries who need to be
> approached themselves. In short, when intermediaries are dependent
> on me or obliged to me already, then I can rely on them. If it is a one-
> way favour, one cannot be sure of anything. [19]

In mediated relations, indebtedness was embedded within each
specific link or dyadic relationship, not diffused all along the chain.
That is to say, each person in the chain would only be indebted to the
next person to whom she or he made a request, not necessarily to the
one who actually granted the favour. The dyadic relations were
personal and thus horizontal, but in the long chain they were
composed in such a way that the result could be achieved at the very
top level:

> If I ask for my friend, she will be treated as I would be, which means
> that she can actually transcend her own limited social circle and have
> the possibilities which I would have had. But I will only provide this
> possibility to those I respect or consider as useful. [3]

It is important to see this flexible and enabling aspect of *blat*. It was not simply a static and status-bound system of exchange.

### *The regulation of blat transactions*

Intermediaries regulated *blat* transactions, particularly in situations which were not routine and habitual for people, where transactions were not self-regulating and ruled by the practical sense of participants. In complicated deals, intermediaries were indispensable to obtain relevant information, to ascertain the donor's competence and willingness to help, to find a diplomatic way of presenting the problem, or to vouch for the recipient's reliability and responsibility. An intermediary who had better personal ties could 'test the channel', for example a cadre, by inquiring into how responsive the cadre might be to his friend. He could ask what kind of gratitude or return would most likely win him over, or whether the position or jurisdiction of the cadre would enable him to fulfil the particular request:

> For example, an acquaintance of mine who was a director of one enterprise came to see me. He had problems with privatisation of his enterprise. He came because 'he was advised to consult me'. Basically he wanted me to ring the regional administration and ask whether or not his enterprise would be given a status of the state enterprise. I knew him as a respectable and reliable partner and I told him that I would call to ask the view of the regional administration, their assessment of his enterprise and their interest in cooperation. I also told him that for his part he had to prepare a concrete and convincing proposal for cooperation. This did not mean that my call could change their decision. I could introduce a person, test the possibilities but I could not influence the decision-making. [34]

Intermediaries were able to put the request in appropriate form, connecting people diplomatically, providing the parties with necessary information about each other – thus, for example, saving one from the embarrassment of receiving a direct rejection and the other from the embarrassment of rejecting the request, or regulating misunderstandings of mutual obligations.

### The ethics of *blat*

As Yergin and Gustavson remark in their *Russia 2010* (1994: 113):

> the Soviet command economy had a powerful inner logic and language of its own, which made the Soviet system more than just

foreign, but rather like [a] distant civilization. Its customs seemed altogether strange, but they did make sense once you understood them in context.

This might be true about any culture – there is always a gap between the unwritten customs and codes and written rules. The distinction of Soviet-type systems, perhaps, was in that the former were followed, in fact, with fewer exemptions than were formal rules. To explain how they acted, the respondents were asked to explicate the rules or principles they pursued in *blat* relations. Curiously, these questions were confusing for the respondents and were constantly avoided. I had to accept that just as the criminal *blat* code had no verbal 'moral code', so the rules governing *blat* relations cannot be reduced to a few *a priori* principles. They are not like logically extracted ethical codes; rather, they are rules of the kind known as 'to be able to go on'.[6] Using de Certeau's phrase (1984), it can be said that knowledge of *blat* rules is already written in practices, but not yet read. This was noted by one of the respondents:

> The ethics of *blat* are in whether you can use it correctly or not, whether you know how to repay or not, whether you know what is possible to say and what is not, whether you can manage the situation or not, etc. They are difficult to instruct in general terms but one feels if something goes wrong. [19]

The rules governing *blat* should thus be considered as techniques applied in the enactment of social practices. The awareness of such rules, expressed first and foremost in practical activities, is the very core of that 'social competence' which *blat* presumed. Most Soviet people were highly 'skilled' in this way (even if people did not use *blat*, they knew how to react 'appropriately' when others went through the backdoor or obtained something by *blat*). The vast bulk of such knowledge was practical rather than theoretical in character. Knowledge of procedure, or mastery of the techniques of 'practising' *blat*, is by definition methodological. This is to say, such knowledge

---

[6] The most analytically effective sense of such a 'rule' can be transferred by Wittgenstein's example of number games. One person writes down a sequence of numbers 2,4,6,8, . . . , the second person works out the formula supplying the numbers which follow. The formula of the progression is $An = An - 1 + 2$. But to understand the progression is not to utter the formula. For someone could utter the formula and not understand the series; alternatively it is possible to understand the series without being able to give verbal expression to the formula. The 'rule' is simply being able to apply the formula in the right context and way in order to continue the series (Wittgenstein, 1972: 59).

does not specify all the situations which an actor might meet with, nor could it do so; rather, it provides for the generalised capacity to respond to and to influence an indeterminate range of social circumstances (Giddens 1984: 22). This can be illustrated by the metaphor of driving: *blat* was an universal alertness for manoeuvre and capability to find the most effective (certainly not direct and formal) way, avoiding the devastating holes of Russian roads, following both formal and informal rules when needed, following extraordinary curves while moving forward and minding other drivers doing the same.

In most social theory today, social rules are seen as ambiguous, flexible, contradictory and inconsistent. They serve as resources for strategies that vary from person to person and from situation to situation (Edgerton 1985: 14). For example, there was no law against *blat*, but there was an unwritten rule which said that *blat* was amoral, bad, anti-Soviet, as well as an unwritten code which prescribed the ways in which *blat* operated. The very fact that 'implicit principles' or postulates were not made explicit created margins of tolerance and the possibility of setting one against the other. *Blat* practices can be grasped as strategies which 'navigate' among the rules, 'play with all the possibilities offered by traditions', make use of one tradition rather than another, compensate for one by means of another. Strategies do not 'apply' to principles or rules; they choose among them to make up the repertory of their operations (de Certeau 1984: 53). The selectivity of the rules is determined by the conventional system of their exempting conditions, status and the occasions under which *blat* relations are initiated. In what follows I shall focus on the ethical guidelines perceived by my respondents as more or less conventional.

### Selectivity of rules

The strategies of 'misrecognition' – when *blat* transactions are seen as friendly help – are the best example of 'navigating' strategies. It is antisocial to obtain something by *blat*, through the backdoor – for example, sausages – for which people queue, or to get the best lean cuts of meat for the same price as others pay for fat and bones as a part of the purchase. On the other hand, from the perspective of those involved in it, a *blat* transaction implies sociability, good intentions and friendly help (*chelovecheskoe otnoshenie*): a shopgirl's mother will not be queueing for sausages and a friend will be given good meat. One of my respondents, a journalist, remarked that 'if the principles of *blat* were recorded in terms of participants, they would probably coincide with the *Moral Code of the Communist'*, the most important principle of which was 'One is a friend, comrade and brother to another'.[7] [28a] These generally moral, humane – even Christian – principles, however, became applied selectively. Under conditions of shortage and the Soviet command economy, they developed into the *blat* system. Being integrally bound up with the conditions of social life, *blat* ethics cannot be considered as those of interpersonal relations (e.g. ethics of friendship). On the other hand, rooted in personal relations, they cannot be seen as simply formed by specific socio-economic conditions (as the professional ethic of fiddling, for example). Rather, *blat* ethics should be seen as deriving from both formal rules and informal codes. *Blat* relations were regulated according to the logic of informal relations, such as not cheating one's neighbour, not letting the other down, keeping one's word, on the one hand, and the logic of 'beating the system' and violating the rules for the sake of efficiency, cleverness and creativity, on the other. Informal codes, however, always penetrated and enmeshed with formal ones, not only in the sense of violating them.

The socialist distribution system was strongly state-regulated and ideologically based on principles of justice and equality. On the other hand, there was always a room for an exceptional case (see chapter 3), meeting each other's personal interests or friendly help. As soon as the principles of equality were reinterpreted in practice of the state distribution system,[8] the principles of personal relations echoed these changes in their own way. In situations of scarce resources, 'friendly help' (*chelovecheskoe otnoshenie*) could be available only for a selected circle of people. Those who did not possess power or privileges to enable them to live according to formal rules were forced to elaborate

---

[7] *Sovetskii etiket*, Leningrad, 1974: 72.

[8] To understand the principles of Soviet rationing, one should analyse the genesis of Stalinist politics of distribution. The rationing system was introduced from the very conception of the regime as an emergency measure against scarcity, starvation and extreme shortages of food supplies. Under Stalin the rationing system became linked to a worker's productive output and was supposed to guarantee supplies for the working class 'vanguard'. It was emphasised as an achievement of the system that the best was provided for the working class, and additional efforts were made to supply central industrial regions while peasants and declassified groups had to shoulder the burdens of this policy. Hierarchical principles of distribution were introduced also within the working class itself. According to their performance workers were allocated different rations. Shock-workers (*udarniki*) shopped at special stores, had cheaper and better food, received extra supplies and additional tokens for boots and clothes when they exceeded their plan tasks. For skilled workers material incentives increasingly displaced moral incentives (see, for example, Andrle, 1988: 31–66).

a network of acquaintances, personal connections, mutual obligations to each other: 'Ethical principles of *blat* seem to be common human principles. But it is a morality within morality because it is not concerned with everybody, but only with "the people of the circle" (*dlya svoikh*), emphasised a respondent with experience in *blat* deals.' [3]

Moreover, 'morality within morality' implies not only selectivity of rules but also selectivity of people. The 'reverse side' of these networks of support and assistance was that the sense of common morality was substituted for by the morality of a selected circle of people. It is therefore important to trace both stabilising and 'corrupting' implications which *blat*, in fact, combines. Affective relations between those involved created a kind of solidarity and support within the circle. The public side of such inner solidarity was a group egoism, when one's own circle was considered superior to any other. *Blat* relations thus divided as well as united people. Let us consider such inner circle principles guiding *blat* relations in more detail.

### The obligation to help

The unwritten ethical code as formulated by respondents was based on the obligation to help: 'Help another and a stranger's help will come to you,' [45] or 'One has to satisfy the request or at least try to meet the need of the other.' [5] Following this code one initiated contacts and created a kind of reserve to have recourse to in future; established and maintained the relationships; rendered assistance and gave attention to both old and new contacts. This pattern was noted by many respondents:

> Western people, in contrast to us, are very independent. They rely on themselves and do not fancy helping out or accepting help from others. Russians assume that they can always ask for help and will help themselves. I am sure that if I ask I will be helped. And the other way round. If I am asked, I drop everything and help the other person, because I can imagine myself in his place. Indifference or refusal is a psychological trauma. I try not to refuse, giving out everything I can. [13]

> There are people, of course, who try to clear up their obligations immediately but this is not appreciated in the *blat* relationship. There are people trying to be independent. Their principle is not ask and not to give a favour, which is not social as well. [36]

It was socially difficult to refuse a request. In these circumstances, the pressure put on the donor was a moral one – the very fact of acquaintance implied an obligation. The same respondent, a university dean, continued:

> Sometimes I don't even have gratitude or pleasure from helping. It is simply impossible to stop helping out. There were the cases where I knew I shouldn't have done but couldn't help giving a hand. This is my character. It is easier to help than to refuse. I suffer more from rejecting. I have a hard time thinking how to explain that I can't help. I do not want people to say that I did not want to help. I always try even if I know it is pointless. I never say 'no' at once, but rather 'let me think what I can do for you'. Psychologically it is very difficult to say 'no'. [36]

### Orientation towards an indefinite future

The logic of the obligation to help is clear: you helped people unselfishly, it was just a humane and warm attitude to your close friends, but if you were in trouble, all those whom you helped turned to you. *Blat* was always open-ended. It was not necessarily a calculative strategy oriented towards particular aims, but rather a specific ethics which forced people to help each other. Such an ethic can be called calculative: at every particular moment one helped altruistically but also knew that to help was the condition for being helped:

> When I do a favour I know I will benefit from it. Not necessarily in money but in terms of contacts, support, credibility. One has to work for years in order to understand that there is profit, but it is not so important as relationships which one cannot avoid. Every favour will come back to you in the most unexpected way, just when you are particularly desperate,

concluded a former *apparatchik*. [6] 'The more you help, the more people are obliged to you. You may get nothing out of it at a particular moment, but the more people are obliged to you, the easier your problems will be solved in future,' sounded as a refrain in many interviews. An interesting aspect of *blat* was that one could do a favour for someone and get a return years later, when it was least expected.[9] There is a folk saying expressing the need for reservations about future: 'Do not spit into a well, you might need to drink from it'

---

[9] As in the fairy tale about Ivan-the-Fool who, despite his grand mission to liberate Helen-the-Beauty, helped different creatures on his way, sharing food with them and saving their homes or lives. He would have had no chance in his fight with the Deathless (in Russian folklore a bony, emaciated old man, rich and wicked, who

(*ne plyui v kolodets, prigoditsya vody napit'sya*), which was quoted as another general ethical principle applied in *blat* relations.

### Do not expect gratitude in return but be grateful yourself

Conscious or unconscious expectations of reciprocation not only bring social relations about, they also stabilise already existing relations by making them, to a certain extent, predictable. In his famous essay 'Faithfulness and Gratitude' (1950), Simmel analysed the moral and social importance of these two feelings in sustaining reciprocity in human relationships. Simmel considered gratitude as a powerful means of establishing social cohesion. By mutual giving, people become tied to each other by a web of feelings of gratitude. Gratitude is the motive which moves us to give in return, and by this, creates the reciprocity of service and counter-service. Gratitude is, in Simmel's words (1950: 388), 'the moral memory of mankind', and as such is essential for establishing and maintaining social relations. An extremely well-connected academic woman remembered:

> My father, who was a *blatmeister* (*blat* dealer), used to tell me 'One has to learn to be grateful'. He never burdened but always helped others. He helped in the ways which were not obvious, elegantly, with no expectation of return. When he died, they finally realised that what he did was costly and burdensome. When I do something for somebody, I never think about gratitude in return. I just do what is appropriate in every particular situation for every particular person and then simply forget about it. [13]

It follows that one had to repay for *blat* favours (*ne ostat'sya v dolgu*) on the one hand but not to expect repayment on the other. There were certain norms of reciprocity not to be violated. For example, money was not to be given or accepted, for it would deprive the relationship of a personal basis, and insult the recipient. Gouldner (1977) explored the meaning of the 'norm of reciprocity'. He went further than Simmel, by reflecting more explicitly on the complicating role of power in reciprocity relations, and elaborating it theoretically. Reciprocal exchange relationships may be very asymmetrical, with one party being obliged to give much more than the other. The respective level of resources of giver and recipient should be taken into account, as well as the needs/wants of the recipient

knows the secret of eternal life), but because every creature returned his favour, in their small ways in particular moments, in the end with their assistance he managed to kill the Deathless and marry the girl.

**Cartoon 11**
My wife does not request anything. But the youngster demands
a BMW                                    (*Krokodil* 1997, 3: 7)

and the freedom of the giver to give or not to give. To what extent is one's giving compelled by other people, or by strong normative expectations to do so? The qualitative aspects of the norms of reciprocity – expectations and social pressures stimulating the obligation to help - have already been touched upon. The quantitative aspects – how much can be requested or given – were normally so context-bound and morally induced that they are difficult to generalise about. 'Exchange rates' are subordinated to the social relations between actors (Sahlins 1972) and therefore there is no criterion by which a general value may be established. Some guidelines for such evaluation were provided in the interviews, again with reference to conventions and folklore.

### Keep within limits

The reaction to the 'what can be asked' questions were unproblematic: 'The rules are simple, you just know them.' [29] One respondent referred to a fairy tale 'The Fisher and the Golden Fish', which tells a story of a fisher who, forced by his wife, asked the Golden Fish for more and more favours until she took all of them back. The moral of the story is that one has to keep within limits (see cartoon 11).

The limits are important to know but difficult to explicate. Partly, they are externally normed: to obtain something by *blat* – in modest volume, with discretion, normally in situations of urgent need and within a closed personal circle – is a norm, to exceed limits is theft, corruption, etc. Partly, they are interpersonal: the request has to be morally approved both by the donor and by the recipient. The moral limits are flexible though: 'to allocate a flat or to enrol a child for a education course through *blat* is not acceptable to me; but I would use my connection to save him from imprisonment.' [39]

People differ in their attitudes towards *blat*. For some people to ask about lending support or assistance was the natural order of things. For others, however, favours were burdensome. Depending on personal biography and specific psychological make-up, people reacted differently to this 'balance of debt' (the notion introduced by the social psychologist Barry Schwartz, 1967). Some had great difficulty in receiving help or material goods from others, because they considered getting around the formal procedures improper or because they could not deal with feelings of gratitude or indebtedness to another person. The balance of debt could be disturbed in several ways. A very effective means of exercising power, for example, was to keep another person indebted by over-reciprocation, that is, to deliberately go 'beyond the limits'. The balance was disturbed if someone returned a gift too quickly thus violating the 'orientation towards future' principle. According to Schwartz (1967: 8), the balance of debt must never be brought into a complete equilibrium: 'The continuing balance of debt – now in favour of one member, now in favour of the other – insures that the relationship between the two continues, for gratitude will always constitute a part of the bond linking them.'

### The tactics of *blat*

The tactics of *blat* were connected with the form of requests and the form of refusals (whom, when and how). This was a delicate matter, since the request had to be made in such a way that it would be fulfilled or, in the case of refusal, would not jeopardise the whole relationship. It was emphasised in the interviews that tactics 'are situational and cannot be explained or generalised. We were brought up here to feel mutual obligations and to know whom and what is possible to ask. It is an inborn ability. It is just clear whether you can ask or not'. These criteria are implicit – that is, they can be inferred only from behavioural regularities or from reactions that occur after such rules have been broken. Let me give an example, supplied by an administrator of Youth Festivals, who remembered his unfortunate experience:

> An *a priori* call was made: 'The deputy of the mayor rang the head of airlines company, at his home number and said: "Well, Ivan Ivanovich, don't you love our young generation? How about the Festival? Can't you help?"'
> – 'Why not, I am happy to help, but *they ask too much*. I understand their situation, but we don't provide such discounts even to our own people. We agreed already that the rates for their foreign guests are reduced to the internal rates, but now they want discounts for their Russian guests as well. We can't make it, you know. We are poor ourselves.'
> – 'Come on, Ivan Ivanovich, let's help them!' – said the deputy of the mayor in a begging tone.
> – 'OK,' replied Ivan Ivanovich, 'Make him come to see me.'
> When I came, Ivan Ivanovich was on a business trip. I was told to go and see the commercial director of the company, that is, the person whose position is designed to make profit out of tourist firms, etc. He was against any charity in principle. I entered at that very moment when he was discussing the contracts with representatives of tourist firms, negotiating the timing of a stay in Turkey and counting every rouble (a one day difference in stay was the point of a hot discussion). And here I am, asking for discounts for the Festival guests. They all looked at me as a complete idiot, and *I felt like one* myself. [32]

It follows from this example that despite the strong support (the deputy mayor) some basic tactical principles were still crucial and had to be followed: one should ask the right person at the right moment about the right thing – that is, the request must be appropriate and relevant. The criteria of appropriateness and relevance are determined by the particular situation and particular person. 'The space of the tactics,' writes de Certeau, 'is the space of the other' (1984: 35). From respondents' responses I came to the conclusion that 'the other' is taken into consideration in relation to:

(1) the other's personal characteristics
(2) the other's possibilities provided by a person's status or contacts
(3) personal relations with the other
(4) the balance of debt
(5) nuances of situations in which one finds oneself.

*Blat* tactics were coordinated according to all these characteristics of the other and applied selectively:

> For some I lay myself out and even consider it as a pleasure. These are either my friends or those who may prove useful in future. For others I may give out all the information I possess or promise to fulfil the request (though without straining my nerves), but some requests I consider as strange and I won't even promise. It is not a consciously designed strategy, it happens spontaneously. [19b]

> There are characters who have to overcome themselves in order to ask another but it is also quite common for people repeatedly to ask for information or something with no limits. It was a habit to involve friends with one's problems, asking about minor things, especially information, which one was perfectly able to find out oneself. [19a]

The habit of exchanging information was absolutely crucial and the most widespread tactic of *blat*. Conversations were all-important, in the neighbour's kitchen, in the office, at celebrations, parties, etc. One just realised who could do what and then it was easy to get in touch, to find mutual interests:

> One should start everything by seeking the advice of one's friends and acquaintances. The practical moments 'where to go, how to ask, whom to approach' are discussed with colleagues at work, with acquaintances in a bus, with friends in a sauna. All information is delivered by personal channels. Imagine someone comes in and asks whether I know a good dentist. If I know a dentist with a good reputation, I tell him where to go. If I know the dentist personally I may ring and arrange an appointment for this person, given that I find this appropriate, of course. I could go myself to the office next door and, having tea, ask whether anybody could obtain brakes for my Lada. Today one can go and buy everything. Then it was important to catch up with information, opportunities, contacts. [29a]

Sometimes it was not even necessary to ask, people offered themselves. One did not normally ask friends in the same manner as acquaintances. They helped themselves if they knew the problem. It was taken for granted between friends in Soviet Russia that problems were shared and sharing became an invitation for help.

When help was sought, the recommended tactic was to go through one's address book and list people who could turn out to be useful. An energetic businesswoman remarked:

> One shouldn't rely on one particular person. If I am desperate for something I ring everybody and somebody helps. And no problem if

others don't. Refusals happen, but it does not matter that much. I'll ring someone else. If there are three variants, one will work out. [3]

On the other hand, this easy-going manner could result in a sense of resentment on the part of those whose efforts were wasted. A donor complained:

It sometimes happens that I drop everything and help people by giving out my 'last shirt'. Afterwards I realise they did not need it. They asked not only me, but many others, and my help turned out unnecessary. [13]

The address books and other information sources saved time and provided opportunities. It was always easier if contacts were available before the need arose: to accept an offer was easier than to ask for it and to ask friends or acquaintances was easier than to look for contacts: 'One had to keep the contacts, rather than search for them afresh when something was needed.' [17] On the other hand, it was also time-consuming: 'To keep *blat* contacts is hard work. One has to be really energetic. It is an unconscious passion to arrange things.' [6] Some people obtained things and arranged problems just to feel useful to others – they valued people's gratitude, greetings, smiles. They wanted to be known and considered their contacts as social capital. As one *blatmeister* confessed:

*Blat* made my life style, it has become my second nature. It is needed to obtain information, to organise my everyday activities. It is convenient to have contacts all around, from a hair-dresser and doctor to business contacts. [3]

If relations are not close, it is very difficult to ask. Especially, if a request demands a real effort and engagement of people in power: 'These are connections which one can't pull often.' [11] The range of tactics in such relations were explicated to me by the young administrator of the Psychology Lab at the Cadres Centre, who worked in a close contact with the regional administration. He referred to the following advice on informal relations given to him by his more experienced colleagues:

(1) When you make a request, ensure that the person is able to fulfil it. If the request is not adequate, one runs the risk of being refused or even losing the relationship, for the applicant is considered unable to put in a correct request.

(2) The adequacy of a request means also that every deal has to be approached on a certain level. Some deals are easier to decide from below, some need a pressure from above, some need an

intermediary who would inquire about my problem. It is also easier to ask an intermediary, because he is not giving anything himself but just assisting and facilitating the decision.

(3) There are no free favours. To be able to ask I should feel that I may prove useful either myself or as an intermediary. Not necessarily now, but somehow in future. At least I should have an imprint of this favour in my memory. Good memory is an important 'apparat' skill.

(4) With people of status it is important to allow no familiarities, even if relations are friendly. If you mistakenly treat as a friend someone who does not treat you as such, it may cause a loss of the relationship. One should not fall into the illusion of warm and friendly relations but keep one's distance. The ability to feel the distance correctly is an important practical sense in *blat* relations. [12]

Apart from techniques of keeping contacts, the arsenal of tactics included what could be called *blat* style, a skill of approaching people in a pleasant or promising manner. One might not know the necessary person but be able to approach them in the way as if social relations existed and to hint that 'we' can rely on each other. It was not *blat*, strictly speaking, for the relationship did not exist at the moment of request; it was *blat* style, the pretension that they existed. This skill did not need much energy, people say, it was rather a social talent. Such a woman spoke with confidence:

> I arrange everything without much problem. I go to the person in charge and talk to him. I was told there are no places in the art school, but I arranged a place for my own daughter and then for five girls one by one, daughters of my friends. One just has to see the proper person and say the right things. I don't like bothering friends by asking them to ring about me or something. I know I can arrange everything myself without any chocolates or bottles. [10]

This kind of talent was caricatured in the satirical magazine *Krokodil* (1936, 27: 2), which described a person who knew 17,342 anecdotes and knew how and which one was to be told to receive what he wanted. These people were perfect brokers or intermediaries, whose tactics were so smooth and cheerful that, as with any kind of talent, they became socially approved.

### Establishing contacts

*Blat* contacts are established in the process of personalising formal channels. They overlap with personal contacts and intimate relations.

They derive from the vicissitudes of careers, rest on common hobby and leisure activities, and include all kinds of occasional contacts. Some contacts occur spontaneously, some are reached strategically. Let us analyse some techniques of establishing contacts, as reported in the interviews.

The most routine way to establish contacts is to transform the formal contacts one has at work into informal ones. In this case:

> a familiar face and repetitive contacts are important. I used to order a car for different occasions in the regional administration car park. First time I was desperate and rang straight to the deputy of the mayor in charge with apologies, etc. He said, 'No problem.' Afterwards it was enough to ring his secretary who knew me and ordered the car automatically. [12]

A professional career necessarily leads to establishing new relations and making contacts. The person who gets promoted enters new circles and acquires new contacts, acquaintances which allow her or him to solve problems. A party career used to be particularly appropriate for making contacts, because it was part of the cadres' function. One had to have specific personal qualities for this, however: 'I had a mate who became very successful in nomenclatura,[10] he was attractive, athletic, ready to compromise. Career-making makes people acquire a great deal of necessary qualities and practical skills in dealing with people.'[27] Let me illustrate the point by some examples:

> Every enterprise or organisation is first of all a person and his contacts. D was a go-ahead man with charm and irrepressible energy. His character was a complicated mixture: he was poetic and sentimental, he wrote poems, sang songs, liked theatre, played football; at the same time, he was stingy and delved into every detail. He could 'penetrate walls'. He realised that socialist society is a huge distribution system, and one just needed to find as many wires of this system as possible and stay near the socket. His charm and football skills made his search for the 'wires' much easier. He married the third secretary of the regional Komsomol committee while being just an instructor. It was a unprecedented case, people talked about it for a long time . . . The story of my contact with D goes back to my failure in the final year of the University. I wrote my thesis on the basis of materials of the party archives which were strictly confidential those days. The work was known as original and the best in the course, but the topic was 'not ideologically correct' (that year [1987] was the 30th anniversary of the Siberian Branch of the Academy of Sciences). The grades were predetermined and the only excellent mark was given to

[10] A detailed study of nomenclatura careers can be found in Klugman (1989).

a daughter of the secretary of the local party committee. I was hurt and disillusioned and decided to become a professional football player. I had played seriously for the regional team before and decided to drop history altogether. After military service, however, I got married which forced me to find a job in a profession. I worked half a year in a museum, got more and more depressed. Until I met a person who was a Komsomol secretary at my university and then became a secretary of the regional Komsomol Committee. He asked for my telephone number and in a week I was offered a job which doubled my salary, provided a personal office and all the privileges. This was not a job I wanted, I had to deal with political education (*politpros*), but I acquired a lot of experience through it. For nine months I visited 23 out of the 40 regions of our administrative area, made lots and lots of contacts. Once, for some celebration the regional committee staff went to the international tourist campus. I had not even heard about it before then. It looked like a surrealist picture to me: bars, discos, tennis courts, super-soft furniture, sauna, beach. It was a kind of shock for me. We played football there, just for fun. Nobody knew I was a football player at university. *D* approached me asking where I am, what I am. In two weeks he came to my office and proposed a position as his deputy. It was less money, but my predecessor said, 'Come on, you have a state car with a driver, wonderful landscapes around, leisure facilities, five months a year of intensive work only, and a flat in three years.' I agreed. [6]

It was extremely difficult to get recruited into the nomenclatura. Marriage could help a lot. I remember one person who was a foreman of a workshop at the plant, and in half a year became a deputy of the Minister of Industry in such a way. [14]

My sister joined the ballet troop which performed abroad. She was not the best dancer but managed to enter it by a 'marriage of convenience'. She divorced her husband and married the director of the troop. She does not love him, does not want children from him but she has a lot of contacts now. [9]

One should not say, but it is so common that women enter intimate relations if they need something, a flat, a treatment for a child, a promotion. It is very widespread among the military to exempt a son from army service or to promote a husband. I used to give all anonymous letters unopened straight to my husband. Perhaps, it is not *blat*, but it is clearly a channel. [23]

Football is worth mentioning specifically. It is an extremely effective channel. I played in a combined team of journalists in Moscow and we were in close contact with a team of the Office of Public Prosecutor and many others. Having beer after the game one can solve any problem there. [6]

All kind of hobbies may serve as a basis for establishing *blat* contacts:

> Tours abroad were my hobby. Those days people who went to those tours were the cream in their fields. The head of the group was normally someone from the regional Party committee (*obkom*), 4–5 people from the KGB. These contacts lasted, I made friends in such tours. [7]

> It is important to go on holidays to the famous resorts and popular places. I met many of my friends at the sea-coast. Also, people one meets there may turn useful people. [13]

Another *Krokodil* personage, a *blatmeister*, says: 'I am a little man, my place is in the Crimea. This is the place for useful people to have their holidays. As I am able to play chess and volleyball, to swim and to remember 20–25 anecdotes, after the season I know numerous people, which opens many doors.' (*Krokodil* 1936, 31: 10]

# 6  Networking in the post-Soviet period

Do not have 100 friends, have 100 dollars     (A post-Soviet folk saying)

### Has *blat* changed?

The expression 'by *blat*' is still known and understood today. Opinions differ, however, about the forms of its present-day usage. Some argue that *blat* is still essential, even though its uses have changed, while others say that bribery and corruption have taken its place. It is telling that the older generation, particularly those respondents not involved with new sectors of the economy, tends to emphasise the enduring significance of *blat* ('old connections') even though they admit that it now meets new needs in new areas. The younger generation of respondents tends to consider '*blat*' an out-of-date term, inappropriate in market conditions. Moreover, younger interviewees observe that the word '*blatnoi*' has lost its Soviet meaning and returned to its original, criminal, meaning, now related to 'bandits' rather than *blat* patients, clients or students. Such a movement in the meaning of the term – from the 1900s' *blatnoi* meaning belonging to a criminal circle, to the 1930s' *blatnoi* as having access by *blat*, back to the 1990s' *blatnoi* as belonging to a new criminals' circle – implies that *blat* is losing its central significance in the conditions of the post-Soviet world. The idiom 'by *blat*' still holds meaning, but it is referred to less and less often: 'The expression is falling out of use: teenagers do know it (though do not use it), but those born since the late 1980s will not even understand.' [22]

Such a generational difference in usage of the term, however, does not mean that the phenomenon has disappeared completely. Rather, the forms *blat* now assumes stretch beyond the areas in which the term was used before. It is important to consider these changes but also see the continuity of *blat*, for the analysis of the dynamics of *blat* in contemporary conditions is not only a contribution to the

history of the end of the Soviet Union, but also a way of investigating the sources, limitations and consequences of the post-Soviet
reformation.

The post-Soviet reforms aimed at establishing a market economy and
the privatisation of state property. These reforms undermined three
basic parameters of the economic system which constituted *blat* (see
chapter 3). First, functioning markets for goods and capital took over
the economy of shortage, in which everything – foodstuffs, goods,
services, places in hospitals and at cemeteries – had to be bartered for
with a concomitant reduction in the role of money in economic
exchanges. The most frequent point mentioned in the interviews was
that *blat* diminished because there was no longer a shortage of
commodities for personal consumption:

> *Blat* was used to obtain commodities in short supply or to jump
> queues. As long as everything – decent shoes, a medicine, a car, an
> apartment – was in short supply, *blat* was vital. Now there is no
> shortage, and people have stopped talking about *blat* so much. [26]

> Now everything for personal consumption can be bought, if there is
> money. Things are available and there is no point in 'obtaining'
> them. The former value of 'obtaining' has lost its significance. To
> obtain a piece of sausage, to book a place for a tourist trip (even if
> cheaper) is not valued so much when there are people who can
> simply buy these things. There is no need to use the channels of *blat*
> if one is buying shoes or clothes. High-quality medical services are
> available for money, and so is education. There are 'commercial'
> groups at the universities and educational courses can now be
> purchased. In areas which are still not commercialised – for
> example, army service – *blat* has been replaced by bribery. *Blat* in its
> previous forms has come to an end. Nothing is a problem these
> days if there is money. [26]

Second, state property became increasingly privatised which
changed a customary attitude towards 'favours of access' and facilitated the economic interests of those in charge (see cartoon 12):

> the people responsible for rationing or distribution had access to
> resources which they were able to manipulate but which did not
> belong to them and which, therefore, they could dispose of without
> reluctance. This is not the case any more. [26]

Third, the system of socialist guarantees ceased to operate – the
process of privatisation in combination with severe economic

— Предупреждал: уходи от кооператоров, у них каждый кусок на счету!

**Cartoon 12**
I told you to keep away from businessmen: they account for every crumb!                    (*Krokodil* 1990, 11:11)

tendencies of the 1990s, such as the decline of industrial production,[1] the investment crisis and the rise of mutual non-payment, etc. ruled out previously dominant forms of solidarity and mutual help between industrial enterprises, a social security system and care about collectives in organisations, and launched a large-scale re-stratification of population.

The implications of such a restructuring of the economy for *blat* are as follows.

With the expansion of the areas of monetary exchange people say 'money became real', which means that they now are able to purchase goods, to differentiate, to 'make' money and to invest. As a consequence, money has become a 'shortage' and an overall need, at which *blat* connections became re-oriented: 'People use their contacts to obtain money: money for living expenses by making deposits in a bank where good contacts can ensure their safety; money for business by getting a loan on privileged conditions.' [28] At the very least, *blat* channels provide an opportunity to earn money or to arrange a 'good' job. It is not, however, the same '*blatnaya*' job as it used to be when only symbolic work was required for guaranteed salary or privileges. In places (normally in commercial firms) where 'real' money is paid for 'real' work and effort, '*blat*' people are not necessarily the first candidates. *Blat* is often aimed at providing the basis for business and trading activities:

> In business, *blat* is most needed to provide access to bureaucratic decision-making and information, especially where bribery is impossible. Where bribes do not work, *blat* can still be effective. For example, to obtain a licence for the export ofmetals three people may be eager to give a bribe but the licence will be issued not to the one who provides the bigger bribe but to the one who has the most *blat*, who is the friend of the son of the head of the regional administration, for example. [19b]

The emergence of private business brought about a significant change in the division between public and private which allowed people's interests to shift towards the commercial sphere. Asked when *blat* is most important today, respondents usually mentioned the needs of business: for instance, when starting business or attempting to run an existing business more efficiently. Personal interests have become business interests, and the ethics of *blat* have

---

[1] According to the *Russian Economic Barometer*, industrial production in 1996 has fallen 52 per cent in comparison with 1990, and will decrease for another 3–4 per cent in 1997, assuming that economic tendencies remain the same.

come into conflict with a more impersonal and calculating business
ethic: 'Finance, licences, privileged loans, access to business information are the "shortage" of today. The authorities in which *blat* contacts
have become most important are thus those of tax, customs, banking
and regional administration.' [5, 24, 25, 39, 41]

The spread of money has changed *blat* relations so much that *blat*
has almost ceased to be a relevant term for the connections that
characterise the new sectors of the economy. One businesswoman
explained:

> the word '*blat*' is out of use now. I never hear that a bank loan is
> given 'by *blat*'. People still say 'by acquaintance' but this no longer
> refers to '*blat*' as it did before. There used to be no difference in the
> Soviet distribution system: there was a fixed state price for every
> product, and the alternative to obtaining it by *blat* at the state price
> was to buy it at a much inflated black market price. In the Soviet
> system one felt as if one had the right to buy goods at a shop for the
> state price (the black market (*barakholka*) was something despised
> then). In return for providing access to product at the state price, a
> shop assistant would receive a non-monetary surplus (my indebted-
> ness and, possibly, a potential favour). Roughly speaking, this non-
> monetary surplus was taken out of the state's pocket by substituting
> for the principle of equal access the principle of private access for
> 'people of the circle'. Nowadays, there are no fixed prices, there is no
> right to buy at a fixed price, and there is no *blat* in the Soviet sense.
> When I do an acquaintance a favour, for example, if I am a retailer by
> selling something at its wholesale price I violate the business code. I
> earn nothing and know the loss that I have suffered. The acquain-
> tance is also aware of how much it cost me. In this transparency 'by
> *blat*' loses its meaning, its previous connotations have gone. It has
> become a dead metaphor. [19a]

In Soviet times 'helping out' by *blat* was often exercised at the
expense of state property or by deploying the influence given by the
holding of an institutional position. By helping out, people gave out
not goods of their own, but benefits of which the other was deprived.
These resources were to be distributed anyway, and in the rationing
system the very fact of acquaintance could become crucial in determining who got what. The fact of a kindness granted to an acquaintance even bestowed some benefit on the donor, as it earned the donor
gratitude and loyalty, and therefore nurtured a relationship which
could result in reciprocation of favours granted, and thus prove
useful. *Blat* was a complicated, culturally grounded, 'social alchemy'
for turning access to state property to one's own advantage but

without stealing anything. The higher one's position in the social hierarchy the more possibility was provided for such metamorphosis beyond the public eye: if shop assistants or workers could be caught with goods under the shelf or using state equipment for private needs, the decision-making bureaucrats were not so easy to apprehend.

In private business, attitudes towards property and helping out are becoming totally different from how they were before. Material calculations, rather than the fact of acquaintance, count for most. In the current situation of instability the fact of acquaintance does not necessarily ensure that favours will be returned: 'Market conditions have changed personal relationships and ruined many friendships. There is no room for *blat* as it used to be. It looks like *blat* won't be the same and the very word is going into oblivion.' [28]

Can *blat* practices be found nowadays? Or have they largely disappeared with such radical changes? Although in post-Soviet conditions *blat* ceased being a necessity for everyday life to the same extent as before (foodstuffs, goods and some services do not have to be 'obtained' any more), it is still needed for a better life, a higher standard of living, convenience and comfort. Informal contacts still remain primary where money is not accepted as a mean of exchange – that is, at the upper level where there is much corruption and nepotism, or at the very bottom level, where informal networks are used to tackle scarcity. Also, people routinely use their contacts for their business activities as they used to do for personal consumption, which has in some contexts brought about a rise in scale of *blat* operations:

> In the new distribution system, where land, raw materials and finance can be distributed in the same manner as sausages, cars and apartments, the effect of connections is a hundred times stronger. A friend of mine imported equipment and materials to construct a modern warehouse. If he could manage to locate it next to the market in the centre of the city, he would have enough income not to work for the rest of his life. The problem was to get a land lease. He got it through his friend in the regional administration, whom he worked with before or something. This could not be achieved by means of a bribe, but the acquaintance settled the problem. [19b]

The point about scale of *blat* deals today was raised in another attempt to answer the 'continuity' question:

> The state system is changing, and *blat* like everything else in the social organism adapts to new conditions. There are continuities in

this change. If one looks at the new bureaucracy (in administration and commerce, etc.), they are usually the same people; former party leaders, directors and executives, who have migrated into the new 'elite niches'. One real problem is therefore that *blat* patterns rooted in parasitism towards the state still prevail in contexts which render them maladaptive. It used to be the case that instead of buying something in a shop or going straight to a doctor, a person chose (or was forced to choose) a roundabout way to acquire an object or service by *blat* (for example, circumventing the rationing system). The scale of dealings is different nowadays: in the legislature strings are pulled to enact laws in favour of private interests. The logic of action, however, remains similar: to get away with a bigger piece of the common pie. [27]

The point is that one's slice could not be really big under socialism (because there were limits to the privileges available), while now it can be huge. In fact, new market pressures make some people regretful about the previous scale of privileges:

It was important that children inherited neither the wealth nor the positions of their fathers. If someone was expelled from the party or a state post, one used to lose the privileges attached to it. The lack of property rights motivated and disciplined bureaucrats. There also existed a strong party discipline and morals to appeal to, and it was often the case that nomenclatura people were dedicated workaholics. [14]

We had only a few wealthy people but not many. A Party high-up, he had a nice apartment, perhaps a dacha in the country, it was not usually anything splendid, a slightly larger car, he could shop at the hard-currency shops, and that's about it. It wasn't a lot. But there was stability and no millionaires around. What was also important was that we were not that dependent on money. We had basic certain rights, and they were free. Education, health care all through your life, even if its standard often could do better, the right to housing and employment, to being looked after when you are old [interviewed by Parker 1992]

A theatre ticket today is 25,000 roubles. The theatre is my passion but with salary of 150,000 I can't afford it. My salary is hardly enough for food, and everything else, durables and clothes, has lasted from my pre-1990 life. My status as an academic was higher than average: I had 350 roubles a month in comparison with average 150, plus my connections, plus my mother's help. My son asked me the other day why I didn't use this. I could obtain everything I wanted, but normally did it for my friends. We had other values, you know.

There was a kind of fundamental caring by everybody for everybody, all acquaintances helped each other. [13]

As was acutely observed by one of the respondents:

there is a radical difference between getting an urgent medical service by providing a theatre ticket and getting financial support for one's own business. It is not relevant to speak of both as *blat* (the profit-making is not limited by personal consumption as *blat* was). Techniques are however the same – using friendly contacts, sauna companions, 'constructive' drinking – and acquaintances are often too. In this sense we are not 'new Russians', we are 'old Soviets'. [29a]

I have shown earlier that *blat* subverted the Soviet economic system at the same time as it sustained it. In practice *blat* amplified personal relations (providing the possibility of 'mutual help'), but it also softened the rigid constraints of the command economy and the Soviet political system. It was well adapted to as well as restricted by Soviet morality. In the beginning of the transitional period after 1985 *blat* kept being effective by contributing to the establishment of new forms of cooperation. Now, with the expansion of the market and the concomitant decline of Soviet norms and values *blat* no longer follows customary rules nor corresponds to economic conditions. *Blat* practices stretched beyond their Soviet limits tend to be destructive to the national economy. These patterns which were organically connected to and functional for the Soviet social and political system have been carried over into the post-Soviet era with no control of their negative aspects and no attention to their advantageous sides.

In 1996 *Argumenty i Fakty* published a whole list of 'Forgotten Words' (with '*blat*' as one of them) and the 'Vocabulary of our times' (23–24 and 29 1996: front pages). Figure 6.1 is an extract from both lists with some additions, which represents the radical change in everyday vocabulary, current problems and fundamental shifts which took place in the society (from shortage and queueing to the non-payments of pensions and wages, from Party apparatus to nomenclatura business and private protection firms, etc.). Before I move on to consider in more detail contemporary forms of *blat* and its relevance for understanding current trends in economy and society I shall concentrate on the role *blat* connections have played in economic and social restructuring (rise of business and the privatisation processes in particular) and on the feedback of the reforms for personal networks and networking.

**Figure 6.1** *Soviet and post-Soviet vocabulary*

| Soviet | Post-Soviet |
|---|---|
| Bribe | *Diskaunt* (discount=bribe) |
| *Blatnoi* | *Blatnoi* |
| *Ya ot Matil'dy Leopol'dovny* (I am from Matil'da Leopol'dovna) | *Majorchiki* |
| *Zvonok sverkhu* (a ring from above, from someone important) | *Korporativnost'* (corporatism) |
| | New Russians |
| | *Prikhvatizatsiya* (priva-nicked-zation) |
| *Gde dostal?* (where did you obtain?) | *krutit' den'gi* (to spin money) |
| *Zaiti s chernogo khoda* (approach through the back-door) | *shopnik* (shopper) |
| | *chelnok* ('shattler'-trader) |
| *Vzyat' iz-pod prilavka* (to obtain from under counter) | Street trade and *kiosks* |
| *Barakholka* (bazaar of goods not available in shops) | *Plata za zaschitu* (payment for protection) |
| **Shortage: closed system of distribution and privileges** | |
| Spetsraspredelitel' (closed distribution system) | *Razborka* (unofficial way of solving conflicts, negotiations with the use of violence) |
| *Beryozka* (shops selling imported high quality goods for hard currency) | *Bratva* (criminalised brotherhood, bullyboys) |
| *Kremlevka* (food and meals distribution system in Kreml') | *Krutoi* (cool) |
| | *Mafia* |
| | *Gryaznye den'gi* (dirty (criminalised) money) |
| | *Otmyvat' den'gi* (money laundry) |
| | *Banki s plokhoi istoriei* (banks with a mean history) |
| **Shortage: queueing and rationing** | *Nevyplaty zarplaty* (non-payments of: salary, pensions, accounts, taxes) |
| *Talon* (token for foodstuffs or goods in short supply) | Forced holidays |
| *Stoyat' za defitsitom* (queueing for something in short supply), for example: toilet paper, vodka, soap, meat, washing powder, toothpaste, sugar, bed-linen | Financial piramid |
| | Auction |
| | Market |
| | Sponsor |
| *Bol'she kilo (2 butylok) v odni ruki ne davat'!* (No more than a kilo (2 bottles) in one hand!) | Commerce |
| | Shock therapy |
| Communist and Komsomol bosses | Nomenclatura business |

### The role of *blat* in business and privatisation

Radical changes have occurred in Russia since Gorbachev launched the process of democratisation in 1985. These have disrupted numerous established structures, not only breaking the Party system and reforming the national economy and local administration, but also affecting everyday practices, primary communities and personal networks. The political and economic reforms of the 1990s,[2] the so-called 'shock therapy', which resulted in the de-centralisation of planning, the abolition of price control and the privatisation of state property, have caused even more dramatic social changes. These social changes became crucial for the transformation of *blat* but this was not a one-way influence. Analytically, two phases of mutual influence between *blat* (as a Soviet legacy) and market reforms can be distinguished: in the first phase, *blat* facilitated and contributed to the development of market activities; in the second phase, developed market conditions altered the frameworks in which *blat* was embedded.

The first wave of Russian entrepreneurs, which appeared during 1988–91 when cooperatives and commodity and financial exchanges were first permitted, originated in *blat*: 'many tried their luck but only those who had what was then called *blat* were successful. Unlike the second wave of new Russians, who were formed from the upper echelons of the Soviet bureaucracy or the nomenclatura, the vast capital accrued by *blatniki* was linked neither to production nor property.'[3] *Blat* as a source of new entrepreneurship is twofold: it is a source of the connections which provide access to those state resources drawn upon by private business; and it also supplies practical skills in keeping personal contacts, fixing things and knowing ways of settling problems.

Interview data collected in 1991–2,[4] shows that personal contacts played a crucial role in the development of small enterprises. As the

---

[2] Skidelsky (1995:191) describes shock therapy as a three-part cure. First, prices are liberated, the exchange rate is lowered and the economy is opened for competition. Second, credits and subsidies to loss-making industries are cancelled. This immediately cuts back the rate of growth of the money supply, reduces the budget deficit and allows the imposition of fresh taxes based on money transactions. Third, the main source of the excessive money supply growth – the bloated public sector – is shut down or sold off for whatever price it will fetch.

[3] E. Pestrushina, 'Russian's Young Wolves Grow Hungry for Power', *Guardian*, 5 July 1995: 14. Pestrushina writes for *Kuranty* and the *Moscow News*.

[4] The texts of forty interviews were kindly provided by Nonna Barkhatova. The sample in the research covered small enterprises (cooperatives) of different profiles, including services, production of items for everyday consumption, educational and organisational services, all in Novosibirsk.

launching of private businesses had not been attempted before, advice and help – for example, in presenting registration documents – was essential. Most 'pioneers' of Russian business acknowledged that their registration documents were prepared by friends or contacts. Even when a paid service for drawing up documents became available, informal channels were reported to be an essential factor in starting a business. The advice or information obtained through friends and acquaintances was the advice and information considered reliable. Business was bound to depend on informal contacts, for 'the contract system was not yet developed. There were no efficient mechanisms for managing conflict situations or inflicting sanctions on unreliable partners'. Therefore, the informal contacts and relations of trust formed within *blat* networks were the only guarantee one could rely on.

The aspect emphasised by all businessmen was the possibility of overcoming financial difficulties through personal contacts. The range of difficulties which personal contacts could help with was enormous: for instance, the arranging of privileged conditions for loans, the postponing of payments, the freedom to withdraw private money from banks and, perhaps most important, the jumping of queues and the speeding up of bank operations. Only those who could rely on the support of their contacts in banks, in state organisations or in local administration could run their business efficiently. Renting premises was a problem for all firms except firms of the 'sons' which were located within their fathers' state organisations or research institutes. Access to all kind of resources – and, particularly, information – was limited unless proper contacts were available. Respondents stressed especially that essential goods and services for business activities (e.g. tax information) had to be obtained through personal channels. The selection of partners, bankers and guarantors was normally determined by the recommendations and advice of acquaintances. In the post-launch phases of a business, connections in local administration, the militia, customs and transport became vital.

*Blat* was an important source of launch capital, although this is not easy to substantiate. It is a commonplace in accounting for the emergence of the market economy in the ex-Soviet Union to refer to either 'unrighteous' money (illegal capital accumulated in the Soviet period and subsequently injected into the economy through money laundering) or 'unrighteous' power (access to privatisation of state resources by the so-called nomenclatura businesses) (*Kommersant*, 27, 1993). Respondents in business, however, gave some evidence for the role of *blat* in this respect. The co-owner of a trading firm in Siberia concluded:

> To a great extent, the success of launching the business was predetermined by the inheritance one received from the Soviet past. Connections are perhaps the least of this inheritance in comparison to money or power, but very important. Those who entered business in the late 1980s – say, the graduates of the economic faculty of the university – were all clever, all of approximately the same competence. But one can see now that only those who had support (connections or relatives) had a real chance to rise solidly. Most business was supported by or based on what was called 'speculation'. Its success was very much predetermined by whether one had access to cash in necessary amounts and at necessary moments. These problems could be solved only through parents, relatives or, a bit later, through contacts in banks. VIPs' children did not mix with ordinary students before but in business, with their connections, they set a real distance. The most successful of us, now a millionaire, simply started in more favourable conditions: a bit earlier than others, in the period of the 'computer boom' in Russia, and he had a relative in Kazakhstan, a director of the state enterprise, from whom he borrowed money. As he had an opportunity to invest more, his profits were incomparably larger than ours. [19b]

An expert from the regional administration remarked that:

> In the transitional period (1991–2) it was possible to make money by *blat*: there were both places where people could buy goods at the state price, and places where the latter could be resold at the market price. I knew someone, connected with the military, who made his capital buying sugar at 0.8 rouble per kg at the military warehouse and retailing it for 1,500 roubles per kg. [25]

*Blat* was indispensable to the businessmen of the 'first wave', but was particularly conspicuous in the cases of businessmen called '*mazhorchiki*'. They became famous for their meteoric careers and their *blat* implied the protection of their families rather than their own connections.[5]

The role of connections in business of the second wave, formed by the representatives of the upper echelons of the Soviet bureaucracy or the

---

[5] G. York, in 'From Marx to Mammon' (*The Globe and Mail*, Moscow Bureau, 27 May 27 1995) describes the story of Stas Namin which is in many ways the story of Russia's New Rich, the emerging class of high-living bankers and entrepreneurs that dominates Moscow's boomtown economy. Namin is just one example of metamorphosis from Communist protégé into flamboyant Russian millionaire. Many were powerful Communist insiders who profited from the Soviet era.

nomenclatura, was profound. New levels of manipulation of the system, as well as the involvement of the nomenclatura, however, compel us to think in terms of corruption rather than *blat*:

> The 'old guard', the nomenclatura – directors of the enterprises and of regional, city, local administration – kept their power and positions in the post-Soviet period. This power and position is now used for private deals. The nomenclatura used to be well connected and they still are. They know each other and always in touch. Younger businessmen often have to find their own way while the 'old guard' decides things collectively. They are well informed and know the conditions of the market. It is no wonder that many firms established by the nomenclatura are flourishing. It is not a secret that some banks and large businesses were founded by the 'old guard'. They put 'their contacts' (*svoikh lyudei*) on the boards of directors and provided starting capital, information and connections. An individual businessman running a firm has to make a fuss to obtain information, whereas nomenclatura-run businesses are supplied with access to regional economic statistics, data on demand and supply and information on foreign investment projects, not to mention moral and material support. This is not to be called *blat*, but mechanisms are similar, just at a different, more organised level. [27]

The dissolution of the Communist party and attempts to reduce the influence of the former nomenclatura do not mean that such a strong and well connected apparatus has disappeared. A former deputy of a regional party committee argued that the former nomenclatura is objectively more capable of handling management problems and that their personal qualities, their experience and their connections are needed in post-Soviet conditions:

> It is fair that they found jobs in line with their ability: the mayor is a former party leader and local administration is formed by those who have experience in management. I am an expert on the previous system, as I worked at the state enterprise, in Komsomol, in the Party and in the Soviets at their local, city and regional levels. I know every step of the nomenclatura career. I know how decisions were made, how directives were sent down and how the tasks were fulfilled. As I understand now – the core element of it all was a system of selection of personnel. You may call this 'connections' and you may say that the system worked because of informal contacts. Yes, these were important, say, 50 per cent important, but there was also responsibility and practical skills. These are still required. Thus, instead of the Higher Party School which has been abolished, we have the Siberian Cadres Centre. They do the same thing under a new name: they train cadres for municipal services and for management. [34]

Before *perestroika* the party apparatus was professionally engaged in regulating and sorting out the problems of the command economy. To maintain informal contacts, smoothing the rigid constraints of the system was part of their function. With such experience these people, particularly the Komsomol elite (sometimes called the 'young businessmen's club'), are objectively more adapted to and active in today's situation. Their starting conditions were immeasurably better than others:

> Ex-party leaders and former Komsomol activists are comfortable in their places in the new system. Positions are not bad, big bosses have moved to governing bodies, to bank consultancies, and to the organisation of large-scale corporations. Former state foreign trade associations, through which all export–import contracts were enacted, such as the *Soyuzraznoexport*, *Mashimport*, were converted into joint-stock companies, headed by their former chairmen. They function now as private enterprises with the support of all their former connections. [22]

Problems arise, however, when state property becomes involved with private business activities, and *blat* methods acquired in the Soviet system are transferred into the market economy. In order to get finance in the socialist system one had to arrange 'through Party connections' that one's initiative would be included in the party decree or programme which was relevant and financially supported: 'For example, the tourist centre "Sibiryak" was included in the Decree of the Central Party Committee "On the Development of Oil and Gas Area", even though Novosibirsk, where it is located, is far away from these areas. The criteria for distribution now are different. The nomenclatura started trading their favours: they either want real money in return for favourable decisions or they launch their own businesses.' [6] An example of the latter was reported by *Izvestiya* (25, 1992):

> The decision to register of the firm 'Nord', which was organised by nine state organisations of St Petersburg, was signed by the first deputy of the chairman of the Executive Committee of the City. The governing body of this firm was headed by the same person, who afterwards also provided the starting capital: two buildings in the very centre of the city, on the Nevsky prospect, and two more in a nice location near the park. In fact, these buildings were given to the firm: the seven-floor building was estimated at 174,000 roubles, at a time when the auction price of a single flat was above a million roubles.

That was the present the first deputy made from the state department of which he was in charge to the firm he was heading. Interestingly, these houses did not even belong to the Executive Committee, but to the City Soviet, so usual is it to dispose of others' property. The main activity of the firm, designed to develop foreign tourism, contained even more violations and after two years was closed down by the Office of the State Prosecutor. But most of the VIPs involved evaded prosecution and, as the reporter concludes: '"Nord" will reappear under another name.'

The mixing of *blat* practices with the new opportunities provided by the market economy resulted in even more dubious activities, particularly to do with privatisation. After a new chairman was appointed to the Committee for the management of City Property in St Petersburg in 1991, he sacked 80 per cent of the employees; nevertheless there have been five prosecutions of employees in this Committee and the Property Fund in the two years since that time. These included the deputy director of the Property Fund. Investigation prior to his arrest in 1993 revealed a shortfall of 130 million roubles in vouchers and counterfeit privatisation cheques, understatement of the value of property by 16 billion roubles, and understatement of the amount received from purchasers by 7.8 billion roubles. In addition the intimidation of bidders at auctions was rife. As the reporter for *Izvestiya* commented: 'our public auctions long ago turned into stage plays with roles assigned in advance. The directors are criminal "authorities" and corrupt bureaucrats.'[6] According to information from law enforcement agencies, 'as much as 70 per cent of the real estate put up for sale at auctions winds up in the hands of individuals who are agreed upon beforehand. Before a public auction begins, the information is conveyed to everyone that an "authority" is interested in this piece of property, and that if anyone takes the risk of competing for it, he shouldn't complain later that he wasn't warned' (*CDSP*, vol. XLV (51) 1993: 15).

Many such cases are reported in the mass media all over Russia, where enterprises, land and buildings are privatised in the interests of 'people of the circle' (*svoikh lyudei*): 'The Tyumen oil and gas resources are being privatised. A former deputy gas industry minister Rem Vyakhirev is now chairman of a privatised Russian gas monopoly Gazprom, conservatively estimated to be worth 170 billion pounds.'[7]

---

[6] The Current Digest of the Post-Soviet Press, 1993: 14, 45, 51, quoted from R. Mellor, 'Authority in a Contemporary Russian City – St Petersburg', unpublished article.

[7] J. Meek, 'Moscow Gold', *Guardian* 20 September 1995: 12.

Someone called Vasily Timofeev bought 210 million 'Gazprom' shares, for which he had somehow made available 2 billion 100 million roubles. 51 per cent of shares of the gigantic enterprise "Uralmash" has been bought by one person.[8] On a smaller scale, those who were in charge of state property and had appropriate skills and connections managed to turn the privatisation campaign to their advantage whereas others given a share (*voucher*) sold it cheap or lost it in new financial structures (investment funds, commercial banks, etc.). It also happened that a worker was given a share but either not given the right to sell it under the threat of dismissal or pushed to sell it by share-hunters.[9]

A notorious contribution to these processes is provided by organised crime. To a large degree shareholders are defenceless in the face of organised racketeering. Their vulnerability allows criminal business to get hold of shares of many privatised enterprises, the 'gangster holding company's share', so to speak. These criminal businesses are by no means the kind of property owners who intend to boost production. Their objective is to buy cheap and sell for many times what they paid. For this reason, one of the gangs intended to acquire controlling blocks of shares in 53 major enterprises undergoing privatisation in St Petersburg and Murmansk in 1993). 'The "expropriation" of controlling blocks was planned and carried out like a combat operation . . . A genuine intelligence network (including bought-off bureaucrats and bankers) was set up, and it reported to "headquarter". Then Khomschuk's gang "bullyboys" would show up at a plant: "We are distributing humanitarian aid. Give us the addresses of your retired workers!" After that, a call would be paid to every retiree, and, for a symbolic sum of money or after a brief intimidation session, the shares to which he was entitled would migrate into Khomchuk's coffers' (*CDSP*, vol. XV (51) 1993: 15).

Organised crime and the so-called 'Russian Mafia' have received a lot of attention in the literature,[10] but one aspect seems to have been underestimated. Organised crime in the 1990s should be viewed as an expanding network of recruits who did not receive any legacy from the Soviet past: no money, no power, no connections, and were forced to use violence to make money:

---

[8] 'The Goals of Privatization', 'RT'–2, 24 January 1995.
[9] Enterprise management is often involved in the purchase of shares through a third party.
[10] See, for example, Chalidze (1977); Zemtsov (1976); Vaksberg (1991); Hendelman (1994); Kampfner (1994); Follain (1995); and J. Lloyd, 'The Russians are coming', *London Review of Books*, 11 May 1995.

The economic and social situation pushed many towards a criminal path. Bandits are just one of the traumatic consequences of the reforms. Just think of those who did not study thinking it was pointless when easy money could be made; who did not have wealthy or influential parents able to back them up in the harsh post-Soviet reality; who did not acquire any profession, and who valued nothing but money. They wanted money at any price, and having no connections for a decent business turned bandits. [13]

We'll have to deal with this for a long time. Half of the school graduates, for whom opportunities are closed, go to . . . a hairdressers shop. They cut their hair 'crew-cut' style, buy 'Adidas' sportswear, a leather jacket, and later, if everything goes 'well', cashmere coats (in colours of claret or emerald) and a BMW. [8]

Bandits created their own solidarity, a net of connections they call *'bratva'* (brotherhood). They comply with their own, *blatnoi*, code. Their code is, however, not the same as a criminal *blatnoi* code: 'It is penetrated by the "economisation" of relationships, they do "business". They have new ideals, they value wealth and comfort. In criminal circles money was always important, but these "new bandits" are different. They demonstrate their coolness (*krutost'*) publicly. Their type of car (and their weapon) are normally reliable indicators of their status. They know who is cool, and treat each other accordingly,[11] says the head of the information office at the Department of Struggle with Organised Crime in Novosibirsk. [35]

Acquaintances and connections with bandits are necessary for many businessmen. For example, all those who run *kiosks* have to face the demand of payment 'for protection' (*za zashchitu*), to ensure that their kiosks are not attacked or burnt overnight. Again, a person has to pay or to have proper contacts among bandits able to release him from payment or cut down the sum. Other problems may also be solved by appeal to a criminal acquaintance. Bandits can be very useful in influencing official decisions by local authorities, for they establish their own contacts in the state structures: 'To receive the support of an influential bandit is, however, no easier than in any other place. It is all a matter of connections and recommendations again.' [8] The most recent data (autumn 1996) indicate that the state

---

[11] The failure to distinguish who is who regularly results in traffic accidents, for the actual traffic rules are enmeshed with indigenous knowledge and understanding as to whom one must let go first. A simplified version of the order of things is expressed in the following joke. A passenger asks a driver: 'Why did you pass the traffic lights on red?' 'Because I am cool,' says the driver. Then he stops at the crossing on the green. 'It's green now, why did you stop?' asks the passenger. 'Look, a cooler one is crossing.'

police has become more and more able to re-establish the monopoly of legitimate violence. This is definitely happening in Moscow and is developing in other places. The growth of efficiency of the tax police has also contributed towards strengthening the state. These tendencies do not necessarily mean that a strong police or tax police are completely free from the legacy of *blat*. According to respondents, however, it is much better to pay the police than bandits. *Blat* has hence been substituted for by new 'business ethics', by the criminal codes of 'bandits' and a more straightforward corruption of the state apparatus.

## The social consequences of the post-Soviet reforms

### Confidence in the future

The economic forms of the Soviet period, such as a stable monetary system, the state system of distribution and price control and the system of division of labour guaranteed a stable, even if limited, level of consumption and state provision of goods and services. Post-Soviet economic and political reforms brought into being new realities not experienced before, i.e. problems in labour markets, 'free' prices and inflation. The most radical change, recognised both in the press and in social research, is a feeling of instability and unpredictability in the social environment. People are forced to face a reality, the complexity of which is difficult to handle. Things routinely taken for granted (for example, stable currency and prices, which meant that the lending and return of a borrowed sum were non-problematic), became matters for everyday monitoring and special attention; situations of risk penetrated everyday life.

Massive signs of distrust of the Soviet state appeared after the campaign of *glasnost'* which revealed the 'dark spots' of the past and such distrust was strengthened by eventual disbelief in Gorbachev's promises (*govoril'nya*). 'Tired' from the political and informational booms of the late 1980s people lost their concern with public matters and turned to their private everyday problems. At this point, particularly in 1991–2, the economic crisis undermined their last illusions. The lack of a change for the better resulted in the utter loss of trust in the state. According to a sociological survey by the Centre of Public Opinion conducted in May 1993, trust in social institutions in Russia is well below that of established democratic societies. The most trusted institutions are the church and army, but even these are trusted by less than 40 per cent of Russians [Salmin *et al.* 1994: 23). The percentage of those who fully trust in state institutions fluctuate from 5 to 15 per cent, depending on the institution. Another survey by the Centre of Public Opinion, conducted in Moscow, showed the following distribution of answers to the question: 'For the sake of whom and in the interest of which social groups do the authorities in Russia act?' Only 9 per cent of Muscovites selected the prompt 'for the sake of all people'. 34 per cent responded 'for the sake of themselves, power holders', 6 per cent 'for the sake of the rich and entrepreneurs', 5 per cent 'for the sake of the mafia', 5 per cent 'for nobody' and 38 per cent had difficulty in answering this question (*Izvestiya*, 3 February 1993).

The problems of the new economic sector has altered the everyday life of the ordinary population. The lack of adequate economic laws, the insufficiencies of contract law and tax policy caused the emergence of a ramified network of informal control and forced sanctions (gangs, bandits, safeguards and protection teams), based on the principle 'fear is the best insurance' (*strakh – luchshee strakhovanie*). The criminalisation of the social environment was expressed by the phrase 'we run a risk simply by living in this country'.

The Chubais campaign of privatisation,[12] called 'a deception of the

---

[12] There were three programmes or schemes of privatisation, differing in speed and sequence of measures. The first scheme by Chernomyrdin, the Prime Minister, representative of large-scale industrial interests (defence, heavy engineering industry) was most conservative, suggesting a slow privatisation of large-scale enterprises. It implied rather formal privatisation, where 51 per cent of shares belonged to the Ministry, 30 per cent to the management of enterprises, and less than 20 per cent to employees, who in practice were not allowed to sell their shares under the threat of dismissal. This maintained an existent vertical scheme of interaction 'Ministry – Director – Collective' and corresponding distribution of power. Corporate responsibility was based on the distribution of state income (every director was appointed by a Minister whom he obeyed thus gaining more resources, fewer plan tasks, etc.), now it is based on shared property (51 per cent is still owned by the state, but 30 per cent already belongs to the directors), but the scheme of dependence is the same. This scheme was aimed at maintaining state control and gradual privatisation in the long run.

The second variant of privatisation was suggested by Gaidar, Minister of Economics for a short time before the beginning of 1994. It was an intermediary scheme, implying privatisation of most enterprises, except a group of strategic enterprises subject to the same type of privatisation as proposed in the first scheme.

The third scheme of privatisation by Chubais, the youngest and most radical vice-premier, Chairman of the Federal Commission of Securities and former Chairman of the Government Committee on Privatisation, included two campaigns: (1) Enterprises were ordered to privatise (through 'voucher' auctions until the end of 1994, and through 'money' auctions after 1994). (2) There was formed a group of strategic enterprises 'privatised' but with 51 per cent of shares belonging to the state, while the others were ordered to further privatise through 'money' auctions. The second stage whole nation' by Gorbachev,[13] failure to guarantee the indexation of people's savings, the bankruptcy of commercial banks and share-holding companies (i.e. MMM), and other dramatic changes of recent years have changed the social atmosphere completely. People have been forced to change their habits and attitudes, lifestyles and careers, plans and orientations.

Confidence in the future was a valued aspect of socialism. For most of the population it has gone together with socialism, followed by the *orientation towards the future* (see p.164), which was one of the assumptions of *blat*. Nobody is protected from inflation, revaluation of money or exchange rate fluctuations. The scale of non-payments of pensions, wages and salaries continuously reported to be the indicators of the financial misuse and corruption in banking has been overwhelming throughout the 1990s. The new realities demanded new skills and efforts which have gradually taken the place of bygone skills and knowledge, such as how to obtain things by *blat*.

### Mutual help

According to a study of Russian directors' 'business ethics' (Kharkhordin and Gerber, 1994):

> the shock therapy conditions of 1992 – which put the phenomenon of the directors' ethics into the foreground – have already passed. 1993 witnessed two primary and related developments which affected industrialists' ethics – a decline in the rhetoric of 'mutual help' (if not a decline in the extent of activities comprised by this concept) and an increase in the number of enterprises breaking away from the *krug*[14] (circle). Many directors cited strong financial pressures as the main reason for the decrease in what they perceived as 'mutual help':
>
> In 1992 we all found ourselves in the same situation – like horses driven into the same corral – and we had to unite to save ourselves.

means that a real privatisation of property will be brought about. See also A. Chubais and M. Vishnevskaya, 'Privatization in Russia: An Overview', in Åslund (1994: 94–100).

[13] Meeting with students of the Novosibirsk University, March 1995.

[14] Relations with other directors were extremely important in 1992 because, as a rule, directors tended to maintain old ties with major partners from the days of centralised planning These personal ties now seem to have become pervaded by a sense of loyalty, mutual help and joint responsibility. In the extreme, the rhetoric of mutual help demanded a continuation of deliveries to a partner even when that partner did not have any funds to pay for the supplies . . . The terms from the vocabulary of the Russian peasant commune, *krug* and *mir*, were used to account for the ethic . . . predicated on familiar features of communal life, i.e. on the mutual control of those who deviated from the established code of behaviour and on joint help for failing members of the commune (Kharkhordin and Gerber 1994: 1076).

Now the rouble has started to function again and we just cannot help everybody [said a director of the heavy industry plant]. We are still friends with our colleagues, but when it comes to dividing money, our ways part.

The study, conducted in 1993, indicated that 'mutual help' did not disappear altogether, but that each enterprise chose 'the essential few' with whom it would sustain these demanding relationships. [p.1077]

The same tendencies were identified in my research. Not only the nomenclatura, but also businessmen, academics and people of various occupations emphasised the decrease in 'mutual help' and the 'narrowing of the circle': 'If in 1991–2 business could be based on relations of friendship, 1993 has ranked everything and stratified us severely. Many people who tried business, have dropped it. Many of those fared badly. Those who stayed afloat became tough,' remarked a businessman. [19b] According to an expert of the Analytical Centre of the Siberian Stock Exchange, in the crisis of August 1995: 'banks were ranked in the same way, it became known who was and who was not reliable, and those who stayed afloat became much more cautious and harsh.' [50] 'Both in banking and in business, the approach is ruthless, especially in bargains and partnerships, not just overnight loans.' [19b] The motto of prison camps 'don't trust, don't fear, don't ask' has become a motto of business.[15]

Many people reduced their business contacts to family connections, especially in small cities. Even though relatives supported each other, this does not mean that they did so with no eye to profit: 'I work with five superstores headed by my mother, her sisters and other relatives. They take nothing on which they cannot turn a profit, just what can be retailed with a gain. However, I have the privilege of immediate payment so that my money is not stuck in circulation.' [3] As a rule, the relations of mutual help tended to cover a more and more restricted circle of people. This meant, above all, that people started identifying themselves with the interests of their business rather than anything else.

The dynamics of friendship, reported by many respondents, suggest a tendency towards the breaking of social ties. In 1991–2 friends were considered the most reliable business partners, by 1994 the rhetoric of friendship stood on its head – 'friends must be excluded from business, otherwise friendship is lost':

[15] Artem Tarasov, in an interview on Russian TV, autumn 1994.

> It is part of my strategy – not to do business with my friends. Business activities, connected with income, profit, shared responsibility, etc. should not be enmeshed with personal emotions of friendship. I still value my intimate relations with friends, we get together, drink, go to the sauna, we talk and support each other morally. But it has been so often the case that two friends running a business have turned into enemies and suspected each other of fraud. One really has to separate business from personal sympathy today. Everyday tensions – sharing a company car, incomes, whatever – may destroy friendship. Envy, hatred are very widespread emotions at the moment. [3, 6, 10]

The resentment about success deeply shook up old patterns of loyalty. One of the most successful businessmen remarked that when his old colleagues ask him how he did it, he can read between the lines that they think he is stealing something. There is some truth in this.[16] Later in the interview he said:

> One has to hide one's money from the state and from racketeers. Everything needs a bribe – getting licences, reducing taxes or custom duties. Our taxes, theoretically, are up to 80 per cent. It would be impossible to operate a business with that. This country is not ready for civilised business. There are no laws, no principles, no traditions.[17]

In such conditions one should not be surprised by the ruthlessness and crudeness of the class of businessmen: 'Now I understand,' continues this 28-year-old banker, 'that Russia is becoming a different country, the mentality of the people is different. Business here is very cynical. It's not quite the jungle, but it's close to it. How do you make money in this country? You kill somebody, you steal, you bribe.'[18] Even if this is too much of a generalisation, it has its implications for the character of relations between businessmen and its dynamics:

> It is most dangerous to have business contacts with friends. The objective difficulties are such that there is always a risk of letting the friend down. Generally, if business is run by friendship, it is not a business. It is abnormal and it is coming to an end. Business is business, and formalities must be fulfilled. The contracts must be signed even with friends, which is difficult: 'don't we trust each other?' [11a]

[16] There is a notion of the 'first million', the origins of which are never questioned. It is the use of it that becomes definitive of business.
[17] York, 'From Marx to Mammon'.      [18] *Ibid.*

Help provided for the sake of friendship in conditions of state property becomes problematic where a market economy and private property come into play. Moreover, the character of friendship itself changes:

> The former understanding that one has to sacrifice one's own interest for the sake of friendship has not gone completely, but will disappear in the next few years for sure. One could 'give one's last shirt' to a friend, now one won't even give one's next to last shirt. The reasons for this are clear. Money was not valued so much (prices were fixed, friends had approximately the same income), rather friends and connections were important. Not only for emotional reasons. Through friends one could have the access and opportunities indispensable for survival in a system in which most matters were solved by mutual help or barter. The proverb 'Do not have 100 roubles, have 100 friends' was an apt one. Social contacts could provide much more than money in the socialist system. Everyone had, roughly speaking, 120 roubles, differentiation resulted from privileges and opportunities provided by social status. To be able to buy cheaper, without queueing and from a wider range were real criteria of differentiation. Now money has come to differentiate opportunities. If there is money, one does not need contacts that much. In a practical sense friends have ceased to be so important. There is no need for *blatmeisters* any more. [11a]

> There are more possibilities not to be obliged to anybody. As long as there is money, of course. There are many firms providing reliable and paid services, almost anything. Therefore, when people appeal to me, it means they just don't want to pay, which is stingy. [19b]

> People used to help each other easily. Asking a neighbour to look after a child, a stranger to carry something, friends to help moving houses was a common thing. Now it is much more difficult: people calculate more and are not always willing to be obliged. [30]

> When there was no equivalent, everything was settled by barter, by 'mutual help'. Now there is an equivalent, the US dollar. People do help each other, but not as before. I won't claim help myself, because it costs money. It used to be easy to ask and to expect money for help was ridiculous. If I received a favour, next time I would do a favour. If my favour was not enough, I would do another. While now, I pay and there is no headache. Today is more like: 'Don't have 100 friends, have 100 roubles.' Or 100 dollars, to be precise. [43]

> Everything is simpler in a way: like the stage when money took the place of barter. This caused other problems though. It is impossible to borrow money from friends now, which used to be the most

common helping out.[19] On the one hand, who else can I borrow from? On the other, inflation makes the return inadequate, while it is awkward to offer interest. There is, of course, the possibility of borrowing dollars, but this introduces a new element into relationships. [22]

The general trend is clear: from a situation in which *blat* was an enforced practice, a crucial and often the only feasible way of getting things done, to a situation with more than one option. Even relationships between parents and children are undergoing big changes now. Post-Soviet children are brought up differently. From five, children are aware of prices and prestige, have their pocket money; from eight some of them earn money by selling newspapers, chewing gum, etc. Teenagers came to understand that they could not depend for money only on their parents. This is the reality which Soviet children did not know. They were very much 'parasites' (*izhdiventsi*) around the necks of their parents and the state. Post-Soviet conditions brought into being the rationalisation of relationships even with the very closest.

A tourist firm boss complained that acquaintances, whom he did not regard his friends, came to his office seeking discounts, or free service, for favours. 'Friends would not allow themselves such requests,' he says, 'while these people, particularly women whom I knew long ago, come shamelessly pretending to be my friends. Those I have to turn down.' [6] *Amikoshonstvo*, a familiarity established in a rather one-way manner, is often remarked on by those who have achieved some success. It remains to be seen whether such complaints are aimed at protecting their business, their 'circle', from impoverished customers, or whether they are indicators of a cutting-off of former friendships. In any event the complaints seem indicative of a process of polarisation and deepening stratification of society. The breakdown of social ties, reported by businessmen, was also emphasised by academics:

> Market conditions broke academic collectives and schools into small temporary teams formed around those able to obtain finance. Instead of the atmosphere of cooperation and open exchange of ideas we experience an atmosphere of secrecy. People conceal information

---

[19] The mutual financial support between friends, colleagues and neighbours was one of the most significant aspects of Soviet private life. According to some data, up to three-quarters of Soviet people regularly borrowed money from each other. See V. Pavlov, 'Razvitie kollektivizma v bytu rabochei molodezhi', in L. Kogan and A. Sharova (eds.), *Issledovanie i Planirovanie Dukhovnoi Kul'tury Trudyashchikhsya Urala*, Sverdlovsk, 1975: 115.

about grants, sources of financing and the ways of obtaining these
and keep in secret their foreign contacts and partners. [49]

All personal networks in which mutual help was rendered underwent such processes of stratification:

> People separate when there is a material barrier. All my friends are
> now businessmen, and they turned their backs on me. Not at once,
> they gradually distanced themselves. They are always busy, and we
> do not see each other often. This is understandable. But somehow
> they imply that they are the elite, whereas I am plebeian. [28]

> Companies of old friends break up. Our company of 30 people or so
> used to celebrate everything collectively. Now these feasts collapsed.
> Strangely, I have much more money now, and drinks and foodstuffs
> are available at any time, but those good days have gone. [38]

As was bitterly summarised by one respondent: 'there are jobs
where people earn 15million roubles a month and others where they
earn 100,000 roubles a month. As this has happened, one should not
be surprised at the rest.' [31] It is worth mentioning that in the
beginning of 1994, 19 million people (13 per cent of the population)
lived at a level of minimum subsistence, 40 million (27 per cent) below
minimum subsistence, 8 million (5 per cent) below the level of
survival. The concentration of incomes is self-explanatory: in March
1994 the richest 10 per cent of Russians appropriated 30 per cent of the
gross money income, the poorest 10 per cent only 2 per cent of the
gross money income.[20] By some estimates, there are 300,000 or more
of the New Rich, living a lifestyle of almost surreal wealth. The gap
between the rich and poor has become increasingly wide. In 1995, the
income of Russia's wealthiest 10 per cent is about 14 times greater
than the income of the poorest 10 per cent. In Moscow, the most
affluent group is 60 times richer than the poorest.[21] Apart from
general polarisation, all social strata are now becoming clear-cut.
Everyone is strongly attracted to their own strata: 'people socialise
within their own strata and find it embarrassing to see those of much
higher or much lower status.' [19b]

Tendencies towards a decrease in mutual help, the narrowing of
circles and the break-up of personal networks, as outlined above,
should not be understood to imply that connections no longer

---

[20] The dynamics of the polarisation of wealth is normally measured by Gini coefficient.
The speed of this process in Russia is unprecedented: from 0.256 in 1991 to 0.333 in
1994 (index for Great Britain is 0.333, the USA 0.490). See A. Livshitz, *Ekonomicheskaya
Reforma v Rossii i ee Tsena*, Moscow, 1994: 101.
[21] York, 'From Marx to Mammon'.

function. They are necessary and maintained, but their 'social' charge (implied by *blat*) seems to have been overtaken by their 'functional' (calculated) one. In other words, connections in the socialist economy were predominantly 'value-oriented' (rhetoric of friendship, requests for others), while now they are driven by considerations of self-interest and mutual profit. In this context the changes in the 'institution of acquaintance' are indicative.

### The transformation of the role of acquaintance

It has already been mentioned that the mere fact of acquaintance has lost its significance in comparison to the Soviet period when the phrase 'by acquaintance' was identical in meaning to *blat*: 'As a matter of fact, people act more rationally now. Even acquaintances do not help any more. They tend to react more formally these days.' [28] The decline of the role of acquaintance is an indicator of the decline of *blat*. Nowadays personal contact is still a necessary but no longer also a sufficient condition for getting things done. Let us illustrate the direction of changes in the role of acquaintance by looking at the business sector, which is perhaps most susceptible to social change:

(1) Acquaintance still facilitates the solution of problems through information. For example:

> if one goes through cargo custom control procedures for the first time, one will have troubles until one grasps the optimal way of passing through the eight customs departments. If one has a classmate working there, he won't help directly but he will give tips about the correct order in which to pass through the departments, the times when processing will not be jammed, the most benevolent clerk, and he will give clues about what makes a custom declaration acceptable at once. [19b]

The transfer of inside information was widespread before, acquaintances exchanged information on what, when and where goods will be on sale, or whom one could ask about a favour. It was not, however, a favour to pay for while now information has a real value and has become an object of business exchange to be entered into the account:

> Between us businessmen I often provided information to acquaintances, saving their time and trouble. A wide range of questions about travel passports, visas, firm registration, tax evasion and the

contract system are in my sphere of competence. I know how to solve problems and always share my knowledge with friends. I can introduce to some useful people. But there is a change. Times go mad now. One and a half years ago I could appeal to my acquaintance in the bank for a loan, now I feel awkward asking my best friend for business information. [19b]

(2)   Acquaintance as intermediary, introducing one to useful people remains very important. Such a service is not necessarily included in contracts, but it tends to be paid for in one way or another. The latter is particularly true where giving or taking a bribe is involved:

> In critical cases, one has to find an intermediary, whose guarantee will be relevant in this case. This is a complicated matter. It does not mean looking for a good acquaintance or drinking partner or friend of the person to bribe. An intermediary must be willing to guarantee the reliability of the giver, on the one hand, and has to be tied by mutual obligations and dependence with the taker. [19b]

The search for an intermediary of this kind is extremely difficult. As a rule, it occurs not among those in higher positions (asked for from above, one would feel reluctant to accede, for fear of acquiring no subsequent promotion) but rather among those in parallel (often criminal) social structures.

(3)   Another role played by acquaintance is that of providing informal recommendation. Recommendations have notably changed their character in post-Soviet conditions. The responsibility for issuing a recommendation has increased. First, due to the need to account for favours received. Second, because people have started identifying their interests with the interest of their business, the philosophy of their banks or the strategy of their institution: 'To let my bank down is to let down myself. I can't give any fake bank acceptances.' [11a] Nothing can be done for an acquaintance at the expense of the business. Even if not at the expense of a business, an acquaintance is not necessarily the first choice for dealing with because bargains with formal partners can be stipulated more firmly, sanctions can be more severe, etc.

(4)   The tendency of relationships with acquaintances in power structures can be described as a move from patronage towards corruption. What could be done in the Soviet system simply from loyalty or sympathy is now calculated in terms of short-run costs and benefits:

> When I decided to run a *kiosk*, I was able to simply because I had an acquaintance who wanted his son to work in it. He had an acquaintance in the trade department of the local executive committee, who supported me in getting a permission. Others had to wait in the queue which did not move until they realised they had to pay. [8]

Commissions, percentages, securities and shares in businesses are now common forms of favour repayment. The income of people in the bureaucracy in the Soviet period was not really high, but it was compensated for by the state system of privileges. Today privileges are nothing in comparison with what one can get for money. Money has become the most urgent need for everybody. Bureaucrats extort (*vykolachivat'*) money by conjuring up obstacles (see cartoon 13):

> To give a bribe to a businessman today is like buying cigarettes. It has simply become a norm. Nothing happens for free. It's understandable: if state officials helped every entrepreneur, the latter would benefit from it while the decision-making people would stay where they are, with no cars, flats or incomes. [8]

These mechanisms spread over the new economic sector as well: 'In the Central bank, to get a licence for banking one has to pay "on the left" (*levye den'gi*). One has to have a good contact to be able to get it without charge or cheaper, or at least some contact to prompt why the decision is suspended and to inform whom, how and how much has to be offered.' [50] A recent shift in the vocabulary is telling: alongside many foreign words adopted to describe market activities, the word 'discount' was coined without translation (*diskaunt*) to refer to the 'bribe':

> Nobody asks for bribes, but rather ask for and propose discounts. The term is foreign enough to be intelligible only to the 'initiated' and to euphemise the essence of the deal. 'To offer a discount' sounds western, extremely up-to-date, but an its post-Soviet sense it is nothing but an all-too-familiar bribe.' [48]

### The new Russian hero

'New Russians are pragmatic. They value success, individualism, efficiency. They are professional, decisive, business-like,

**Cartoon 13**
50% – racket, 50% – bribe for fabric, bribe for building, bribe to fireman, bribe for equipment, bribe to sanitary inspection, cost price, other bribes . . .                              (*Krokodil* 1990, 4: 5)

practical, persistent, even aggressive, and able to handle difficulties.'[22] This stereotype is particularly associated with 'the third wave
entrepreneurs', 'the children of the wild market' or 'the young
wolves':

> They are all over Russia. Aged between 25 and 40, they started from
> scratch in conditions of a fiercely competitive market, but managed
> to make their fortunes. The young wolves are proven warriors, more
> flexible and more imaginative than their predecessors, and much
> hungrier. Life has taught them to use all available methods, including
> violence, to defend their interests. (*Guardian*, 5 July 1995: 14)

Such an outlook is largely predicated upon the changed nature of
risk in society. The place of ethical principles governed by emotions
('he couldn't have acted so') is taken by the calculation of risks – a
'specific ethic without morality' (Beck 1992). If in stable Soviet conditions responsibility for the failure to satisfy the demands of the other
could be personalised, now there appear objective factors reducing
the responsibility of the partner. Modern situations encourage one to
think not in terms of trust in the person but rather in terms of the risk
he or she is running. Taking objective circumstances into account
helps to avoid excuses, such as 'I was let down, so I let the other
down'. Letting the other down is not just something happening by
accident, rather it becomes an element of strategy. The ability to
manipulate, to violate codes, to open new ways into the unknown,
becomes a fetish for youngsters. Russia, with dramatic changes at all
levels of society, becomes an experimental ground for those inclined
to take a risk. Many are tempted to run a risk in anticipation of
'waking up rich': 'Sometimes one has to violate one's own principles,'
noted one of the really successful businessmen, 'it is just another rule
of the game. Everyone cheats, I just win more often. The formula of
success is to calculate plus to be able to overcome one's own limits.'
[1] The ethics of calculativeness was emphasised by many businessmen:

> Questions of equivalence and balance in relationships have become
> central. Everything can be calculated nowadays, all costs are clear.
> People have learnt the language of opportunity costs. What used to
> be free of charge (*nakhalyavu* ) now has its price. Calculativeness has
> an impact on sincerity. People used to be open and shared their
> problems with others. Now problems are excluded from talk –
> everything must be fine, especially if this is related to business

[22] V.V. Kramnik (1995).

problems. One has to take into account all the reactions and consequences of such a request.[23] [19b]

Attitudes to time form another aspect of post-Soviet change: 'People finally realised why "time is money." People are so busy these days, that it is very difficult to burden someone with my problem. It is even difficult to catch people at home.' [31] 'Real business means 16 hours working day, after which one is dead tired. There is no time for socialising.' [11c]

Socialising was often connoted with drinking: 'People used to say: you do not drink – you are not part of the circle (*ne pyosh' – ne nash*).[24] Now drinking is out of fashion. If one is rich, there is no point in drinking. Drinking is the destiny of the poor.' [43] Only five years ago drinking was considered a significant influence upon cooperation. Some firms adopted *tolkachi* methods (see chapter 3), hiring a special person for negotiating who could overdrink (*perepit'*) a partner. But this has gone. The executive of a commercial bank remarks:

> People still drink but, shall we say, in a more civilised manner. It is often a physical need, just to be able to relax after sixteen hours of work. I come home late and can't fall asleep until I have a bottle of wine or couple of beers. My work in the bank is a different matter, everything is done soberly. There is occasional drinking at work, but this is normally a social event, reception or celebration. When we drink we do not talk about work. It is considered now as bad taste, while real work starts with documents and contracts which can't be mixed with drinking. [11a]

> 'Heavy drinking is clearly out of fashion,' concluded the financial expert of the Stock Exchange talking about her experiences of contacts with New Russians, 'in business and banking fresh heads and office-type suits are required. A healthy life-style – tennis, jogging, swimming – is now in vogue and demonstrated publicly. It could be an imitation of the West again, but this is a useful imitation.' [50]

No wonder *blat* is considered obsolete by New Russians. It is just not efficient enough with its impecunious favours, long-term obligations, 'mutual help' rhetoric and 'socialising techniques' of drinking. The ethics of *blat* (obligation to help, orientation towards the future,

---

[23] On the other hand, problems are sometimes exposed on purpose. A so-called 'complex of the poor' has come into fashion. People pretend they have problems (*pribednyayutsya*) to conceal their income or to avoid awkward situations with friends and relatives.

[24] Now they say: 'You do not take bribes – you are not part of the circle' (*ne beryosh' – ne nash*).

gratitude and modesty in demands) grounded in Soviet realities, seem incongruous in post-Soviet conditions. It is also understandable that other people feel nostalgic. Experiencing relative impoverishment, they miss the non-monetary opportunities provided by *blat*: the humane spirit, stability of life and lack of pressure.

### *Blat* in contemporary Russia

The previous sections were concerned with how political and economic reforms and the consequent changes in the social climate diminished the significance of *blat* and the degree to which institutional relationships were personalised. This section focuses on the present state of *blat* relations and their relevance for post-Soviet conditions.

For a long time market relations, which were forbidden by the Soviet state, did not operate in a sphere of their own, so they became symbiotic with a culturally accepted form of relations, namely *blat*. Lack of resources and lack of wealth also made it necessary for people to use whatever they had access to: their jobs, their friends, and so on, to strengthen their material and social positions. This does not mean that once people were given possibilities to become more prosperous, and the market became legitimate, *blat* networks dissolved. The fact that *blat* can work only through a non-market ethic and informal human relations does not rule it out from the market-oriented economy either. Rather *blat* was transformed in order to function in the new conditions, and this transformation is of particular interest for understanding of the type of 'market' economy in the new Russia.

To discover the current forms of *blat*, we will consider its role in terms of three economically distinct categories: goods, services and income. In the Soviet economy of favours *blat* covered all of them: goods were obtained and services were delivered 'by *blat*', access to jobs and education, in the final analysis oriented on income or privileges (an indirect income), could also be arranged in this roundabout way. All these were rationed by the state but redistributed by *blat*. When goods and services, even if costly, became available, *blat* lost its significance in these two spheres but its role in the sphere of income remained significant and even relatively increased. In procedures directly or indirectly connected with the distribution of income, *blat* matters a lot.

*Blat* is still deployed in the spheres of state education or employment. According to Ashwin (1996), workers at Kuzbass mines complain that *blatnye* are more often and better paid than 'simple workers'. Any paid job is not easy to get in fact; most of them are still sought and offered by acquaintance even where market tendencies are supposed to take over. Western companies working in Russia try to resist and block *blat* employment, quite often with no success. Some, however, look for the ways to turn *blat* relations to their advantage. Let me provide an example of the employment policy adopted at the Samara chocolate factory, which has been privatised with more than an 80 per cent share held by Nestlé. In 1995 Nestlé launched the programme of modernisation and reorganisation of management and marketing. As a result, the factory became one of the most prestigious enterprises in the city and consequently a 'closed' enterprise. To get a job there one has to have a connection to the factory, either a relative working there or an influential person who could recommend a recruit:

> Blat or protection used to be needed when one wanted a particularly prestigious or well paid place at the factory, otherwise the factory employed openly through the personnel department. Today this department has a note on the door 'No vacancies'. It doesn't mean of course that there are no vacancies, it means that nobody is taken 'from the street'. One has to be a relative or relation of somebody already employed[25]

This arrangement has been accepted as the employment policy. The head of the personnel department said:

> I can tell you directly we do not take outsiders. We are a small shareholding enterprise and we want 'our' people to work here. We want the factory to become a family business. That's why we only take people by recommendation. People work really well here, as they are not only under administrative control, but also under the social control of their relatives. It is not that we take anybody who is somebody's relative. We have a waiting list of all relatives of our workers who are interested in employment with all their details. They are people of different age and profession, doctors and militiamen, teachers and workers, graduates of higher schools and colleges, students, schoolchildren, qualified specialists and those who do not have a profession yet, many of them with knowledge of a foreign language. We can chose. When a vacancy comes up I start with this list, see who fits well, invite a few for a talk. We do not have

[25] The example is quoted with the kind permission of Pavel Romanov from his case study 'Shokoladka', conducted by the Samara branch of the Institute of Comparative Labour Studies, 1996.

any problem with filling in our vacancies. They literally get torn into pieces.

Modernisation of this factory undertaken by western managers has started with the most intimate sphere of every enterprise – informal relations. Employment by *blat* has been rationalised and bureaucratised, given the shape of a somewhat formal procedure. An attempt to combine the customary ways with new formal procedures (competitive principle of employment for specialists and managers, jobs are advertised in a local press etc.) has been made.

As has already been mentioned, *blat* operates most efficiently in situations of the distribution of limited resources, particularly where formal criteria are not sufficient to make a choice from a few candidates satisfying all of them. Formal criteria and procedures are in fact organised in the way that allow informal ones to creep in. A great deal of transgression still takes place routinely in the most significant matters of the Russian economy: in the distribution of the state budget and of state subsidies, the application of export–import duties and the execution of tax policy, etc.: 'Despite the changes in society which reduced the role of *blat* in daily life and business activities, *blat* endures in the state sector, where the principles of distribution have not been changed radically.' [26] 'The psychological parameters of state management and control remained the same,' concluded the director of a large industrial complex. 'And old methods are effective: for example, "luring" secretaries, going to dachas, etc.' [21] 'There are still niches of state distribution system (collective farms, mines, large enterprises) where one can approach the director and arrange a personal deal.' [41]

*Blat* often serves the needs of business in the spheres of the state budget and of state information. According to an expert involved with state auditing, the abuse of the budget is elaborate. It is now distributed through state funds, say, the Fund for the Development of Small Enterprises, etc. There are no subsidies but rather state loans on privileged conditions or bearing no interest. They must be paid off, but taking inflation into account, it is all the same subsidy. Interest is paid to the fund, and normally 30–40 per cent of it is 'black money' (*chernymi na lapu*) paid to the fund administration. [11c] The obtaining of state money for private commerce has become a matter of clear-cut corruption. Corruption is severe – from 10 per cent to 50 per cent can be levied as a so-called 'discount'.

New horizons for the use of information makes the use of it more corrupt: '*Blat* used to be the way to gain access to the state distribution of goods, services and honours. Now that the role of the state in the economy has been radically reduced, *blat* is found mostly at work in the distribution of information, mainly related to status or income.' [50] Information becomes both the channel and the filter of distribution of income in a 'market' (but not quite 'market') society. Well connected firms are able to build their marketing strategies on the basis of information about budget distribution. For example: 'Having inside information, they offer their products to those possessing finance which is non-transferable to the next financial year.' [47]

Because of the lack of formal channels of information or habits of using them, if they are available, the obtaining of information from acquaintances is still often considered efficient. A bank executive emphasised the necessity of contacts today:

> The more acquaintances, the more information. This is very important. Five executives of currency departments in different banks are my friends, not to mention managers, assistants, etc. I ring them every morning just for a chat, but of course we discuss exchange rates, sources and problems in currency operations. It is not secret information, but I have to know it. Until the formal channels of information are available, we use our informal contacts. I could ring to those banks where I have no contacts, but this puts me in the position of a beggar. While in a friendly chat, I obtain information without asking for it directly. Information exchange is important because it also constructs a kind of community. I want to belong to it, and it is much easier to penetrate the community through personal channels. [11a]

*Blat* always implied information obtained through contacts and exchanged within a certain circle of people. Yet the character of information nowadays has changed: 'It used to be information about what, where and how things could be obtained. Now it is information about money, business, laws and regulations, tax evasion, etc.' [26] The privatisation of enterprises through cheque auctions has produced another sphere where information is really costly: 'Information about the variant of privatisation to be chosen, about the administration of share sales and the intentions of the collective, about the position of the trade union and the possibilities of purchasing shares is in great demand. Most of the information required by foreign investors is inside information and cannot be obtained without good contacts.' [22] Within networks of businessmen information plays the role of sanction: 'Sanctions can be positive if additional information is provided for the sake of corporatism and shared interests. As a potential negative sanction, information on the family, friends, lovers and contacts of every significant businessman is held by the others.' [47]

The coexistence of state and commercial structures is often governed by horizontal contacts which create a niche for mutual favours. They have no formal mechanisms to press one another, so informal contacts are sustained to solve everyday problems:

> For example, the formal cooperation of the chairman of a state airport and the head of a commercial airline company allows each of them to exchange favours informally. This basically means that one recommended by the chairman of the airport can fly with this airline without paying full air-fare or paying at all. The post-Soviet difference is that now these favours are calculated much more carefully at every link of the *blat* chain. People think twice before asking a favour and getting into an obligation. [32]

Horizontal contacts can be effective where they can be used for mutual advantage:

> I had many contacts at resorts, as I organised many conferences there. Now they are commercialised but this has not broken my relationship with the administration. They welcome me as before, and I feel at home there. I am sure they will always help and won't charge me commercial prices. They know I have a limited budget for the conference and can't pay a full rent for their conference room and they will accept what is available. I have no budget to pay full price, but I help them with providing clients, advertising and other benefits. [13]

To conclude, the decreasing role of the state feeds two mutually exclusive tendencies. On the one hand, most informal relations, especially those involving exchange, are becoming separated from state property and thus increasingly deprive *blat* of its institutional basis. On the other, *blat* has also contributed to the formation of corporate interests which involve and intertwine with state institutions. In the financial and business spheres, 'corporatism' (*korporativnost'*), another term coined in the post-Soviet period, has two implications: 'First, the term is used to denote a criterion for the choice to be made: "whom an opportunity will be given to." Second, corporatism implies trust, as it is aimed at reducing the complexity of an unstable and high-risk environment. The logic is recognisable – to protect and to deal with "people of the circle"' [50]:

The forms of relationship maintained in *blat* networks did not disappear completely. All large-scale operations – financial swindles, non-paid loans, investment projects, in which millions vanished in unknown directions – are mostly based on former connections. Real business requires informal networks, even in the West. If old contacts turn bad, new but similar ones arise. What has changed is that the selection of people is more severe and demands are harder. [22]

The informal networks, networks of interests and networks of control, ensuring trust and reduction of risks are in fact indispensable in today's Russia where, according to an expert in commercial law: 'it's crucial to remember that banks are not banks, money is not money, and insurance is not insurance.' It is not surprising that smaller banks form their clientele on an informal basis, selected entrepreneurs receive bank loans on privileged conditions, and the whole institution of 'people of the circle' ('*svoi lyudi*') functions no less effectively than *blat* networks did in the Soviet era. Similar as it may seem, the solidarity of informal networks nowadays is based on different principles and ethics. Grown out of old *blat* ties and connections, corporate networks are 'profit-oriented'. According to experts from the special departments in charge of combating organised crime and corruption, the modification of *blat* patterns in the transitional period had serious implications:

> *Blat* prevalent in the Soviet Union was not a matter of material–financial significance. It was based on moral and ethical foundations. Together with these foundations *blat* was bound to change. The essence remained the same – the use of connections (family, friends, acquaintances) in solving all sorts of problems – but this form has been filled up with a new, material–financial contents. Now if some questions are to be solved 'by *blat*', via acquaintances, they imply, hint or even tell you directly how much it is going to cost. The deal, they say, has to be '*greened*' (colour of US dollar) or '*crocodiled*' (*nado pozelenit' ili okrokodilit'*). Therefore, everything which used to be by *blat* now takes the form of bribery, all sorts of bribery. Because bribery sounds unacceptable, it happens in the form of presents, gifts, payments for children's education, payments for holidays and 'business' trips abroad, offering engagement in commercial firms, banks, etc. – that is, all forms of corruption. What used to be the matter of morals and ethics based on modest norms of Soviet society and notions of kinship, friendship and other social ties, now, in the transitional stage of 'wild', as we call it, capitalism – involves material and financial capital. It is not surprising that the Anti-Corruption Law in Russia keeps slipping off the agenda. The spread of corruption is not dissimilar to the spread of *blat* in the Soviet era.

The scale, however, is different. Even if *blat* - providing access to the people of the circle at the expense of other citizens – meant a certain degree of relevant deprivation, it was nothing in comparison to the degree of polarisation and the impoverishment of the population today.

Not only the Soviet past but also the unbalanced democratic reforms in Russia are to blame for these corrupt tendencies: pre-occupied with the 'state', with privatisation of its property and marketisation of the command economy, the reforms were not orient-ed to (or did not ensure adequate transformation of) customary law, civic responsibilities and civil justice ('which always had been alien concepts in Russia' (Kampfner 1994: x). Most cultural, domestic or personal issues were reduced to questions of monetary influence. Changes which should have been considered in terms of civil society thus often had the familiar stamp of the state upon them, inherited from Soviet conditions. Parliamentary deputy Vladimir Lepyokhin, author of a book on lobbyism in Russia, laughed when asked whether there wasn't an imbalance between the interests of big capital and society as a whole: 'There is no balance. Society doesn't exist. What society is there in Russia? Have you seen one? How does it express itself? What does it look like? I don't see one. You can see some weak political parties. You can see the authorities. That's it. There aren't any other institutions' (*Guardian*, 20 September 1995).

I have already mentioned that the Soviet command economy had a powerful inner logic and language all its own: 'Two generations of Russians were raised on that logic and language, and the whole economy was built on them. That is why it is so hard to undo the legacy and to build what amounts to a completely new civilization,' emphasised the authors of *Russia 2010* (Yergin and Gustavson 1994: 113–14). *Blat* patterns have been strongly internalised by the culture of older Soviet generations, but even the Newest Russians have a weak spot for this kind of 'Sovietness'. Given that some processes, such as the privatisation of state property, the accumulation of capital and the re-emergence of class divisions are all shaped in a culturally specific way, it might be argued that post-Soviet society is never going to resemble Western societies. In his *The World After Communism* (1995), Skidelsky describes the end of the 'age of collectivism' as a lapsing into a 'gangsters' capitalism and nomenclatura expropriation and rent-seeking' (1995: 168). Pervasive bribery, corruption, the so-called 'nomenclatura businesses', a criminal 'second' society and active

**Cartoon 14**
Instructions versus laws

interpenetration of big business with politics are all part of the criminalised legacy of the economy of favours.

As for the legacy of *blat* practices, 'how can it all be undone?' is perhaps not the right question. Rather, the problem is how to make use of *blat* today, to limit its weaknesses and not to lose its virtues. *Blat* still plays a role in a variety of contexts including the large-scale barter economy where 'old methods', unwritten codes and networks are crucial. Understanding the advantages of *blat* can help to combat its negative implications. The fundamental issue underlying these practical concerns is how to deal with society in which loyalty to one's connections means more than loyalty to the state and where unwritten codes and social conventions dominate the law. The outcome of the changes now under way in Russia will depend on how far the constructive effects of informal networks and *blat* practices can be recognised and integrated into a new Russian order.

# Appendix 1: list of respondents

M = male, F = female.

[1] M/34, St. Petersburg, businessman, single. Russian, privileged background, Degree in Economics, solid business, involved in City politics, extremely well connected.

[2] M/22, Moscow, sportsman, single, Russian.

[3] F/32, Akademgorodok, businesswoman, single. Russian, family connections in trade, Degree in Economics, well connected. Witty, clever, cynical.

[4] M/20, Akademgorodok, student, single. Russian, intelligentsia background, having no experience of *blat* of his own, felt inhibited to talk about parents'.

[5] M/30, Novosibirsk, massage service, single. Russian, dealer.

[6] M/33, Novosibirsk, president of a tourist company, married. Russian, working-class background, Degree in Humanities, nomenclatura career. Idealist, party-member in the past.

[7] F/59, St. Petersburg, doctor, re-married. Russian, rural background, married to a construction worker. *Blatmeister.*

[8] M/32, St. Petersburg, property agent, widower. Russian, former waiter, failed businessman.

[9] M/30, Pskov, worker (*electrogazosvarshchik*), highly qualified, married, Russian.

[10] F/44, Pskov, independent trader ('*chelnok*'), married, Russian.

[11a] F/31, Novosibirsk, an executive of the currency department of the bank, divorced. Russian, nomenclatura background, Degree in Economics.

[11b] F/33, Barnaul (Altai), an independent trader, divorced, Russian.

[11c] F/45, Akademgorodok, chief accountant of a small firm, married. Russian, Degree in Economics, wife of a military man, lived all over Russia and abroad.

[12] M/35, Novosibirsk, head of the laboratory of psychology and media studies, advisor on political image, single. Russian, Degree in Economics, experience in working with nomenclatura.

[13] F/50, Moscow, administrator of the Certificate Committee of Scientific Degrees, single. Russian, privileged background, PhD in Chemistry, open and cheerful character, well connected.

[14] M/60, St. Petersburg, professor of Physics, married. Russian, intelligentsia background, intellectual with ideals.

[15] F/24, Akademgorodok, young academic. Russian, middle-class background, Degree in Sociology, married, no personal experience in *blat*, family connections.

[16] F/20, Novosibirsk, unemployed 'free artist'. Russian, working class background, privileged school, bohemian life style, no personal experience in *blat*, family connections.

[17] M/19, Novosibirsk, unemployed, 'underground existence', single, Russian.

[18] M/40, Novosibirsk, executive of International Business organisation, Siberian branch, former Head of the City Council. Russian, middle-class background, nomenclatura career, party-member in the past. Elusive, inhibited to talk.

[19a] M/30, Novosibirsk, businessman, married. Russian, middle-class background, Degree in Economics, company co-owner, well connected.

[19b] F/32, Novosibirsk, businesswoman, married. German, rural background, Degree in Economics, company co-owner.

[20] M/43, Kurgan (Ural), deputy director of a large industrial enterprise, married. Russian, working-class background, professional career, party-member in the past.

[21] M/60, Akademgorodok, academician, the director of the research institute and industrial complex in micro-biology, remarried. Russian, Academic career, self-made man, extraordinary character.

[22] M/38, Novosibirsk, businessman, remarried. Russian, privileged background, Degree in Economics, Lecturer at the High School of National Economy, well connected.

[23] F/55, Akademgorodok, administrator of a closed distribution system, widow. Russian, rural background, self-made person, a widow of the top boss in trade.

[24] M/24, Ulan-Ude, Republican treasury officer, single. Buryat, strong clan background, Degree in Economics, well connected.

[25] F/42, Novosibirsk, head of the International Affairs department at the regional administration, single. Russian, middle-class back-

ground, Degree in Humanities, nomenclatura career, well connected, party-member in the past.

[26] F/43, Akademgorodok, teacher of the elite school, married. Russian, intelligentsia background, Degree in English, former people's deputy of the local Soviet, party-member in the past.

[27] M/46, Akademgorodok, businessman, single. Korean, Degree in Technical Sciences, former head of the Research Department at the Institute of Automatic Systems.

[28a] F/45, Akademgorodok, aerobics coach, married. Russian, involved with organisation of sport events, active.

[28b] M/47, Akademgorodok, sports coach, married. Russian, constantly involved with trade union rationing activities up to 1993.

[29a] F/27, Novosibirsk, journalist, organiser of cultural events, single, Russian.

[29b] M/25, Novosibirsk, journalist. Russian, middle-class background, privileged school.

[30] M/65, Akademgorodok, pensioner, married. Russian, rural background, former worker.

[31a] M/40, Novosibirsk, worker, highly qualified, married, Russian.

[31b] F/39, Novosibirsk, housewife, Russian.

[32] M/30, Akademgorodok, organiser of political and musical youth festivals, single. Russian, middle-class background, former Komsomol leader.

[33] M/70, Akademgorodok, senior scientist, widower. Jewish, privileged background, dedicated party-member in the past.

[34] M/46, Novosibirsk, vice-president of the bank, married. Russian, 'apparatchik', self-made man, nomenclatura career, party-member in the past.

[35] M/39, Novosibirsk, police detective, a head of the information office at the Department of Struggle with Organised Crime, Russian.

[36] M/59, Akademgorodok, Dean of the Faculty at the University, married. Armenian, a wise man.

[37] M/61, Novosibirsk, Professor of Economics, the rector of the Independent University, married. Jewish, a well known independent scholar.

[38] M/41, Chita (Eastern Siberia), TV and radio repair technician, married. Russian, working-class background, well connected.

[39] M/46, Novosibirsk, independent dealer, married. Russian, working-class background.

[40] F/43, Novosibirsk, shop assistant, married, Russian.

[41] M/29, Novosibirsk, dentist. Russian, privileged background, well connected.

[42] M/49, Novosibirsk, head of Department of History at the University, single. Russian, former Komsomol leader and party-member, a close friend of the 'nomenclatura circle'.

[43] M/38, Moscow, businessman, remarried. Russian, former military man, successful business, well connected.

[44] M/29, St. Petersburg, businessman, married. Russian, provincial background, Degree in Mathematics, self-made man.

[45] M/44, Moscow, sculptor, married. Russian, working-class background, former military man.

[46] F/56, Novosibirsk, administrator of Higher Party School, married. Russian, middle-class background, career in education.

[47] M/31, Novosibirsk, New Rich, remarried. Korean, Degree in Economics, fast-track career in business, well connected.

[48] M/49, Akademgorodok, businessman, married. Jewish, intelligentsia background, senior scientist in chemistry, business in production of ecological equipment.

[49] F/65, Moscow, Professor of Sociology, widow. Jewish, intelligentsia background, distinguished academic.

[50] F/38, Novosibirsk, head of the analytical centre of the Currency Stock Exchange, divorced. Russian, middle-class background, Degree in Economics, professional career, party-member in the past.

Altogether 50 interviews were recorded. Some of the interviews were conducted with more than one respondent, normally, family or a circle of close friends, and these cases are marked by the same number of the interview as, for example, [19a] and [19b]. Normally interviews were conducted in an informal atmosphere, either at my place or I was invited to visit the respondents' homes. It was always the case that we had tea, a meal or drinks during the interview and discussed a wider range of questions than presented in the scheme of interview. Some of these discussions covered more specialised topics summarised in appendix 2.

# Appendix 2: interview topics

## Basic questions

1. Have you heard the expression 'by *blat*'? In which situations is it normally used? Can you think of an example from your own experience? What, do you think, *blat* is?
2. Do you remember a situation when you obtained something, arranged something for somebody, or helped somehow? What was it? Do you know of others using *blat*?
3. What could you do as a favour for your best friend? Or at least try? What kind of problem you could help to solve?
4. Would you do the same for others? If yes, on what conditions?
5. Who helped you actively in solving your problems? Why?
6. How many people can you rely on in problematic situations?
7. How often do you use your contacts? What for? In which situations? What forces you to ask your friends and contacts for a favour?
8. How often have you helped your friend through another friend? What was the difference when you helped a friend yourself or asked someone else to help him?
9. How did you express your gratitude? Did you give gifts? What kind of gifts?
10. When your request was rejected, something was promised and not fulfilled, what was your reaction? Was it often the case?
11. Do you depend on personal contacts, on support and favours of others:
    – in your everyday life (foodstuffs, goods, services, housing, dacha)
    – in leisure activities (resorts, travel and theatre tickets, hobbies)
    – at work (contacts, promotion)
    – in bringing up children (prestigious kindergartens, schools, clubs, entrance to universities, etc.)?

12. Do you know whether your parents had to use contacts for obtaining something or helping you in any way?

13. In which spheres *blat* was most important?

14. In which situations and in which form it was appropriate to ask for a favour? Could you give an example?

15. How do you know what is appropriate to ask and what is not? How do you decide what would be an adequate level of gratitude?

16. Was it necessary to ask for a favour or would it be offered? Is there a difference if one is offered or asks him/herself?

17. How are *blat* relations connected with personal relationships (kinship, friendship, acquaintanceship, intimate relations)?

18. Do *blat* relations imply the equality of partners?

19. How would you formulate the rules of *blat* relationships?

20. *Blat* relations have undergone significant changes in recent years. What are these changes?

21. What role does *blat* play now?

## More specialised topics discussed

*Origins of* blat

*Blat* and the usage of the term (time–space, contexts, connotations).

The public/private dimensions of the Soviet system (public property and the character of access to resources in the command economy).

How different is the same *blat* favour from three different perspectives: the giver's, the receiver's and the observer's?

*Negative and positive aspects of* blat

Differences between *blat* and bribery, corruption, the informal economy.

The use of public office or work for private advantage (profit-seeking and helping out a friend).

Personalisation of bureaucracy.

Tributes to the party apparatus.

*Blat* as human and warm (trust in *blat* relations).

Specifics of acquaintanceship in Soviet conditions.

*Political and economic factors*

Social implications of shortages.

Specifics of money and its realisation in conditions of shortage.

Soviet privileges and *blat* (what values and symbols are associated with privileges and *blat*).

How is *blat* related to the official ideology?
Legitimacy of *blat*.
Specific attitude towards legality (no final 'no').
What are the rules of rule-breaking (how to make an exceptional case)?

*Stratification and objects of* blat.
What is the symbolic significance of different objects of *blat*?
Are *blat* objects used as symbols of social/political/economic differentiation?
Are *blat* transactions manipulated to improve relative status?
Do *blat* exchanges amplify or sanction gender inequalities?
The periodicity of needs and fashion.
Information as an object of *blat*.
Types of networks in correspondence with *blat* objects.

*Ethnographic inquiry*
Aspects of reciprocity in *blat* relations (whether *blat* relations are always reciprocal).
The vertical/horizontal dimensions of *blat* (are goods redistributed from the rich to the poor)?
What is the measure in non-monetary *blat* exchanges?
Is there an external criterion for evaluation of exchange or any standardised value?
How do we know whether an exchange is fair? What does it depend on?
What is ethical code of *blat* relations?
What are the tactics of *blat* (how to learn 'to go on' in *blat* situations).

Blat *in post-Soviet conditions*
What are the everyday implications of the market reforms?
Changes of use-contexts of *blat*, new areas of application.
Transformation of personal relations between people (trust, confidence, mutual help).
Attitudes of different generations to *blat*.
New Russians (values, fashion, stereotypes, new attitudes to time, money, drinking, etc.).

# Bibliography

Alapuro, R. (1993). 'Civil Society in Russia', in J. Iivonen (ed.), *The Future of the Nation State in Europe*, Aldershot: Edward Elgar, 194–218

(1996). 'Categories, Social Networks and Civil Society: Social Ties of St. Petersburg Teachers', in *Civil Society in European North*, Centre for Independent Social Research, January 1996

Alessandrini, S. and Dallago, B. (eds.) (1987). *The Unofficial Economy: Consequences and Perspectives in Different Economic Systems*, Aldershot: Gower

Allan, G. A. (1979). *A Sociology of Friendship and Kinship*, London: Allen & Unwin

Anderlini, L. and Sabourian, H. (1992). 'The Economics of Barter, Money and Credit', in C. Humphrey and S. Hugh-Jones (eds.), *Barter, Exchange and Value: An Anthropological Approach*, Cambridge: Cambridge University Press

Andrle V. (1988). *Workers in Stalin's Russia: Industrialisation and Social Change in a Planned Economy*, Brighton: Harvester

Appadurai, A. (ed.) (1986). *The Social Life of Things: Commodities in Cultural Perspective*, Cambridge: Cambridge University Press

Arendt, H. (1951). *The Origins of Totalitarianism*, New York: Harcourt Brace Jovanovich

Åslund, A. (1995). *How Russia Became a Market Economy*, Washington, DC: Brookings Institution

Åslund, A. (ed.) (1994). *Economic Transformation in Russia*, London: Frances Pinter

Baker, R. N. (1982). 'Clientelism in the Post-revolutionary State: the Soviet Union', in C. Clapham (ed.), *Private Patronage and Public Power: Political Clientelism and the Modern State*, London: Frances Pinter, 36–52

Balzer, H. D. (ed.) (1991). *Five Years that Shook the World*, Boulder, CO: Westview

Barber, J. (1980). 'Notes on the Soviet Working-class Family, 1928–1941', *Second World Congress for Soviet and East European Studies*, Garmisch-Partenkirchen, Federal Republic of Germany, 30 September–4 October

Bauman, Z. (1990–1). 'Communism: A Post-Mortem', *Praxis International*, 10 (3–4), October–January

Beck, U. (1992). *The Risk Society*, Cambridge: Polity Press

222

Berdiaev, N. (1946). *The Russian Idea*, London: Geoffrey Bles

Berliner, J. S. (1957). *Factory and Manager in the USSR*, Cambridge, MA: Harvard University Press

Blau, P. M. (1964). *Exchange and Power in Social Life*, New York: Wiley

Blau, P. M. and Meyer, M. W. (1971). *Bureaucracy in Modern Society*, New York: Random House

Boissevain, J. (1966). 'Patronage in Sicily', *Man NS*, I, 18–23

(1974). *Friends of Friends: Networks, Manipulators and Coalitions*, New York: St Martin's Press

Boltanski, L. (1990). *L'amour et la Justice comme Competence: Troir Essais de Sociologie de l'action*, Paris: Metailie

Bomton, M. (1965). *The Relevance of Models for Social Anthropology*, ASA Monographs, 1, London: Tavistock Publications

Bourdieu, P. (1977). *Outline of a Theory of Practice*, Cambridge: Cambridge University Press

(1979). *Algeria 1960*, Cambridge: Cambridge University Press

(1990). *The Logic of Practice*, trans. R. Nice, Cambridge: Polity Press

Boym, S. (1994). *Commonplaces: Mythologies of Everyday Life in Russia*, Cambridge, MA and London: Harvard University Press .

Breslauer, G. (ed.) (1990). *Can Gorbachev's Reforms Succeed?* Berkeley: Centre for Soviet and East European Studies, University of California

Brzezinski, Z. and Friedrich, C. (1956). *Totalitarian Dictatorship and Autocracy*, Cambridge, MA: Harvard University Press

Burke, P. (1992). *History and Social Theory*, Cambridge: Polity Press

Cambpell, C. (1964). *Honor, Family and Patronage* , Oxford: Clarendon Press

Campbell, J. K. (1977). 'Honour, Family and Patronage: A Study of Institutions and Moral Values in a Greek Mountain Community', in S. W. Schmidt, J. C. Scott, C. Lande and L. Guasti (eds.), *Friends, Followers and Factions*, Berkeley: University of California Press

*CDSP* (various issues). *Current Digest of the Post-Soviet Press*

Carlitts, M. and Hall, P. (1994). *Technopoles of the World*, London: Routledge

Certeau, M. de (1984). *The Practice of Everyday Life*, trans. S. F. Rendall, Berkeley: University of California Press

Chalidze, V. (1977). *Criminal Russia*, New York: Random House

Cheal, D. (1988). *The Gift Economy*, London: Routledge

Cherednichenko, G. and Shubkin, V. (1985). *Molodezh Vstupaet v Zhizn'*, Moscow: Mysl'

Clapham, C. (ed.) (1982). *Private Patronage and Public Power: Political Clientelism and the Modern State*, London: Frances Pinter

Clarke, M. (ed.) (1983). *Corruption: Causes, Consequences and Control*, London: Frances Pinter

Cohen, H. (1981). *Connections: Understanding Social Relationships*, Ames: Iowa State University Press

Cohen, S. and Taylor, L. (1978). *Prison Secrets*, London: NCCL and RAP

Collins, R. (1980). 'Erwing Goffman and the Development of Modern Social Theory', in J. Ditton (ed.), *The View From Goffman*, London: Macmillan

Crankshaw, E. (1956). *Russia Without Stalin*, London: Michael Joseph

Craven, P. and Wellman, B. (199 ). 'The Network City', *Sociological Inquiry*, 43 (3/4), 57–88

Dallago, B. (1990). *The Irregular Economy: The 'Underground' Economy and the 'Black' Labour Market*, : Dartmouth

Dallin, D. J. (1951). *The New Soviet Empire*, London: Hollis & Carter

Davis, J. (1977). *People of the Mediterranean: An Essay in Comparative Social Anthropology*, London: Routledge & Kegan Paul

(1992). *Exchange*, Buckingham: Open University Press

Dicks, H. (1960). 'Some Notes on the Russian National Character', in C. E. Black (ed.), *The Transformation of Russian Society*, Cambridge, MA: Harvard University Press

Ditton, J. (1977). *Part-time Crime: An Ethnography of Fiddling and Pilferage*, London: Macmillan

Djilas, M. (1957). *The New Class: An Analysis of the Communist System*, London: Thames & Hudson

Douglas, M.(ed.) (1988). *Constructive Drinking*, Cambridge: Cambridge University Press

Dovlatov, S. (1993). *Sobranie prozy*, vol. 2, St. Petersburg: Limbus Press

Dunham, V. (1976). *In Stalin's Time*, Cambridge: Cambridge University Press

Edgerton, R. B. (1985). *Rules, Exceptions, and Social Order*, Berkeley: University of California Press

Eisenstadt, S. N. and Lemarchand, R. (eds.) (1981). *Political Clientelism, Patronage and Development*, London: Sage

Feige, E. L. (ed.) (1989). *The Underground Economies: Tax Evasion and Information Distortion*, Cambridge: Cambridge University Press

Feldbrugge F. J. M. (1989). 'The Second Economy in a Political and Legal Perspective', in E. L. Feige, *The Underground Economies: Tax Evasion and Information Distortion*, Cambridge: Cambridge University Press, 301

Fischer, C. S. (1977). *Networks and Places: Social Relations in the Urban Settings*, London: Collier Macmillan

Fisher, D. and Vilas, S. (1996). *Successful Networking: The Key to Personal and Professional Success*, London: Thorsons

Fitzpatrick, S. (1992). *The Cultural Front: Power and Culture in Revolutionary Russia*, Ithaca and London: Cornell University Press

Fleron, F. J. and Hoffman, E. P. (1993). *Post-Communist Studies and Political Science: Methodology and Empirical Theory in Sovietology*, Boulder, CO, San Francisco and Oxford: Westview

Follain, J. (1995). *A Dishonoured Society*, London: Little, Brown

Friedrich C. J. (1966). 'Political Pathology', *The Political Quarterly*, 37 (1), 70–85

Fukuyama, F. (1995). *Trust: The Social Virtues and the Creation of Prosperity*, London: Hamish Hamilton

Gabor, I. R. (1979).'The Second (Secondary) Economy', *Acta Oeconomica*, 22 (3–4), 291–311

Gambetta, D. (ed.) (1988). *Trust: Making and Breaking Cooperative Relations*, Oxford: Basil Blackwell

Gellner, E. (1973). *The Concept of Kinship and Other Essays*, Oxford: Basil Blackwell

(1980). *State and Society in Soviet Thought*, London: Duckworth

(1988). 'Trust, Cohesion, and the Social Order', in D. Gambetta (ed.), *Trust: Making and Breaking Cooperative Relations*, Oxford: Basil Blackwell

Getty, J. A. and Manning, R. T. (eds.) (1993). *Stalinist Terror: New Perspectives*, Cambridge: Cambridge University Press

Giddens, A. (1984). *The Constitution of Society: Outline of the Theory of Structuration*, Cambridge; Polity Press

Goffman, E. (1959). *The Presentation of Self in Everyday Life*, New York: Doubleday

Gorer, G. and Rickman, J. (1950). *The People of Great Russia: A Psychological Study*, New York: Chanticleer

Gouldner, A. (1977). 'The Norm of Reciprocity', in S. S. Schmidt (ed.), *Friends, Followers and Factions: A Reader in Political Clientelism*, Berkeley and London: University of California Press

Graziano, L. (ed.) (1975). 'A Conceptual Framework for the Study of Clientelism', *European Journal of Political Research*, 4(2), 149–74

Gregory, C. A. (1982). *Gifts and Commodities*, London: Academic Press

Gregory, C. A. and Altman, J. C. (1989). *Observing the Economy*, London: Routledge Grossman, G. (1977). 'The Second Economy of the USSR', *The Problems of Communism*, 26 (5), 25–40

(1992). 'The Second Economy in the USSR and Eastern Europe: A Bibliography', *Berkeley–Duke Occasional Papers on the Second Economy in the USSR*, 21 (July)

Gudeman, S. (1986). *Economics as Culture: Models and Metaphors of Livelihood*, London: Routledge

Habermas, J. (1976). *Legitimation Crisis*, London: Heinemann

Handelman, S. (1994). *Comrade Criminal: The Theft of the Second Russian Revolution*, London: Michael Joseph

Hanson, P. and Kirkwood, M. (1988). *Alexander Zinoviev as Writer and Thinker: An Assessment*, London: Macmillan

Harding, P. and Jenkins, R. (1989). *The Myth of the Hidden Economy: Towards a New Understanding of Informal Economic Activity*, Philadelphia: Open University Press

Heidenheimer, A. (1970). *Political Corruption: Readings in Comparative Analysis*, New Brunswick: Transaction Books

Held, D. (1990). *Political Theory and the Modern State: Essays on State, Power and Democracy*, Cambridge: Polity Press

Henry, S. (1978). *The Hidden Economy: The Context and Control of Borderline Crime*, Oxford: Martin Robertson

Henry, S. and Mars, G. (1978). 'Crime at Work: The Social Construction of Amateur Property Theft', *Sociology*, 12, 245–63

Herzfeld, M. (1987). *Anthropology Through the Looking-Glass*,

(1992). *The Social Production of Indifference*, New York and Oxford: Berg

Hingley, R. (1978). *The Russian Mind*, London: Bodley Head

Holmes, L. (1993). *The End of Communist Power: Anti-Corruption Campaigns and Legitimation Crisis*, Cambridge: Polity Press

Hough, J. F. (1988). *Russia and the West*, New York: Simon & Schuster

Humphrey, C. (1983). *Karl Marx Collective: Economy, Society and Religion in a Siberian Collective Farm*, Cambridge: Cambridge University Press

Humphrey, C. and Hugh-Jones, S. (eds.) (1992). *Barter, Exchange and Value: An Anthropological Approach*, Cambridge: Cambridge University Press

Inkeles, A. and Bauer, R. A. (1959). *The Soviet Citizen: Daily Life in Totalitarian Society*, Cambridge, MA: Harvard University Press

*Istoriia SSSR v Anekdotakh: 1917-1991*, Riga: Everest (1991)

Jowitt, K. (1974). 'An Organizational Approach to the Study of Political Culture in Marxist–Leninist Systems', *American Political Science Review* (September)

(1983). 'Soviet Neotraditionalism: The Political Corruption of a Leninist Regime', *Soviet Studies*, 35 (3) (July), 275–97

Kagarlitsky, B. (1995). *Restoration in Russia: Why Capitalism Failed*, trans. R. Clarke, London: Verso

Kampfner, J. (1994). *Inside Yeltsin's Russia*, London: Cassell

Karol, K. S. (1971). 'Conversations in Russia', *New Statesman* (June), 8–10

Kasianova, K. (1994). *O Russkom Natsional'nom Kharaktere*, Moscow: Institut Natsional'nykh Modelei Ekonomiki

Katsenelinboigen, A. (1977). 'Colored Markets in the Soviet Union', *Soviet Studies*, 1, 62–85

Keane, J. (ed.) (1988). *Civil Society and the State*, London: Verso

Kenny, M. and Kertzer, D. I. (eds.) (1983). *Urban Life in Mediterranean Europe: Anthropological Perspectives*, Urbana: University of Illinois Press

Kharkhordin, O. and Gerber, T. P. (1994). 'Russian Directors' Business Ethic: A Study of Industrial Enterprises in St Petersburg, 1993', *Europe–Asia Studies*, 46 (7): 1075–1107

Kireevsky, I. V. (1911). *Polnoe sobranie sochinenii*, Pod red. M. Gershenzona, 2 vols., Moscow (Farnborough, 1970)

Kirkwood, M. (1993). *Alexander Zinoviev: An Introduction to his Works*, London: Macmillan

Klugman, J. (1989). *The New Soviet Elite: How They Think and What They Want*, London: Praeger

Kordonsky, S. G. (1989). 'Sotsial'naya Struktura i Mekhanism Tormozhenia', in *Postizhenie*. Moscow: Progress

Kornai, J. (1980). *Economics of Shortage*, Amsterdam: North-Holland

(1992). *The Socialist System: The Political Economy of Communism*, Oxford: Clarendon Press

Kotkin, S. (1995). *Magnetic Mountain: Stalinism as a Civilization*, Berkeley: University of California Press

Kramnik, V. V. (1995). *Imidg Reform: Psikhologiya i Kultura Peremen v Rossii*, St. Petersburg: Peterburgskii Universitet Ekonomiki i Finansov

Kristman, L. N. (1925). 'Geroicheskii Period Velikoi Russkoi Revolutsii – Opyt Analiza t.n. "Voennogo Kommunizma"', *Vestnik Kommunisticheskoi Akademii*, 9

Kukathas, C., Lowell, D. W. and Maley, W. (eds.) (1991). *The Transition From*

*Socialism: State and Civil Society in Gorbachev's USSR*, Melbourne: Longman Cheshire

Lampert, N. (1984). 'Law and Order in the USSR: The Case of Economic and Official Crime', *Soviet Studies*, 36 (3), 366–85

Lampert, N. and Rittersporn, G.(eds.) (1992). *Stalinism: Its Nature and Aftermath. Essays in Honour of Moshe Lewin*, New York: M. E. Sharpe

Lane, C. (1978) *Christian Religion in the Soviet Union: A Sociological Study*, London: Allen & Unwin.

Lane, D. (ed.) (1988). *Elites and Political Power in the USSR*. Aldershot: Edward Elgar

   (1990). *Soviet Society Under Perestroika*, Boston: Unwin Hyman

Lapidus, G. W. (1989). 'State and Society: Towards the Emergence of Civil Society in the Soviet Union', in S. Bialer (ed.), *Politics, Society and Nationality Inside Gorbachev's Russia*, Boulder, CO: Westview

Leinhardt, S. (ed.) (1977). *Social Networks: A Developing Paradigm*, New York: Academic Press

Leites, N. (1953). *A Study of Bolshevism*, Glencoe, IL: Free Press

Levi-Strauss, C. (1969). *The Elementary Structures of Kinship*, Boston: Beacon

Lewin, M. (1985). *The Making of the Soviet System: Essays in the Social History of Interwar Russia*, New York: Pantheon

Livshitz, A. (1994). *Ekonomicheskaya Reforma v Rossii i ee Tsena*, Moscow

Los, M. (ed.) (1990). *The Second Economy in Marxist States*, London: Macmillan

Lotman, Y. M. (1994). *Besedy o Russkoi Kulture*, St. Petersburg: Iskusstvo: 44

Luckmann, B. (1978). 'The Small Life-worlds of Modern Man', in Luckmann, T. (ed.), *Phenomenology and Sociology*, Harmondsworth: Penguin

Luhmann, N. (1979). *Trust and Power*, Chichester: Wiley

Luhmann, (1988). 'Familiarity, Confidence, Trust: Problems and Alternatives', in D. Gambetta (ed.), *Trust: Making and Breaking Cooperative Relations*, Oxford: Basil Blackwell

Lyon, L. (1987). *The Community in Urban Society*, Chicago: Porsey Press

Malinowski, B. (1922). *Argonauts of the Western Pacific*, London

Matison, J. and Mack, R. (1984). *The Only Barter Book You'll Ever Need*, New York: Bantam Books

Mars, G. (1982). *Cheats at Work: An Anthropology of Workplace Crime*, London: Allen & Unwin

Mauss, M. (1925). *The Gift*, London: Routledge, English trans. (1954)

Mead, G. H. (1954). *Mind, Self, and Society*, Chicago: Chicago University Press

Millar, J. R. (1988). 'The Little Deal: Brezhnev's Contribution to Acquisitive Socialism', in T. L. Thompson and R. Sheldon (eds.), *Soviet Society and Culture: Essays in Honour of Vera S. Dunham*, Boulder, CO: Westview

Miller, J. R. (ed.) (1987). *Politics, Work and Daily Like in the USSR: A Survey of Former Soviet Citizens*, Cambridge: Cambridge University Press

Misztal, B. A. (1996). *Trust in Modern Societies: The Search for the Bases of Social Order*, Cambridge: Polity Press

Nove, A. (1977). *The Soviet Economic System*, London: Allen & Unwin

   (1982). *An Economic History of the USSR*, New York: Penguin Books

Novozhilov, V. V. (1926). 'Nedostatok Tovarov', *Vestnik Finansov*, 2

Offe, C. and Heinze, R. G. (1992). *Beyond Employment: Time, Work and the Informal Economy,* Cambridge: Polity Press

O'Hearn, D. (1980). 'The Consumer Second Economy: Size and Effects', *Soviet Studies,* 2, 218–34

Osokina, E. (1993). *Hierarchy of Consumption: O Zhizni Lyudei v Usloviyakh Stalinskogo Snabzheniya 1928-35,* Moscow: Izd-vo MGU

Pahl, R. (1984). *The Divisions of Labour,* Oxford: Basil Blackwell

Palmier, L. (1983). 'Bureaucratic Corruption and its Remedies', in M. Clarke (ed.), *Corruption: Causes, Consequences and Control,* London: Frances Pinter

Parker, T. (1992). *Russian Voices,* London: Picador

Parry, J. and Bloch, M. (eds.) (1989). *Money and Morality of Exchange,* Cambridge: Cambridge University Press

Pavlenko, S. Y. (1990). 'O neformal'nykh otnosheniyakh v upravlencheskikh strukturakh', in *Postizhenie,* Moscow: Progress

Peristiany, J. G. (ed.) (1968). *Contributions to Mediterranean Sociology,* The Hague: Mouton

Pipes, R. (1974). *Russia Under the Old Regime,* New York: Scribner's

Polanyi, K. (1944). *The Great Transformation,* Boston: Beacon Press
    (1957). *Trade and Market in the Early Empires* Glencoe, IL: Free Press

Polanyi, M. (1964). *The Personal Knowledge: Towards a Post-Critical Philosophy,* New York: Harper & Row

Portes, A., Castells, M. and Benton, L. A. (1989). *The Informal Economy: Studies in Advanced and Less Developed Countries,* Baltimore and London: Johns Hopkins University Press

Priestley, P. (ed.) (1984). *Social Skills in Prison and the Community,* London: Routledge & Kegan Paul

Propp, V. (1984a). *Russkaia Skazka,* Leningrad: Izd-vo LGU
    (1984b). *Theory and History of Folklore,* Manchester: Manchester University Press

Putnam, R. D. (1993). *Making Democracy Work: Civic Tradition in Modern Italy,* Princeton and Chichester: Princeton University Press

Redclift, N. and Mingione, E. (eds.) (1985). *Beyond Employment,* Oxford: Basil Blackwell

Rittersporn, G. T. (1991). *Stalinist Simplifications and Soviet Complications: Social Tensions and Political Conflicts in the USSR, 1933-1953,* Philadelphia: Harwood Academic

Rose, R. (1983). 'Getting by in the Three Economies: The Resources of the Official, Unofficial and Domestic Economies', *Studies in Public Policy,* 1983, 110, University of Strathlyde, Glasgow

Ruble, B. A. (1990). 'The Soviet Union's Quiet Revolution', in G. Breslauer (ed.), *Can Gorbachev's Reforms Succeed?,* Berkeley: Centre for Soviet and East European Studies, University of California

Sahlins, M. D. (1972). *Stone Age Economics,* New York and Chicago: Aldine–Atherton
    (1976). *Culture and Practical Reason,* Chicago: University of Chicago Press

Salmin, A. M. , Bunin, I. M. , Kapelyushnikov, R. I. and Urnov, M. U. (1994). *Partiinaya sistema v Rossii v 1989–1993 gg.*, Moskva: Nachala Press

Salmon P. (1986). *The Theory of Informal Transactions in Bureaucracies*, Dijon: Université de Dijon

Sassen, S. (1991). 'The Informal Economy', in J. H. Mollenkopf and M. Castells (eds.), *Dual City: Restructuring New York*, New York: Russell Sage Foundation

Schmidt, S. W. , Scott, J. C. , Lande, C. and Guasti, L. (eds.) (1977). *Friends, Followers and Factions*, Berkeley: University of California Press

Scott, J. C. (1972). *Comparative Political Corruption*, Engelwood Cliffs, NJ: Prentice-Hall

(1985). *Power of the Weak: Everyday Forms of Peasant Resistance*, New Haven: Yale University Press

Schwartz, B. (1967). 'The Social Psychology of the Gift', *American Journal of Sociology*, 73, 1–11

Shanin, T. (1988). 'Expolary Economies: A Political Economy of Margins', Agenda of the Colloquium on Alternative Economies, Toronto (May)

Shansky, N. M. (1965). *Etymologicheskii slovar' russkogo yazka*, Tom 1, Moscow: Izdate'stvo MGU

Shlapentokh, V. (1989). *Public and Private Life of the Soviet People*, New York: Oxford University Press

Sik, E. (1994). 'Network Capital in Capitalist, Communist and Post-communist societies', *International Contributions to Labour Studies*, 4, 73–93

Silver, B. D. (199 ). 'Political Beliefs of the Soviet Citizen: Sources of Support for Regime Norms', in J. R. Miller (ed.), *Politics, Work and Daily Life in the USSR*, New York, 100–41

Simis, K. M. (1982). *USSR: Secrets of a Corrupt Society*, London: Dent

Simmel, G. (1950). *The Sociology of George Simmel*, Glencoe, IL: Free Press

Skidelsky, R. (1995). *The World After Communism*, London: Macmillan

*Sovetskii etiket* (1974). Leningrad

Starr, S. F. (1988). 'Soviet Union: A Civil Society', *Foreign Policy*, 70, 26–41

Steele, J. (1995). *Eternal Russia: Yeltsin, Gorbachev and the Mirage of Democracy*, London and Boston: Faber & Faber

Stirling, A. P. (1968). 'Impartiality and Personal Morality', in J. G. Peristiany (ed.), *Contributions to Mediterranean Society*, The Hague: Mouton: 49–64

Strathern, M. (1981a). *Kinship at the Core*, Cambridge: Cambridge University Press

(1981b). *Disembodied Choice*, Cambridge: Cambridge University Press

(1988). *The Gender of the Gift*, Berkeley: University of California Press

(1991). 'New Literary History', *A Journal of Theory and Interpretation*. 22 (3) (Summer)

(1992). *After Nature: English Kinship in the Late Twentieth Century*, Cambridge: Cambridge University Press

Sudoplatov, P. and Sudoplatov, A. (1990). *Special Tasks: The Memoirs of an Unwanted Witness – A Soviet Spymaster*, Boston: Little, Brown

Tarkowski, J. (1981). 'Patrons and Clients in a Planned Economy', in S. N. Eisenstadt and R. Lemarchand (eds.), *Political Clientelism, Patronage, and Development*, London: Sage, 173–90

Timasheff, N. S. (1946). *The Great Retreat: The Growth and Decline of Communism in Russia*, New York

Tolz, V. and Elliot, I. (eds.) (1995). *The Demise of the USSR: From Communism to Independence*, London: Macmillan

Trotsky, L. (1967). *The Revolution Betrayed: What is the Soviet Union and Where is it Going?*, London: Faber (first published 1937)

Vaksberg, A. (1991). *The Soviet Mafia*, London: Weidenfeld & Nicolson

Vasmer, M. (1964). *Etymologicheskii slovar' russkogo yazka*, Pod. red. Larina, Tom.1, Moscow

Voinovich, V. (1978). *The Ivan'kiad, or, The Tale of The Writer Voinovich's Installation in His New Apartment*, London: Jonathan Cape

Voslensky, M. (1984). *Nomenclatura: The Soviet Ruling Class*, Garden City: Doubleday.

Walker M. (1989). *Martin Walker's Russia: Dispatches from the Guardian Correspondent in Moscow*, London: Abacus Original

Weber, M. (1968). *Economy and Society*, Vol. 1, New York: Bedminster

Wedel, J. (1986). *The Private Poland*, Oxford: Facts on File Publications

Weindle, W. (1956), *Zadachi Rossii*, New York

Weingrod, A. (1968). 'Patrons, Patronage, and Political Parties', *Comparative Studies in Society and History*, 10 (3), 377–400

Wellman, B. and Berkowitz, S. D. (1988). *Social Structures: A Network Approach*, Cambridge: Cambridge University Press

Werner, S. (1983). 'New Directions in the Study of Administrative Corruption', *Public Administration Review*, 43 (2), 146–54.

White, S., Pravda, A. and Gitelman, Z. (eds.) (1994). *Developments in Russian and Post-Soviet Politics.*, 3rd edn (first published 1990), London: Macmillan

Willerton, J. P. (1992). *Patronage and Politics in the USSR*, Cambridge: Cambridge University Press

Wittfogel, K. A. (1957). *Oriental Despotism*, New Haven: Yale University Press

Wittgenstein, L. (1958). *The Blue and Brown Books*, Oxford: Basil Blackwell
  (1969). *Philosophische Grammatik.*, Oxford: Basil Blackwell
  (1972). *Philosophical Investigations*, Oxford: Blackwell

Wixman, R. (1984). *The People of the USSR: An Ethnographic Textbook*, Armonk NY: M. E. Sharpe

Yang, M. M. (1994). *Gifts, Favours and Banquets: The Art of Social Relationships in China*, Ithaca and London: Cornell University Press

Yergin, D. and Gustafson, T. (1994). *Russia 2010*, London: Nicholas Bradley

Zaslavskaia, T. (1994). *Kuda Idet Rossiya?: Alternativy Obshchestvennogo Razvitiya*, Materialy Mezhdunarodnogo Simposiuma (17–19 December 1993), Moscow: Interpraks

Zaslavskaia, T. and Ryvkina R. (1989). *Ekonomicheskaia Sotsiologiia i Perestroika*, Moscow: Progress

Zemtsov, I. (1976). *Partiia ili Mafiia? Razvorovannaya Respublika*, Paris: Editeurs
    Réunis
Zinoviev, A. (1978). *The Yawning Heights*, trans. G. Clough, London: Bodley
    Head
    (1984). *The Reality of Communism*, New York: Schocken Books
    (1985). *Homo Sovieticus*, trans. C. Janson, London: Gollancz

# Index

References in **bold type** indicate the main discussion of a topic.

second economy 3, 4, **47–52**
'second' society 212
shock therapy 184, 184n.2, 194
shock-workers 93
shortage 10, 11, 22, 28, 36, 40, 52, 69, 71,
    78, 86, **87–92**, 93, 106, 107, 124, 127,
    134, 137, 162, 176, 178, 179, 182
  economy of 33, 88, 92, 176
social alchemy 179
socialising 45, 74, 84, 120, 140, 205
socialism 16, 68, 70, 76, 87, 96, 100, 101,
    181, 194
  paradoxes of 72
speculation 23–4, 49, 186
*Stakhanovtsy* 74, 93n.7
Stalin, J. 10, 11, 16, 27, 54, 74, 75, 76, 85,
    93, 96, 97, 98
suspended punishment **77–9**, 132n.4

tactics of *blat* 63, 167–71

theft 12, 48, 49, 50, 114, 135, 167
Timasheff, N.S. 75
*tolkach* **25–7**, 44, 50, 86, 119, 205
totalitarianism 3, 43, 73, 74, 77, 84
Trotsky, L. 74–5
trust 10, 24, 34, 39, 40, 85, 86, 101, 115,
    125, 128, 141, 142, 147, 149, 158,
    185, 192, 195, 196, 204, 210, 211

useful people 32, 118, 119, **121–5**, 174, 201

*voucher* 189, 190, 193n.12
*vynos* (*see also nesuny*, theft) 49, 50

Wittgenstein, L. 34, 38
workers 23, 49, 57, 58, 61, 64, 66, 75, 88,
    93, 97, 100, 101, 112, **132–3**, 137,
    180, 190, 206–7
  workers' cooperatives 94
  workers' departments of supply 94

# Cambridge Russian, Soviet and Post-Soviet Studies